JUDICIAL ACTIVISM IN INDIA

JUDICIAL ACTIVISM IN INDIA

With Special Reference to the Quest for Social Justice

Nilanjana Jain

KALPAZ

Judicial Activism in India
With Special Reference to the Quest for Social Justice

ISBN: 978-81-7835-954-0

Published in 2013 in India by
Kalpaz Publications,
C-30, Satyawati Nagar
Delhi-110 052

Phone: 9212142040

E-mail: Kalpaz@hotmail.com

Laser Typesetting: Awadhesh Computer, Delhi

Printed at: G. Print Process,Delhi

To

Prof. Hari Mohan Jain

My Role Model, Ideal, Guide

and Legendary whom

I Shall Miss the Whole Life.

Contents

Preface

The credit for activating the Supreme Court in the cause of Social Justice goes back to the creative judgements of Justice V.R. Krishna Iyer and Justice P.N. Bhagwati.

The trail set ablaze by them was also joined in by Justices D.A. Desai, Chennappa Reddy and M.N. Venkatachallaya, and in recent years by such Justices as J.S. Verma and K.G. Balakrishnan.

These Justice felt it necessary "to evolve a strategy..... in order that justice may become availableto the lowly and the lost". The new strategy was the public interest litigation in place of the traditional rule of standing and adversarial litigation in enforcement of fundamental rights.

PIL is a form of participatory or cooperative litigation in which the petitioner, the state and the court cooperate to secure the end of Social Justice. PIL also entails inquisitorial or inquisitionary process whereby the court takes upon itself the investigative duty by appointing commissions, social activists or experts to ascertain facts of the case, suggest immediate remedial steps and collect prima facie evidence.

As Bhagwati J. explained in the Bandhua Mukti Morcha Case,

"Where one of the parties to a litigation belongs to a poor and deprived section of the community, and does not possess adequate social and material resources, he is bound to be at a disadvantage as against a strong and powerful opponent under the 'adversary system of justice' because of his difficulty in getting competent legal representation, and more than anythnig else, his inability to produce relevant evidence before the court".

(1984) 3 SCC 161.

In S.P. Gupta case he said, "procedure is but a handmaiden of justice and the cause of justice can never be allowed to be thwarted by any procedural technicalities."

(AIR 1982 SC 189)

Similarly Justice Krishna Iyer noted in Ratlam Municipality case, "the centre of gravity of justice is to shift from traditional individualism of locusstandii to the community orientation of public interest litigation.........At issue is the..... court's power to force public bodies, under public duties, to implement specific plans in response to public grievances............in the exercise of such power, the judiciary must be informed by the broader principles of access to justice necessitated by the conditions of developing countries and obligated by Article 38 of the constitution."

(AIR 1980 SC 1628)

In this process the courts seek gradual improvement in the administration and compel the government to be responsive to law and constitutional values.

The judicial departures from the traditional pattern of litigation and admission of innovative strategy for providing easy access to justice to the weaker sections of society made judicial activism the focus of interest and attention of the press, people and parliament alike. Parliament has debated twice in the past (7th Dec., 2006 and 3rd Dec. 2007) the growing encroachment of, the judiciary into the legislative and executive domain, thus upsetting the principle of separation of powers which is the corner-stone of our constitutional democracy.

No doubt the Judiciary has provided a salutary check on executive sluggishness, insensitivity and atrocities and the judiciary has directed it to perform its duties and responsibilities to the great relief of the citizens, specially the poor and the helpless. But the judicial interference in legislative and administrative spheres has made it the controller and master of these two branches of government and not their coordinate in the division of power. It is the loss of legislative supremacy that has caused the greatest discontent and resentment against the judiciary and evoked sharp criticism of "government by judiciary".

The judicial interference in legislative affairs extends judicial function to policy making which is essentially political function. The function of the judiciary is to apply the law and not to make the law and then seek to apply it. Its function is to control and check the executive in the discharge of its functions and, to pull it up or push it where it is overbearing or sluggish.

As the Supreme Court stated in Chaitanya Kumar vs. State of Karnataka (1986), "...... the court cannot close its eyes and persuade itself to uphold publicly mischievious executive actions which have been so exposed, when arbitrariness and perversion are writ large and brought out clearly, the court cannot shirk its duty and refuse its writ."

In the S.P. Gupta case (1981) Bhagwati J. held that, "any member of the public having sufficient interest can maintain an action for judicial redress for public injury arising from breach of public duty or from violation of some provision of the constitution or the law and seek enforcement of such public duty and observance of such constitutional or legal provision".

It is conceded that in course of application of law some degree of law making is inevitable Lord Denning said that it is an illusion that the Judges do not make law, that they only interpret it. He said, "this illusion is now being discarded everywhere. Every new decision or every new situation is a development of law. Law does not stand still. It moves continuously. The Judge .... must consciously seek to mould the law so as to serve the needs of time."

Krishna Iyer J. admits that judicial law making, though interstitial, is needed. Judges may interpret the law, expand it to cover new situations and fill gaps, even if the Judge may apply his own choice of values in a case when there is no clear legal answer. The judge may transform the law to meet the end of Social Justice." But, they have no right to hold that the law is unconstitutional. The determination of constitutionality of laws is a political question. It ought to be outside of the purview of judicial review. There is no reason to suppose that Judges, are better equipped to interpret the Constitution than the Parliament. Why should the interpretation of Judge be taken as, valid. Why should the interpretaion of parliament be not taken, as valid? It is not that the court is Supreme because it is right. It is right because it is Supreme. There is no mathematical finality or objectivity in the court's opinion. One court may differ from the other on the same point of law. Even the same court may be divided between a majority and a minority, the majority often exceeding the minority by one.

However, this does not mean that any finality attaches to a legislative Act in so far as its compatibility with the constitution is concerned. What is to be underlined is that the constitutionality of a law or constitutional amendment is a political question and therefore not justiciable.

It is therefore, suggested that the power of judicial review should be so restructured as to preclude the judicial review of legislative Acts as well as decisions of the political executive. While the courts may review the legality of administrative acts, omissions and lapses and enforce the constitutional provisions relating to rights and freedom of the people, the power of deciding questions of constitutionality of laws and acts of the political executive should be vested in a quasi-judicial organ like the Constitutional Council of France or Federal Constitutional Court in Germany.

Since the Supreme Court in a number of cases has held that any curtailment of the power of judicial review will mean impairment of the basic structure of the constitution, such curtailment of the power of judicial review will be impermissible.

In view of the basic structure theory it may be necessary to recreate the primary constituent authority to bring about the restructuring of judicial power so that it may be beyond any judacial challenge.

This is in brief the substance of this book.

The book is divided into three sections.

Section I deals with the theoretical aspects of judicial power and contains three chapters namely:

1. The myth of Judicial independence,
2. Judicial Power: From Judicial Review to Judicial overreach.
3. Judicial Activism and its dimensions.

Section II, deals with Judicial activism in action, with separate chapters on : (1) Police, Prisoners and Under Trials, (2) Women arid Children, (3) Labour, Poor, helpless indigent, denizens, (4) Weaker Sections of Society: Judicial activism versus political activism, (5) Urban development, health, hygiene and sanitation, (6) Environment and pollution.

Section III deals with the restructuring of judicial power in two chapters namely:

1. Judicial overreach and
2. Restructuring judicial power and judicial reforms. It is the opinion of the author that almost every chapter of this study can be the subject of a fullfledged doctoral dissertation.

I was spurred to take up this study by a Major Research Project grant of the University Grants Commission although the current political debate in the country during the last few years has sufficiently motivated me to work out this theme. Without the U.G.C. grant it would not have been possible for me to undertake this study and therefore I am grateful to the U.G.C. for the financial support.

I am grateful to the Principal of my college, Dr. Rita Purwar for motivating me to apply to the U.G.C. for this Research Project and helping me in completing it.

I thank Mr. Suresh Chandra Varma, Advocate, High Court Allahabad, Administrator, Arya Kanya Degree College, Allahabad for his cooperation.

The members of the staff of the Political Science department, of the University and in particular the Ex Head of the department Prof. Alok Pant, former Head of the department Prof. M.P. Dube, Professor and Head Dr. Mohammed Aslam, Dr. Krishna Gupta and Dr. Anuradha Kumar have been consistently encouraging and supportive to me in the endeavour. No words will be adequate to convey my gratitude to all of them.

In the end, I thank all my colleagues, the office staff, especially for their help, guidance from time to time.

I must also express my gratitude to my cousin brother, Mr. Rajeev Jain for making my stay in Delhi, for pursuing the project related work at the U.G.C. and various other offices, comfortable and convenient.

I am also grateful to Mr. Akhilesh Pandey, Advocate Hight Court for the legal assistance, scrutiny and support, he provided to me. He not only helped me with his wide knowledge of case law but also put at my disposal the services of his staff and also the facility of his rich library and its allied electronic equipment.

The book is very interesting and useful for academicians, researches, judges, advocates, social activists, political leaders, policy makers and the students specially appering in competitive examination.

Lastly, I thank Kalpaz Publications Delhi, for his active support and endeavor for bringing the book in the market. I hope to carry on this line of research further and shall be greateful to any critic for suggestion, advice or comments.

Nilanjana Jain

PART–I

1

The Myth of Judicial Independence

Not until Montesquieu (1689-1755) does one come across in the history of political thought: any suggestion that judiciary is or ought to be, a separate and independent organ of government. There is no place for it in the greek political thought.

Plato's *'Republic'* is admittedly a treatise on justice, but in Plato Justice or its 'delivery, is not in anyway related to any institutional form. In fact in the 'Republic' the Philosopher King is all in all.

In Aristotle, as in the entire Greek political thought, no distinction is made between the State and Government. What is described by Aristotle as classification of states is as a matter of fact only a classification of governments. Therefore, there is no question of any consideration of division of governmental power in Greek thought. Aristotle does discuss the conception of law and government and justice but there is no reference to division of powers within the government.

Roman Period

The Roman political thinkers are known for their passion for law and justice. But with the exception of polybius (204-122 B.C.) no Roman political thinker attempted any classification of governments or division of power within the government. Polybius is the only Roman thinker who advocated a 'mixed form of government' which exerted a considerable influence down to modern times. Political theorists in the seventeenth century evolved from it the theory of the 'Separation of powers.'[1]

The Middle Ages

The middle ages were typically "unpolitical". The medieval political thought is largely rocked by church–state controversy. In the early years the farthest approach to politics is the doctrine of "two swords". In the later half of this period Dante's *De-Monorchia* and Thomas Aquinas's four fold classification of laws are notable contributions. Towards the end of this period Marsilio of Padua wrote about the stat and government.

He regarded law as a rule of reason or of intrinsic justice, emanating from a constituted authonity. In his view, the legislator is the people or whole body of citizens, or a prevailing part of it. The executive and judicial part of government "Marsilio regards as set up or elected by the body of citizens. It is essential that this authority should be exercised in accordance with law and that its duties and powers should be such as the people determine".[2]

English Constitutional Theory

This line of constitutional theory is carried forward in the English constitutional theory of the 17th century, notably in the writings of Harrington and Locke (1632-1704).

Harrington

This pattern of thought found its clearest theoretical expression in James Harrington's 'Oceana' (1656). He conceives of the legislative powers being vested in a combination of the 'natural aristocracy' and the 'common people'. Together they constitute the legislative power. Of necessity there must be a third order, "to be executive of the laws made, and this is the magistracy, magistracy then meaning the judiciary primarily."[3]

The magistracy is primarily for executing the laws. "In constructing a free government he thought it essential to secure a separation of powers. Harrington's division of political powers, however, did not correspond precisely to that later-mader familiar by Montesquieu but followed a line suggested by his study of city-state.

The deliberative or policy-forming function he regarded as necessarily aristocratic, in the sense that it must be performed by a few persons who have experience and expert knowledge. The acceptance or rejection of a proposed policy he regarded as popular function which ought to be performed by a large body elected for that purpose and having no power to deliberate. Rather curiously, in view of English experience just prior to the civil wars, he had nothing to say about the independence of the judiciary."[4]

John Locke (1632-1704)

Locke is the pioneer of the theory of constitutional government. Constitutional government means Limited Government. The most important contribution of Locke to Political theory was—

(*i*) The idea of Limited Government and

(*ii*) Functional differentiation of governmental powers, though not their organic separation.

The essentials' of his theory are—

(1) The government is limited because it is brought into being by the people and holds power in trust for the people. It has "only a fiduciary power to act for certain ends", its authority is confined to securing these ends. These ends are the security of life, liberty and property of the individual.

(2) Locke not only propounded the concept of limited government he also conceived of the division of

governmental power into three parts. These are the legislative, the executive and the Federative.

(3) It is notable that in the theory of Locke the executive includes the judicial power. Judiciary is not a separate or independent organ of state power. It is merely an extension or extended part of the executive.

(4) In Locke the three organs of government are not co-equal in power and authority. They are no coordinate branches of government. The legislative is unquestionably the superior most power.

(5) The third branch of government, according to Locke is not judiciary but, what he calls, the federative power that makes treaties and is concerned with the state's external relations.

"The legislative, though it be the supreme power in every commonwealth, is not, nor can possibly be absolutely arbitrary over the lives and fortunes of the people.

Rationale of Functional differentiation

The functional differentiation between the legislative and the executive authority is explaind byLocke, as by Harrington before him, on the well-known ground that it is necessary for the maintenance of liberty. Their view was that liberty suffers when the same human beings make the laws and apply them.

This view was canonized by Blackstone in his 'commentaries on the Laws of 'England' (1765) : "In all tyrannical governments, the Supreme Magistracy, or the right both of making and enforcrng the laws is vested in one and the same man, or one and the same body of men; and whereever these two powers are united together, there can be no public liberty.[5]

Similarly Locke writes — "It may be too great temptation to human frailty, apt to grasp at power, for the same persons who have the power of making laws to have also in their hands the power to execute them, whereby they may exempt themselves from obedience to the laws they make, and suit the law, both in its making and execution, to their own private advantage, and thereby come to have a distinct interest from the rest of the community, contrary to the end of society and government." He further– writes - "In all cases whilst the government subsists, the legislative is the supreme power. For what can give laws to another must, needs be superior to him, and since the legislative is no otherwise legislative of the society but by the right it has to make laws for all the parts, and every member of the society prescribing rules to their actions and giving power to execution when they are transgressed, the legislative must needs be the supreme, and all other powers in any members or parts of the society derived from and subordinate to it."[6]

While Locke declares that men in the state of nature resolve to form civil society because of want of "the want of an established, settled known law", the want of a "known and indifferent judge", the want of "an executive power to enforce just decisions", he does not provide for any judiciary as a separate, independent branch of government. Perhaps he assumes the judiciary to be subsumed in the executive. In doing so he may have been influenced by the institutional growth of judicial bodies in the English constitutional history.

In England the courts separated from the 'Witangemote to form judicial bodies to exercise judicial function on behalf of the king. The House of Lords is the highest court of appeal in England. Its presiding officer, the Lord, Chancellor, is a senior member of the British Cabinet. The king or the queen is the fountain of Mercy with the right to grant pardon, reprieve and amnesty in all cases.

MONTESQUIEU (1689-1755)

The French thinker, Montesquieu is said to have of J-F "mistaken" the functional differentiation of powers within the British government for "organic separation" of powers. It is on this "error" that his famous theory of separation of powers is believed to rest. Montesqliieu was primarily interested, as a result of the contemporary situation in France, in the problem of how to secure liberty. He saw in the independence of judges a guarantee or assurance of individual liberty. He was therefore led to formulate the concept of "judicial power" and place it as a separate organ of government. He made another change in Locke's scheme by joining federative power to executive power. The executive power in Montesquieu's description was to execute the laws and maintain internal and external peace, and "by thus, assimilating the police functions to the functions of defence and foreign policy, Montesquieu constructed the modern executive power."[7]

Montesquieu formulated the concept of judiciary as an independent and separate branch of government.He also laid down the doctrine of separation of powers between legislature, executive and judiciary. Contrary to Lock he regarded the three branches of government as coordinate units of a single entity (government), equal to each other, and autonomous in their own sphere of authority and power. The separation of the three branches of government, and their balancing he regarded as essential to individual liberty.

His scheme may be recorded in his own words as follows—

"In every government there are three sorts of power: the legislative, the executive and..... the judiciary...... when the legislative and executive powers are united in the same person, or in the same body of Magistrates, there can be no liberty Again, there is no liberty if the judiciary be, not separated from the legislative and executive, were it joined with the legislative, the 'life and liberty of the subject, would be exposed to arbitrary control, for the judge would, then be legislator were it joined to the executive, the judge might behave with violence and oppression."

There would be an end of everything were the same men or the same, body (whether of nobles or of the, people) to exercise all three powers.....[8]

In this way Montesquieu made the separation of powers into a system of legal checks and balances between the parts of a Constitution. Moreoverhe raised the judiciary to the status of a separate and independent, branch of government. Therefore, it may be said, that the rise of judiciary as a separate organ of power in the government begins with Montesquieu.

American Constitution

Montesquieu's theory of separation of powers and checks and balances found a faithful translation in the American Constitution (1789); The American system of government is based on the theory of, separation of powers between the legislature, executive and judieiary. Moreover, it raises the judiciary to a status of supremacy unknown anywhere in the European continent, or in the world at large, except perhaps in India where the judicial power can be seen expanding itself by leaps and bounds since the commencement of the Constitution.

In the United States there is a clear cut separation of powers in the three branches of government. "All legislative powers shall be vested in a Congress of the Unites States." (Art. I)

"The executive power shall be vested in a President of the United States of America." (Art. II)

"The judicial power of the Unites States, shall be vested in one supreme court, and in such inferior courts as the Congress may from time to time ordain and establish." (Art. III)

However, the Constitution not only makes a division of powers into three separate branches of government but also provides for mutual check and balance between one branch and another. For example, the President or his Cabinet Secretaries may not be members of either House of Congress and are debarred from participating in its proceedings, but no bill (ordinary or financial) can become the law without receiving the assent of the President.

While appointments and treaty making are within the jurisdiction of the President, the appointments recommended by him, including judicial appointments and treaties made by him require the concurrence of the Senate.

The Congress may from time to time ordain and establish inferior courts, and the Judges both of the Supreme Court and inferior courts may be removed by the process of impeachment.

In U.S.A. the judicial power expanded beyond the limits of the Constitution as Chief Justice John Marshall formulated the doctrine of judicial review in the case of Marbury V. Madison (1803).

Marshall declared that a law repugnant to the Constitution is void and that courts, as well as other departments, are bound by that instrument.

Judicial Independence: What it Means: What it Does't

While separation of powers is designed to safe guard the liberty of the individual the principle of checks and balances purports to secure coordination in government and efficiency and expedition in administration.

In any case the insistence is on free and fair administration of justice. Therefore, the independence of judiciary is the highest value in a democracy. It is necessary that the Judges should be able to function without fear or favour and for this their appointment and service conditions (Promotion, Posting, Transfer, pay) should be uninfluenced by the prevaling political power. This is the meaning of Judicial independence.

In the U.S.A. Supreme Court Judges are appointed by the President subject to confirmation by the Senate. In their case there is no age of superannuation. Their emolumens and conditions of service cannot be varied to their disadvantage.

These devices are aimed at securing the independence of the judiciary. These measures have more or less been adopted in democracies all over the world.

In India Judges of the Supreme Court and state High Courts are appointed by the President. The number of Judges in the Supreme Court is prescribed by law, by Parliament, and in the High Courts, it will be such as may be prescribed by the President from time to time. Besides, the President has the power to appoint additional Judges for a temporary period not exceeding two years and also ad-hoc- Judges to fill in vacancies in the Supreme Court or in a High Court.

The Judges are appointed by the President of India. The Constitution provides that "every Judge of the Supreme Court shall be appointed by the President after consultation with such of Judges of the Suprem Court and of the High Courts in the states as the President may deem necessary for the purpose........provided that in the case of appointment of a Judge other than the Chief Justice, the Chief Justice of India shall always be consulted." (Art. 124).

However, in the case of High Court Judge the President shall make the appointment "after consultation with the Chief Justice of India, the Governor of the State, and, in the case of appointment of a Judge other than the Chief Justice, the Chief Justice of the High Court." (Art. 217)

In this context D.D. Basu comments, "the above provision, thus, modifies the mode of appointment of Judges by the Executive – by providing that the Executive should consult members of the Judiciary itself, who are well qualified to give their opinion in this matter."[9]

However, the Supreme Court in interpreting these provisions has held that consultation would actually mean consent and subsequently the Court has ruled that the initiative for appointment of a Judge should come from the Chif justice. In this way the Executive, contrary to the will of the Constitution makers, has lost initiative and the discretion in the matter of appointment of a Judge to the Judiciary itself. This has resulted in a situation that obtains no where in the world, and in no other administrative organisation. This, to say the least, is not judicial independence; it is the very reverse of it. The result is that a large number of vacancies have remained unfilled and a Parliamentary Panel has blamed the judiciary itself for these vacancies.[10]

The panel also criticized the lack of transparency in the present procedure for appointment of Judges and long delays in their recruitment, specially for subordinate courts. The panel pointed out, "The root of the problem is the closed system of appointments in the Higher Judiciary. The entire process is kept so secretive that it gives rise to suspicion".

The committee recommended a review of the entire procedure for appointment of Judges of the Supreme Court and High Courts.

It has asked for inclusion of members from outside the judiciary in the committee that decides on appointments.

Eminent members of the public, a government representative, a leader from the opposition and a member of the Bar Council should be part of the panel, along with senior judge, to clear judicial appointments, the committee said,[11]

Chairman of the Bar Council of India, S.N.P. Sinha told the media that the BCI would soon forward a proposal to the Central Government regarding the procedure for appointment of Judges. He maintained that there should be the highest degree of transparency in appointment of Judges of the Supreme Court and the High Courts, which was so far being done by the Judges themselves. The Judge's selection panel should also include members of Bar and persons of highest repute and experience."[12]

Ramesh Abhishek, a Joint Secretary in the department of Justice admitted that, "The initiation process is entirely in the hands of the Chief Justice of India for Supreme Court appointments and Chief Justice of High Courts for High Courts appointments."[13]

However, the ex-chief of BCI and presently the President of Allahabad High Court Bar Association, Mr. V.C. Mishra, reacting instantly to the statement of House Panel said that the inclusion of members from outside the judiciary in the committee that decides on appoinments, "is an attempt to erode judicial independence". He said judiciary is at liberty, to consult whom soever it so desires for making appointments in the judiciary. The three wings of the Constitution, the Judiciary, the Legislature and the Executive are independent of one another and the same be maintained for proper functioning of the Constitution.[14]

It is obvious that Mishra has exaggerated notions of judicial independance. A cursory perusal of major democracies, U.S.A., Germany, France, U.K. will easily disprove Mishra's apprehensions. How will the association of eminent public figures in the appointment procedure of Judges will erode judicial independence is difficult to guess? Judicial independence does not mean judicial autarchy. It does not mean a closed, secretive, internal selective process. Moreover it is wrong to say that the three branches of government are independent of each other. Even Montesquieu, who may be said to be the father of the theory of separation of powers, agreed that there has to be mutual check and balance among the three branches of government.

The former Law Minister Mr. H.R. Bhardwaj has repeatedly criticised the present procedure for appointments and transfers of Supreme Court and High Court Judges. The Minister said, "In a bid to maintain its supremacy, the judiciary tried to rewrite the law through a Supreme Court judgement in 1993", which laid down that the recommendations for appointment should be made by committee of judges (collegium), consisting of the Chief Justice and two senior most Judges of the High court (4 in the supreme court). In this way, "the judiciary wrested the control of judges appointments and transfers.

The Minister said, "there was no problem till 1993 when the judiciary tried to rewrite the Article of the Constitution dealing with appointments. They created, a new law of collegium which was wrong. In a democracy, the primacy of Parliament cannot be challenged.[15]

The House panel as the Law Minister vehemently criticised the collegium system. The minister said, Collegium systerm has failed. Its decisions on appointments and transfer lack transparency and we feel courts are not getting judges on merit. It has become a give and take system." The House Panel said, "The collegium system has been a disaster and needs to be done away with."[16]

The Minister said, in criticism of the collegium system that "Merit has been ignored.... the quality of some judges selected by the collegium system over the years has been questionable. The judiciary's insistence on showing itself superior has not helped the country."[17]

Former CJI, V.R. Krishna Iyer in an article in the Hindu (February 19, 2009) has condemned the collegium systems "the trade unionist feature of capturing management power through collective pressure", arid "constitutionally unwarranted". He writes, "The executive power to appoint judges is wrested from abinet and exercised by the collegium. This is a novel conquest, unique in any democracy. The selection of judges is an expert job, but judges, senior or junior, are untrained and without investigative tools and unfit for this non judicial technical operation."

In criticism of the collegium phenomenon, lyer writes, "the collegium would often seem to have no conscience or not done any investigation before an appointment is made. The selection process is kept secret from the Bar, the legislature and the people." (The Hindu, 19.2.09).

The government has maintained that there was no explicit direction that in appointing an additional judge, of a High Court permanent judge, the Chief Justice of India should consult the collegium. In an affidavit filed before the supreme Court the center said, "From January 1, 1999 to July 31, 2007, a total of 351 additional judges were appointed permanent judges; in these cases the Supreme Court collegium was not consulted. The records indicate that successive, CJIs have not consulted the collegium while considering the cases of appointment of additional judges as permanent judges."

In 2007, Justice Ashok Kumar of the Andhra High Court was appointed permanent judge by the CJI without consulting the collegium.[18]

The former Chief Justice of India J.S. Verma, speaking at a public function, called for more transparency in judicial appointments to ensure judicial accountability and independence. He said, "the entire correspondence on judicial appointments, should be made public at least after the appointments are made so that people would know what type of judges they are.... people must know why a certain person was recommended and why certain person were not recommended".[19]

Recently the recommendation by the Supreme Court collegium for elevation of three High Court Chief Justices (Madras, Patna and Kerala) to the Supreme Court, by passing sum of the senior most judges in the country, has raised a storm of controversy and prepared the ground for confrontation between the government and the judiciary.

"The PMO instead of forwarding the file to the President for her assent, has referred back the file to the Law Ministry. The PMO is reported to have recorded on the file, "when senior judges from M.P. and J & K were available, there was no reason to ignore them.[20]

Ministry officials said the PMO's observation would now be shared with the CJI and there is little role for them in the process, "we have no role in the recommendation process, so we are out of the picture even when these are referred back," the official said.[21] The ministry returned the file to the Supreme Court to reconsider the points raised by the government.[22]

However, the Supreme Court collegium declined to reconsider its decision and returned the file to the government, sticking to its recommendations. There was some speculation that the government may not forward the names recommended by the collegium to the President. But the government lacked the courage to confront the judiciary and quietly cleared the collegium recommendations for the President's approval which she accorded early this month (9.12.2008).[23]

The collegium system has continued to draw irritation and criticism from the knowledgable section all over the country and inside the Parliament. The then Union Law Minister H.R. Bhardwaj speaking on the sidelines of a conference on 23.2.2009 reiterated that "the collegium system for appointment of Judges has failed." As has the in-house procedure for dealing with complaints against the Judges. He expressed his helplessness in changing the system and said, "I would have changed the system if could but there is need to evolve broader consencus on the issue in Parliament (The Times of India, 24.2.2009).

During the debate on the Judges (Salaries and conditions of services.) Amendment bill, 2009, the Minister disclosed that there was a plea for making the appointment of Judges more fair and objective and for setting up a broad based National Judicial Commission. Sevral members, during the debate sought changes in the appointment procedure of Judges. Arun Jaitely (BJP) said, "the government needs to improve the quality of judges by evolving foolproof criteria for appointment. Discretion of the collegium in appointment of judges would be restricted through a legislative procedure" (The Hindu, 25.2.2009).

E.M. Sudarshan, Natchippan, Chairman of the Parliamentary Standing Committee on Law and Justice, delivering the keynote address at the third state conference of the Indian Lawyers congress on March 8, 2009 disclosed that there was consensus in the committee that the pre 1993 system of appointing High Court and Supreme court Judges was the better option as it was in consonance with the provisions of the constitution". He said the committee favoured the restoration of the pre- 1993 situation where both the President (executive) and the judiciary were involved in the consultative process to appoint the judges. But an "interpretation of that constitutional provision by the Supreme Court in 1993 led to a situation where the executive's decision in the appointment of Judges has been totally negated."

He suggested that a committee, comprising representatives of the executive legislature, and judiciary plus one member from the Bar could initially screen the names for the appointment of Judges and refer them to the National Judicial Commission proposed in the Judges (Inquiry) bill 2006, for final recommendations (The Hindu, 09.03.09).

The recommendation made by the collegium (27.08.09) to elevate Karnataka Chief Justice P.D. Dinakaran to the Supreme Court has again brought the collegium system into the whirlpool of controversy. A number of prominent jurists and bar leaders have opposed the recommendation for his promotion for "doubtful integrity" with this, the demand for scrapping the collegium system is reaching fever pitch. The Supreme court and Delhi High Court Bar Association said, "some of the appointments made in the high courts and now even the present selection of this controversial judge to the apex court—all show that the collegium system is worse than the previous system of the executive selecting the Judges."

The worst example of the failure of the collegium system was the appointment of Soumitra Sen as Judge at Calcutta High Court in 2006, even as he faced allegations of having misappropriated Rs. 50 lakhs while serving as a court appointed lawyer in 1993 in a dispute between two public sector companies. "How is it that the collegium which cleared him for appointment did not even bother to check his credentials when the entire record was available in the court itself', asked Prashant Bhushan, a senior lawyer.

The Parliamentary Standing Committee on Law and justice had slammed the "veil of secrecy" surrounding the entire process. (Hindustan Times, 18. 09.09).

A scathing commentary on the collegium system is presented by the Supreme Court annulling the appointment of Justice N. Kannadasan as the Chief of State (T.N.) consumer panel. His name Was cleared by the collegium in 2003 for High Court Judgeship. The collegium thrice recommended N. Kannadasan for appointment as additional judge in the Madras High Court in 2003, despite the government's objections. Both the NDA government and President A.P.J. Abdul Kalam returned his name as he faced corruption charges. But the collegium insisted and he was finally cleared.

In 2005, however, it refused to make him a permanent judge. "How can two collegiums arrive at two conclusions, asked former S.C. Judge P.B. Sawant. The Tamil Nadu government made Kannadasan President of the State Consumer Forum last year which was challenged in the High Court. The court declared his appointment "illegal".

Kannadasan moved the Supreme Court which on May 06, 2009 retified the High Court decision. The former Law Minister, Shanti Bhushan comments, "the Supreme Court declared illegal an appointment cleared by top judges. This system is not working". (Hindustan Times, 28.09.09).

At a gathering of legal luminaries including Fali S. Nariman and former CJI J.S. Verma, Senior Apex Court Lawyers, Anil Diwan and Ashok Desai, the system of appointment of Judges on the recommendation of the collegium came in for severe criticism. It was denounced as a total failure. Led by veteran Jurist Fali S. Nariman and former CJI, J.S. Verma, they said that "it was a result of the collegium system's failure that controversial Karnataka High Court Chief Justice P.D. Dinakaran was recommended for promotion and the delay in deciding the matter of his promotion' while the gentleman should have been dropped like a hot cake," the moment serious allegations supported by documentary evidence surfaced against him. Nariman said, "I have no faith in the collegium system. It's members do not do their homework on the names of judges being promoted. Justice Dinakaran's name was recommended by a coterie and nobody bothered to check the antecedents.

Former C.J.I. J.S. Verma said, "what is important is the institution and not individuals. In case of a reasonable doubt, when you are being forced to order a probe the best course of action would have been to drop the doubtful name," Justice Verma said.

Justice Dinakaran was recommended by the collegiums on August 27, 09 for promotion to the S.C. It had to be put on hold following objections by top jurists about alleged land grabbing and disproportionate assets. (Hindustan Times 29.11.09)

The Government, bowing to the persistent criticism of the collegium system, asked the Supreme Court on April 4, 2011 to reconsider its 1993 verdict that gave primacy to the judiciary over the executive in appointment of Judges in the apex court and High Courts.

During hearing of Suraj India Trust's petition seeking a review of the 1933 ruling that led to the collegium system under which a panel of top SC judges select judges for the higher judiciary, Attorney General G.E. Vahanvati supported the petition.

Maintaining there were certain apparent inconsistencies in the 1993 SC Advocate-on-Record' Association case judgement, Vahanvati said the appointment process needed to be reconsidered.

Vahanvati told the court that the government was in the process of bringing in a bill for necessary changes in the appointment procedure of judges but its enactment would take a long time and, therefore, the SC could refer the matter to a bench for reconsidering it, he added. (H.T. 5 April 2011).

What it Doesn't

It is the wrong and exaggerated notions of judicial independence that have completely disturbed the harmony between the three branches of government established by our constitution makers. The Prime Minister Dr. Manmohan Singh and the former Lok Sabha speaker Mr. Somnath Chatterjee have had, to publicly warn the judiciary to keep within limits and not to overstep its limits. Even Supreme Court Justices, notably Mr. Markandey Katju has in several of his (recent judgement advised the judiciary "not to try to run the government."

The U.P. Government's decision to build Kanshi Ram Research Institute in the land allotted for Ambedkar Park in Lucknow caused a split in the Supreme Court bench comprising J.J. Altamas Kabir and Markandey Katju which was to decide on its order vacating the Allahabad High Court stay on changing the landuse of 35 acres area of the park. Justice Katju questioned the legal basis of the opposition to the project and said— "It's a democratically elected government and it can take up construction activities, you can vote them out if you are not happy with it". Justice Katju observed, while stating that there was nothing wrong in the U.P. Government's decision, as it did not violate any statute or rule.

Justice Katju, asked the Mahasamithi's senior counsel Abhishek Manu Singhvi to spellout the rules, guidelines or any law that has been violated by the U.P. Government "we (judges) are not political. We are neutral" Justice Katju observed.

Judges Should Know Their Limits

Corning down heavily on judicial activism, the Supreme Court deprecated the tendency of courts to rule on issues like nursery admissions and autorickshaw overcharging and said Judges should know their 'limits' and notary to run the government.

In a judgement that did a lot of self-introspection, a two member Bench said, "......, we are repeatedly coming across cases where juages are unjustifiably trying to perform executive or legislative functions."

"In our opinion, this is clearly unconstitutional. In the name of judicial activism, Judges cannot cross their limits and try to take over functions which belong to another organ of the state."

The apex court also looked inward when it held the directions given by it in the Assembly proceedings in Uttar Pradesh in 1998 and Jharkhand in 2005 as "glaring examples of deviations from the clearly provided constitutional scheme of separation of powers,"

Justice A.K. Mathur and Markandey Katju listed a number of local issues like unauthorised schools, criteria for free seats in schools, the size of speed breakers on Delhi roads and enhancing of road fines, dealt with by the Delhi High Court which, they said, were" matters pertaining exclusively to the executive or legislative domain".

If there is a law, judges can enforce it. But judges cannot create a law and seek to enforce it", they observed.

The observations came in a 22 pages verdict with the court setting aside a Punjab and Haryana High Court order directing ereation of posts of tractor driver to accommodate two gardeners employed on daily wages at a golf club run by the Haryana Tourism corporation and were asked to perform the duties of tractor drivers.

In this context, the Bench recalled the observations of the then Chief Justice of India A.S. Anand, "that judicial activism does not become judicial adventurism, the courts must act with caution and proper restraint".

It said that policy matters, on fiscal, educational and other issues, are thus best left to the judgement of the executive. "The danger of judiciary creating a multiplicity of rights without the possibility of adequate enforcement will, in the ultimate analysis, be counter productive and undermine the credibility of the institution", the Bench observed.[24]

Actually, the function of judiciary is only to adjudicate disputes of all kinds and categories. The judicial function should be limited strictly to adjudication. The judiciary should not be allowed to "review" the constitutionality of laws or constitutional amendments. That is plainly a political function. The extension or encroachement of the judiciary into the political domain, reserved for Parliament exclusively, results in the kind of unseemly controversy about judicial independence that we are witnessing in India today.

Judiciary Under Liberal Democracies

In continental Europe or in England, this pattern of Separation of powers has not been accepted or adopted. However, it is accepted as universal principle that the judicial power should be separate and independent and judges should be empowered to act without fear or favour.

With the triumph of liberalism in the 18th century, the ideal of independent judiciary became the norm of civilized states. Independent judiciary is regarded as an essential element of a liberal democracy. The thesis of judicial independence may be formulated as follows:

Liberal democracy postulates limited government. Limited government involves Rule of Law. Rule of Law demands independent judiciary. "To construet the law" Bryce wrote of the American Supreme Court, "that is, to elucidate the will of the people as supreme law giver, is the beginning and end of their duty".

Bryce then adds in a footnote: "Suppose, however, someone may say that the court should go beyond its duty and import its own views of what ought to be the law into its decision as to what is the law, this would be an exercise of judicial will? Doubtless, it would, but it would be a breach of duty, would expose the court to the distrust of the people, and might, if repeated or persisted in a serious matter, provoke resistance to the law as laid down by the court."

A final quotation from Bryce: In America the constitution is at all times very hard to change: much more then must political issues turn on its interpretation. And if this be so, must not the interpreting court be led to assume a control over the executive and legislative branches of government, since it has the power of declaring their acts illegal? [25]

The American and the Indian experience, both suggest that the Supreme Court exercising its power to interpret the Constitution and the laws and to over rule the interpretations of legislatures and executives, may go too far. The *Dred Scott;* decision (1857) or the decisions overruling the New Deal laws in the mid 1930's are American examples. The Indian cases are the Golaknath Decision (1967), Keshwanand Decision (1973), Minerva Mills (1980), I.R. Coelho (2007). In U.S.A. the result of the Dred Scott decision was the Civil War (1861-65), and of the anti New Deal decisions, the court packing plan."[26]

In India it is notable that the interpretation of one and single article, Art. 31 (read with 31 A, 31 B) has triggered the 1st, 4th, 17th, 24th, 25th and 42nd constitutional amendments generating nation wide political tension and controversy, besides involving massive expenditure. (The fees of the lawyers alone running into millions of rupees).

Judicial review of Laws often slips into and takes the form of judicial activism. The court in this role does not hesitate to nullify the actions of the legislature and issue directives to the executive.

In nullifying laws and, in India, constitutional amendments as well, the court may often appear to run counter to the people's will as expressed by their elected representatives in the legislature, When that happens the court's decision appears to be negation of democracy.

During the debate on 42nd amendment Bill many members pointed out that in cases involving socio-economic reforms, the judicial intervention has been sought only by the vested interests and these interests were backed by those who failed to make it at the polis.

The judicial decisions have been to the advantage of the vested intersts and the propertied classes. It is these groups who have been relying on judicial review to frustrate the electoral verdict. 'They have found in the court a convenient counter balance to the political process. As Dr. M.R.Vyas put it "for twenty years or twenty five years, they tried, in vain, to come to power by means of elections. When they did not succeed, they thought that the means of judiciary would be good means to supersedes the representatives of the peopleas represented by Parliament.[27]

He continued, "The worst aspect of this point is that they have looked upon the courts and specially the Supreme Court is a kind of means to come to power over the head of Parliament."[27]

The judicial process has been employed to defeat the social policy of the government, to bypass the decisions of the parliament, to frustrate the electoral verdict of the people. The judiciary, has taken on the role of *Super*

Parliament or of the *Third Chamber* of *Parliament,* which Jawaharalal Nehru had repeatedly denounced:

During the Lok Sabha debate on 42nd constitutional amendment bill, C.M. Stephen was at pains to point out the helplessness of the Parliament in the face of judicial assaults on its sovereignty. He'said,.... you go on asserting that you have got the power, they can go on denying it. Assertion and rebuttal can go on *ad infinitum.* It started 1967 and it is going on."[29]

The point of debate is as to who should have the supremacy in deciding the nature and pace of social change and the means to achieve it. As Prime Minister, Smt. Indira Gandhi said, "It is the Parliament and not the judiciary which should be the custodian of the nation and its future."

On the other hand the judiciary should not be involved in such matters, and the reasons are—

(1) The judiciary does not represent the people. It is not elected by them nor it is accountable to them.

(2) The determination of the validity of a law or constitutional amendment is a political question, not a legal one. The judicial review in such matters is bound to drag the court in unseemly political controversies.

(3) The judiciary itself has shown to be divided and shifting on vital constitutional issues, often deciding by a majority of one. In such cases the judicial decision is pitted against the near unanimous decision of the Parliament.

For example—the Keshwanand ruling by a majority of 7 to 6 had the effect of vetoing the portions of 42nd amendment adopted by 550 members of Parliament representing as many millions of people.

In this way the 'sovereign' parliament has been unable to debar judicial review of constitutional amendments. It has found it impossible to curb or curtail judicial review in the face of the Supreme Court's insistence on the basic structure theory. On the other hand the reactionary and vested interests have so to say a 'reserve power' in the Supreme Court to defeat and frustrate the people's verdict at the polls.[30]

The position is that whatever political party or ideology the people may vote to power, the ultimate power remains in the hands of the Supreme Court. Richard D. Heffner notes a parallel phenomenon in the appointment of John Marshall as Chief Justice of U.S. Supreme Court in the face of Republican victory in the election of 1800. He writes "To Jefferson's chagrin and intense anger, however, in at least one branch of government, the federal judiciary, defeated federalists were able to limit the Republican triumph at the polls."[31]

The power of judicial review is to give primacy to the undemocratic element of the Constitution over the democratic process. The Indian experience is that if any attempt is made to restructure the judicial power so as to reinstate the principle of 'sovereignty of Parliament and debar the judiciary from 'reviewing' parliamentary decisions, it is treated as erosion of judicial independence.

Judicial independence does not mean that the judiciary is above the law and the Constitution or above the people and the Parliament.

Judicial independence only means that the judges are able to act without fear or favour within the parameters of law and Constitution as amended from time to time.

References

1. Carl J. Friedrich *Constitutional Government and Democracy*, 1974, p. 173.
2. Sabine: *A History of Political Theory*, 1959, pp. 257 258.
3. Friedrich: p. 173.

4. Sabine: p. 428.
5. *The citation from Blackstone is found in his 'commentaries'*, 1765 (ed. T. Cooley, 1876) Vol. I, p. 146.
6. Locke: *Two Treatises of Civil Government, Everyman's Library, London*, 1949, pp. 190-193.
7. Fedrick p. 176
8. W.T. Jones: Masters of Political Thought, Vol. II; George G. Harrap, 1961, p. 245.
9. D.D. Basu : *Introduction to the constitution of India,* Prentice Hall, 1990, p. 269.
10. Report of the Parliamentary Standing Committee on Law and Justice, H.T. 18, April 2008.
11. *Ibid.*
12. *Hindustan Times,* May 7, 2008.
13. *Hindustan Times,* Feb. 21, 2008.
14. *Hindustan Times,* April 20, 2008.
15. *Hindustan Timgs,* Oct. 20, 2008.
16. However making an about turn the Law Minister speaking at the Law day (26.11.2008) celebrations back tracked on his earlier statements and declared that the present system has worked well and there was no complaint. He said; "the recommendations for appointments are made by competent. persons in the collegium and-there is transparency in the procedure. The minister said that he had reservations on the setting up of National Judicial Commission to deal with appointments and errant judges; as that would mean delay and deadlock, He disfavoured the setting up of a National Judicial Commission with outsiders as members.' (*The Hindu,* 27.11.2008).
17. *Hindustan Times,* Sept. 26, 2008.
18. *The Hindu,* Oct. 24, 2008.
19. *The Hindu,* Nov. 11, 2008.
20. The collegium had over looked the case of their senior the Delhi, M.P. and Uttarakhand High Court Chief Justices, *The Hindu* 12.11.08.

21. *The Hindu*. 12.11.2008.
22. H.T. 14.11.08.
23. *The Hindu*, 10.12.2008.
24. *The Times of India*. Dec. 11, 2007.
25. *Nathan Glazer*, "Towards an Imperial Judiciary?" in the American Commonwealth, edited by Nathan Glazer and Irving Kristol, Basic Books, Newyork, 1976, p. 122.
26. *Ibid*, p. 105.
27. Rajya Sabha Debates 5 Nov. 1976, Col. 15.
28. *Ibid*, col. 17.
29. Lok Sabha Debates, 26 Oct., 1976, Col. 81.
30. Richard D. Heffner, A Documentary History of the United State, A Mentor Book, 1952, P. 71.

2

Judicial Power: From Judicial Reveiew to Judicial Over-reach

Judicial power is the power to judge, under the prevailing law, the lawfulness of a plea or petition between two parties in dispute over any question of law or fact.

It is but natural to expect and insist that the judge, whether an individual, a court or a tribunal must be impartial objective and independent.

The judge must decide according to the law but:

(*i*) It is possible that the dispute be such that it is not covered by the existing law or

(*ii*) The law may be uncertain and ambiguous and ambivalent.

In such circumstances it is open to the judge to interpret the law, or, even create the law by analogy or circumstantial evidence and other well-known methods. This is called Equity law.

In interpreting the law the judge inevitably is led, to create law. There is a very harrow line between interpreting the law and creating new law and this way the judge in applying the law may be led to create new law and to that extent the judicial function takes on the form of legislative function. To this extent the intrusion of the judge into law making domain is accepted universally, but it is necessary that the interpretation should flow from the existing law and, in no case, should be contrary to the written law. In brief the function of the judge is the adjudication of disputes between opposite parties on the basis of law and uninfluenced by extraneous circumstances. However, a measure of discretion rests with the judge in applying the law and interpreting it.

Judicial Review

Judicial review means that power of the court to decide whether a law or an executive act is, or is not, consistent with the Constitution and the law of the land. In the event of a repugnancy between the two, the Judge must uphold the Constitution or the law and must void the impugned law or the executive action. This power was first formulated and applied in the U.S.A. by the then Chief Justice, John Marshall in the well known case of Marbury V. Madison.

However, in continental Europe the courts do not exercise the power to interpret a Constitution, and incidentally to annual acts of the legislature.

K.C. Wheare wrote that "In some countries although the Constitution is silent upon the question whether the courts are entitled to interpret it or not, it appears to be the accepted doctrine that courts should seldom or never embark upon the decision of such questions."[1]

These include the Constitutions of the Third, Fourth and Fifth Republics of France. The French constitutional practice is accepted in a number of continental countries, such as Holland and Belgium, Sweden and Denmark.

K.C. Wheare writes that "it must not be supposed that countries in which the power of judicial review of legislation or of executive action is not practised are indifferent to the supremacy of their Constitutions. In some cases the Constitutions themselves impose no limitations upon the powers of the legislature or executive, and the question of judicial review will not arise. In countries where limitations are imposed, however, it is often held that the only thing to do is to trust the bodies upon which restrictions are imposed to observe these restrictions."[2]

The basic question is why should judge be thought more competent or better equipped to decide these questions than the legislators or administrators? In fact the interpretation of the Constitution or the law is predominantly a political question and not a legal one. The judges who are advised to keep off political controversies are hardly suited to undertake this task.

As the noted Jurist and Law Professor Upendra Baxi remarks, "Justices are not always autonomous agents – autonomous from the deeply embedded logics of the internal and external constraints of the polity and the markets of for legal services".

(Upendra Baxi : quoted in the foreward to O, Chinnappa Reddy's book "The Court and the Constitution of India", O.U.P. 2008, p. xxix.)

K.C. Wheare asks, "should this function be placed upon the courts? It is possible to understand why judges are obliged to take these decisions - it arises inevitably as part of their duty to say what the law is in a case of dispute. But it brings them into the field of political controversy and it means, too, that their appointments are criticized and canvassed and that those who appoint them are inclined to consider what views they are likely to take of the interpretation of the Constitution. Does this not discredit the judiciary?[3]

The Constitution makers in India, notably Jawaharlal Nehru were conscious of these pitfalls of 31 judicial review. Jawaharlal Nehru again and again warned that the court was not to be regarded as a "third chamber" of Parliament and that judiciary could not be allowed to come in the way of the will of the sovereign parliament. But the Constituent Assemibly was dominated by the lawyers like Alladi Krishna Swami Ayyar "with his oceanic depths of learning and a whole knowledge of the constitutional law of the world on his finger tips". B.R. Ambedkar, described as the "Manu of the present age", K.M. Munshi, P.K. Sen were other legal luminaries.

It is possible that progressives like Jawaharlal Nehru were swayed and overwhelmed by the legal acumen and erudition of the lawyer members into submission to acceptance of Judicial Review of laws enacted by the Parliament and the state legislatures. No one would have foreseen at that time the expansion and extension of the power of judicial review into such areas as constitutional amendments. Even in 'reviewing' ordinary laws the judiciary has totally reversed the will and intent of the Constitution makers and imported the doctrine of due process of law in examining the validity of laws touching personal liberty and right to property. Even the distinguished constitutional lawyer D.D. Basu, admits "From Gopalan to Maneka, thus, the judicial exploration has completed its trek from the North to the South pole. The decision in *Maneka's case* is being followed by the Supreme Court in subsequent cases."[4]

Marbury V. Madison (1803)

The power of judicial review was actually 'discovered' by Chief Justice Marshall of the United States, in interpreting the American Constitution. The American Constitution, unlike the British or the Indian Constitutions rests on the principle of separation of powers and checks and balances The Indian Constitution makers had opted for the British Parliamentary System. This decision was nearly unanimous. It may therefore seem baffling and astonishing that the Indian Constitution makers imported the principle of Judicial Review which is the specific feature of the American system of government.

As said above this doctrine of judicial review was enunciated by John Marshall C.J. in 1803. It is not expressly provided for in the Constitution. The Constitution in Art. 6 only provides as follows:

"This Constitution, and the laws of the United States which shall be made in pursuance thereof and all treaties made, or which shall be made, under the authority of the United States, shall be the supreme law of the land; and the judges in every state shall be bound thereby:anything in the Constitution or laws of any state to the contrary not with standing.

From this provision Marshall deduced the doctrine of Judicial Review. The logic and reasoning of this enunciation deserve detailed description, and are given below:

(1) The government of the United States is a government of laws, and not of men. It will certainly cease to be so, if the laws furnish no remedy for the violation of a vested legal right.

(2) The Constitution vests the whole judicial power of the United States in one Supreme Court and such inferior courts as congress shall from time to time ordain and establish. The powers of the legislature are defined and limited and that those limits may not be mistaken or forgotten, the Constitution is written.

(3) If an act of the legislature repugant to the Constitution is void, it does not bind the courts and obliges them to give it effect.

(4) It is the province and duty of the judicial department to say what the law is. Those who apply the rule to particular cases must of necessity expand and interpret that rule. If two laws conflict with each other, the courts must decide on the operation of each.

(5) So if a law be in opposition to the Constitution, the Constitution and not such ordinary law, must govern the case to which they both apply.

(6) A law repugnant to the Constitution is void and that courts, as well as other departments, are bound by that instrument. This principle is essential to all written Constitutions.

Judicial Review in India
Sources of the Power

In the Indian Constitution there is no express provision empowering the courts to invalidate laws. However, the power of judicial review flows from various features of the Constitution.

(1) The Constitution has created the organs of government with definite limitations. Any transgression of these limitations invites the court to void them.

The direct source of court's intervention is Art. 13

(2) Which declare, that any law, which contravenes any of the provisions of the fundamental rights shall be void, In the Romesh Thapar Vs. State of Madras[5] the Supreme Court laid down two other rules:

(*a*) Even without the specific provision In Art. 13 (2), the court would have the power to declare any law, which takes away or abridges any of the fundamental rights, as invalid.

(*b*) Supreme Court will have the original jurisdiction in cases alleging breach of fundamental rights.

(2) Federal polity and the division of powers between the Union and the States. Art. 254 says that in case of inconsistency between Union and state laws in certain cases, the Union law shall prevail.

(3) The limitations imposed by the Constitution upon the powers of legislatures are (i) Fundamental rights (ii) Legislative competence and (iii) Specific provisions imposing limitations relating to particular matters.

(4) The basic structure theory enunciated by the Supreme Court in the Keshvanand Bharathi case (1973) debars the Parliament from adopting Constitutional amendment, which may violate or infringe the basic structure of the Constitution.

In this way, although the Constitution has not conferred the power of Judicial Review on the courts, the judiciary has *ipsofacto* the jurisdiction in all cases involving the breach of the Constitution. The Supreme court, therefore, is regarded as the guardian of the Constitution and protector of the Fundamental Rights of the people.

It is notable that until 1961 no case in original jurisdiction involving Union-State relations had been filed before the Supreme Court.

The cases alleging breach of provisions of fundamental rights filed in original jurisdiction in the Supreme Court have been numerous and many of them a landmark. There already exists a voluminous body of case law dealing with this subject. In one of the earliest cases filed before the Supreme Court, Romesh Thapar Vs. State of Madras (1950), Supreme Court entertained the writ petition alleging violation of the fundamental rights to personal liberty under Art. 21 and said, "under the Constitution the Supreme court is constituted the protector and guarantor of fundamental rights, and it cannot, consistently with the responsibility so laid upon it, refuse to entertain applications seeking protection against infringement of such rights, although such applications are made to the court in the first instance without resort to a High, Court having concurrent jurisdiction in the matter"[6]

The wording of Art. 32, shows that the Supreme Court can be moved to grant a suitable relief in respect of the Fundamental Rights mentioned in part III of the Constitution.

The court said that since the right to move the Supreme Court, in case of violation of the fundamental right, is itself a fundamental right, the Supreme Court is constituted the protector and guarantor of fundamental rights, and it is the duty of the Supreme Court to grant relief under Art. 32. Where the existence of the fundamental right and its breach is prima-facie established, the Supreme Court cannot refuse a petition under Art. 32 on the ground that such application has been made to the Supreme Court in the first instance, without resort to the High court under Art. 226.

In the interpretation of fundamental rights provisions the Supreme Court has extended the metes, and bounds of every provision. This process can be seen in relation to Art.14 where the Supreme Court has held that the right to equality does not preclude the state from classifying persons for legitimate purposes provided the law deals equally with members of any well defined class.

In numerous cases it has held that the reservation of posts and seats in Educational Institutions in favour of schedule castes and Tribes and other backward classes is no breach of equality provided the reservation does not cover more than one half of the posts and seats and the creamy layer of the caste is excluded from the benefit of reservation.

By way of illustration the interpretations of Art. 21 in numerous cases may be noted which have had the effect of expanding the scope of Art. 21 guaranteeing the right of life and personal liberty of every person, immensely. The right to life which is the most fundamental of all is also the most difficult to define. Certainly it cannot be confined to a guarantee against the taking away of life; it must have a wider application.

The Supreme Court held in 1981 in Francis Coralie's case. "....... the right to life include the right to live with human dignity and all that goes along with it, namely, the bare necessities of life such as adequate nutrition, clothing and shelter over the head and facilities for reading, writing and expressing one self in diverse forms, reely moving' about and mixing and co-mingling with fellow human beings."?[7]

Both right to life and personal liberty have been given the ardent and the most liberal interpretation by our courts. Notable among them are enumerated below:

(*a*) ***Rights of Prisoners:*** have been recognised by the courts in several cases. These range from a bar on hand cuffing, wrongful detention torture unreasoable prison restriction to solitary confinement.

(*b*) ***Right to legal aid :*** An accused has a right to free legal aid at the cost of the state if he cannot afford legal services for reasons of poverty, indigence or incommunicado situation. It is, a part of fair, just and reasonable procedure under Art. 21.

(*c*) ***Right to Speedy trail :*** This right came up in a series of cases involving undertrials, who were in jail for a period longer than the maximum sentence that could be imposed on conviction.

(*d*) ***Natural Justice:*** It is implicit in Art. 21 and comprises two important principles, one being, no one should be condemned unheard and secondly no one should be a judge in his own cause. It was the Maneka Gandhi's case (1978) where it was said in unequivocal terms that Art. 21 includes the basic principles of natural justice, even if not said in so many words:

(*e*) ***Compensation:*** Right to claim monetary compensation for the violation of the rights in Art. (21 has been recognised.

(*f*) ***Right to know:*** It has been recognised in Art. 21 as a necessary ingredient of participatory democracy.

(*g*) ***Environment:*** The right to life, public health and ecology, have been held to have priority over unemployment and loss of revenue.

Of late several new rights have been recognised, which include:

- Right to shelter
- Right to potable water
- Right to education
- Right to electricity
- Right to pension

Right to Pension

In November 2008, the Madurai Bench of the Madras High Court ordered the Payment of Pension and other retirement benefits to one, N. Sunthi of the former sweeper with the Aruppu Kotti, Municipality who since her retirement on July 31, 1977 had been struggling to get the monthly pension and other emoluments for more than 30 years. The reason given for denial of these terminal benefits to her was that her service records were misplaced. On the High Court's intervention her service records were recreated and the proposal for disbursing monthly pension processed with in a prescribed time frame.[8]

In a landmark judgement, the Bombay High Court held (December 2008 that pension is a vital aspect of social security and that the right to receive it constitutes parts of the right to life under the constitution. It held that pension must be paid regularly in first week of the month. It did not accept the argument of the Solapur Municipal Corporation that it was in financial difficulties and could pay by the 15th and not the first. The court said, "Deprive a pensioner, of the payment and you deprive him or her of the right to life. Delayed pensionary payments place a pensioner in a position of uncertainty and dependence which impinges on the quality of life under Article 21, and the right to dignified existence of the aged."

It directed the transport undertaking of Solapur Municipal Corporation to deposit, the pension of 13 retired employees on the first day of the succeeding month or latest by the 7th day.[9]

Art. 31 Right to Property

The interpretations of Right to property in Art. 31 have been so controversial that as and when a judicial ruling was handed down, a constitutional amendment had to be made to counter it. At last, in 1978 Art. 31 itself was deleted from the chapter on Fundamental Rights, by the 44th constitutional amendment.

The validity of this amendment itself has now been challenged in a PIL petition resting on the Basic Structure Theory, more than three decades after its enactment.[10]

In nutshell, it may be said that the provisions of the fundamental rights were explained, elaborated and expanded by the process of judicial review. It is not possible to understand the constitutional provisions without reference to the relevant case law. As a result, there are today whole treatises on individul rights such as Equality, Liberty, Property, Religious freedom etc.

Abuses of Judicial Review

However Judicial Review has not been an unmixed blessing. It has had its darker sides which show the wisdom and foresight of our Constitution makers who endeavoured to limit it as much as possible.

(*a*) They adopted such a detailed Constitution that there was left not much scope for judicial interpretation.

(*b*) They expressly barred judicial review in specified Articles of the Constitution.

(*c*) The 25th, 39th and 42nd constitutional amendments were directly aimed at excluding judicial review.

(*d*) They in preference to the doctrine of due process of law opted for procedure estabiished by law in depriving any person of life, liberty or property.

(*e*) They prescribed the rights and liberties of the people and also the permissible limits on them, rather than leaving it to court to deduce these limitations by way of interpretation.

(*f*) The Constitution leaves no scope for applying the vague and indefinite principle of natural justice in defining rights and duties.

With remarkable intelligence and ingenuity the superior bench and bar in India have been able to circumvent and supersede the design of the Constitution makers to delimit the power of Judicial Review, so much so that judicial review is presently regarded as an element of the Basic structure of the Constitution, or an essential feature thereof. Any attempt to exclude judicial review of any constitutional provision, as in the 25th, 39th and 42nd Amendments, has proved to be abortive.

Undoubtedly, the Judicial Review has been of vital importance in protecting the civil liberties and fundamental rights of the people even of the prisoners and detenues and of the under trials, specially during the period of Emergency (1962-1976). It has held out safeguards against such draconian laws as MISA,TADA,. FERRA and the like. But sadly, enough, the judicial intervention has been of the greatest benefit to the criminals, gangsters, Mafia dons and even terrorists.

In the economic sphere judicial review appears to be opposed to progress and economic reforms. It has stood in the way of alteration of property relations and thereby hampered the course of social engineering by peaceful and constitutional means. Thus, it has had the effect of delaying land reforms and blocking such measures as nationalization of banks, abolition of privy, purses and introduction of OBC quota in educational institutions and services.

Legal Process:

The legal process in India, as in all liberal democracies, is heavily to the advantage of the affluent sections of society. It is so expensive, cumbersome and time consuming as to be beyond the capacity of the common man so that only the rich can afford it. The lawyer class is the immediate beneficiary and has a vested interest in maintaining it with all its technical superfluities and vestiges of colonial past. It is, therefore, little surprising that judicial review has been largely to the benefit of the upper sections of the society and specially to the financial enrichment of the class of constitutional lawyers.

Judicial Activism

One positive contribution of judicial review is what is popularly called Judicial Activism. Unlike judicial review, judicial activism is not a legal term. It represents only an attitude or approach of the judge handling a case and monitoring its progress. It has its roots in the power of judicial review but it takes on its attributes from the personality and working style of the judge in question. This is why judicial activism is the characteristic of the judge rather than of the judicial system.

Judicial Activism denotes that the judge or the bench, at its discretion, without manifest violation of law, may depart from the norms of standard practice, in the admission and disposal of a writ petition, motivated by considerations of natural or social justice. For instance the judge may admit a petition moved on behalf of the aggrieved person or persons, by some NGO or a public spirited individual. The petition may even be sent by the aggrieved person on a postcard, on plain paper, or even by telegram. The court may even take cognizance of a situation *suo motto*. In every case the purpose should be the protection of a wider public interest.

The disposal of the petition results in what may be called instant justice.

In this way judicial activism has the potential of transforming the courts of law into courts of justice. This accounts for its nationwide popularity.

Judicial Over-Reach

The instrumentality of public interest litigation is now being widely employed to secure public interest and social justice. The danger inherent in this situation is that the judiciary may overstep its limits in which case judicial activism is transformed into judicial over-reach.

Addressing a conference of Chief Ministers and Chief Justices of High Courts at the Vigyan Bhawn in New Delhi, on April 18, 2007, P.M. Mahmohan Singh told the Judiciary not to overstep its limits. He said the dividing line between the Judicial Activism and Judicial Over-Reach is a thin one. A takeover of the functions of another organ may at times become a case of over-reach. He cautioned the Judiciary against substituting its power of mandamus, with the takeover of the functions of other organs.[11]

In practice it may be difficult to divide judicial review from judicial over-reach.

In the Golaknath case (1967), the majority of the judges held that Art. 368 laid down only the procedure of amendment of the Constitution, but did not confer the power of constitutional amendment on Parliament.

On the contrary, many of the judges on the Keshavanand (1973) Bench held that Art. 368 contained expressly the procedure of amendment of the Constitution, and impliedly, the power of amendment of the Constitution.

One may say that the Keshavanand view was a case of Judicial Review, while the Golaknath view was one of Judicial over-reach.

The other examples of the judiciary encroaching into the field of power of another organ, from recent experience, are given below:

(*1*) The Supreme Court issuing the summons to the Loksabha speaker Somnath Chatterjee on the issue of expulsion of 11, M.Ps in the cash-on-camera scandal.

(2) The Supreme Court reversing the pardon granted to congress leader by the Governor in Andhra Pradesh.

(*3*) In the Jain Hawala case, in the 1990's chief Justice J.S. Verma laying down the procedure for appointment of the CBI Director and in a bid to insulate it from politicals pressure, placing the agency (C.B.I.) under the supervision of the central vigilance commission.

(*4*) In the Visakha case, Justice Verma laying down the law for the safeguards that must be provided to women at work places against sexual harassment.

(*5*) In the D.K Basu case Justice K.S. Anand coming up with the law to check misuse of police powers to arrest and detain.[12]

(*6*) The Supreme Court reviewing constitutional amendments and annulling portions of constitutional amendments, such as 25th, 39th and 42nd amendment.

(*7*) The directions given by the apex court in the assembly proceedings in U.P. in 1998 and Jharkhand in 2005.

(8) The Supreme Court denouncing the police firing in, Nandigram on 14th March 2006 "as unnecessary and unconstitutional."

(9) The Supreme Court describing Bihar Governor Buta Singh's report to the centre recommending imposition of the President's Rule in the State under Art. 356, as unconstitutional.

These examples can be multiplied endlessly.

In a recent judgement,[13] a two member, Bench comprising A.K. Mathur and Markendey Katju, J.J. Vehemently deprecated the tendency of courts to rule on local issues like nursery admissions, the size of speed breakers on Delhi road's and auto rickshaw overcharging, and said judges should know their "limits" and not try to run the government. The Bench said, ".......we are repeatedly coming across cases where judges are unjustifiably trying to perform executive or legislative functions."

"In our opinion, this is clearly unconstitutional. In the name of judicial activism, judges cannot cross their limits and try to take over functions which belong to another organ of the state."

The Bench returned to the same theme in another case and said "courts are not a remedy for all evils. People will laugh at us". They further said there are many evils that cannot be solved by courts but (they can be) by the public who can either use their creativity or resort to demoractic methods like holding a peaceful march.This is Democracy, where elections are held. You vote for a better government if you are not satisfied with the governance.[14]

The public and political reactions to the growing cases of judicial over-reach can be seen in the resentment and frustration expressed in the parliamentary debates on legislative executive judicial relations held in the Lok Sabha on 7.12.2006 and 3.12.2007.

In the debates held on 3.12.2087, the MPs cutting across party lines asserted the supremacy of Parliament on the ground that it represented the "will of the people" and warned that judicial "activism" might become "despotism" if not checked in time. The debate was raised on a motion affirming the need of "harmonious functioning" of legislature, judiciary and executive. It brought to the fore the rising impatience of MPs over their turf being curtailed by pro-active courts ruling on lissues on issuse ranging from reservations to road maintenance and water supply. Most speakers invoked the "separation of powers" doctrine to insist that the judiciary was over stepping its mandate.

The MPs reflected the anger of members over recent (2007-2008) showdowns over OBCs reservations in Central Higher Educational Institutions, demolitions and sealings in the capital, ouster of AIIMs Director, P. Venugopal and monitoring environmental norms. Warning that Judicial Activism overtaking the legislature and the executive congress M.P. Kishore Chandra Deo warned,. "It is the worst tyranny that could engulf the system"[15]

References

1. K.C. Wheare, Modern Constitutions, HUL Series, O.U.P. 1956; p. 149.
2. *Ibid*, p. 152.
3. *Ibid*, p. 175.
4. D.D. Basu: Introduction to the Constitution of India, Prentice Hall, 1990, p. 106.
5. AIR 1950 (1950) S.C.R. 594.
6. Romesh Thapar Vs. State of Madras (1950) S.C.R. Vol. 1. pp. 594-605.
7. *Hindustan Times*, Lucknow, 3.12.1998.
8. *The Hindu*, 12.11.2008.
9. *The Times of India*. dated December 24, 2008.

10. *The Hindu,* 28.02.2008
11. *Hindustan Times,* Lucknow, 9.3.2007
12. *Times of India,* 13.12.2007.
13. *Times of India,* 11.12.2007.
14. *Hindustan Times.* 3.4.2008.
15. *Times of India,* Allahabad, 5.12.2007.

3

Judicial Activism and its Dimensions

From Judicial review to judicial activism is partly a matter of temperament and partly a matter of motivation.

The temperament is a habit of mind to look beyond bare law, to be guided by a sense of social morality. The motivation is a social purpose, a wider cause, the cause of social justice.

In the exercise of the power of judicial review two types of behavioural patterns can be seen: (a) judicial self restraint, and (b) Judicial-activism

Judicial self restraint is the classical or traditional virtue of judicial behaviour. It is the other name for standard behaviour. It means that the courts will be careful in defining their jurisdiction and shy in expanding it and will observe restraint in interfering with legislative will or executive action. The Supreme Court in U.S.A. made it a rule not to decide "political cases", so as to keep clear off political controversies of the day. It refused to render "advisory opinion" to the executive in any case. It refused, for instance, to advise as to the lawful duration of Military Occupation in Cuba, holding it to be, the function of the political branch of the government. Of course, the court itself is the judge as to what constitues a political question.

Judicial self restraint, can be seen in the following built in rules in the exercise of the power of judicial review—

(1) Laws are not scrutinised by the courts suo moto but only when impugned in actual litigation.

(2) Laws shall be invalidated only when their unconstitutionality is clear beyond all reasonable doubt.

(3) Law as a whole need not be voided but only those portions of it which are violative of the Constitution unless of course the latter can not be severed from the rest without doing violence to the whole.

(4) The courts shall hot decide political questions, that is, deny itself jurisdietion in cases involving political controversies.

(5) The function of the court is to examine the constitutionality of laws, not to ensure justice or good government. So long as the laws are within the terms of the Constitution, the court does not interfere even if laws are oppressive, unjust or unwise.

Marshall CJ of the USA is said to be the leading exponent of the rule of judicial neutrality. In his verdict in Osborne Vs. Bank of The United States, he said, "the judicial department has no will in any case...... judicial power is never exercised for the purpose of giving effect to the will of the judge, always for the purpose of giving effect to the will of the legislature"[1]

Numerous judicial pronouncements can be cited in support of the view that the function of the judiciary is only to find the law and declare it, and not make the law. In the South-West Africa case, the I.C.J. itself said, "The duty of the court is to apply the law as it finds it, not to make it" (1966). Legislation belongs to the province of the legislature exclusively.

The judiciary must restrict itself to interpreting the law and applying it to the case before it, interpret it in terms of the intention of the law makers. "The intention of Parliament is to be discovered by a body of independent persons, free from any direct interest in the result, and trained by long years of practice to standards of judgment by which that intention may be tested".[2]

In India also, judicial self restraint in the above sense has been accepted as a necessary element in the theory and practice of judicial review. The judges have tended to keep aloof from social life and avoid mixing up with the public. They have scrupulously refrained from taking part in public debates involving political controversies: In the case impugning the constitutional validity of the Tashkent Agreement (1966) the Supreme Court presided over by Mr. Justice Gajendragadkar, CJ refrained from giving any verdict on the ground that it was a political question and the Court will not decide political controversies. These questions, it added, are the exclusive domain of the political branch of the government. It may be recalled here that the Tashkent agreement involved cession of national territory in favour of Pakistan, which had been recaptured from the illegal Pakistani possession.

In an Advisory Opinion given earlier (1960) the Supreme Court had laid down the principle that cession of national territory in favour of a foreign state could not be lawfully made by means of an executive agreement or treaty but required a Constitutional amendment in accordance with the prescribed procedure.[3] Public opinion was greatly dismayed at this abdication of authority and responsibility by the highest court of the land in a matter involving the territorial integrity and, sovereignty of the country. But the Supreme Court stood firm on its resolve not to enter into political controversies. The result was that when five years later the government made a similar cession of national territory under the Shimla Agreement, (1972) no one even cared to approach the apex court. The decision in the case involving the Tashkent, Agreement was the highest water mark of judicial self restraint.

In reference to Art. 143, the Court reserved its right to refuse to give an Advisory Opinion. In re Special Courts Bill, the Supreme Court expressed doubts on whether it should answer references which are vague general and of omnibus character.[4] In re Ayodhya Ramjanmabhoomi case (1993)[5] the court refused to answer the reference made to it, namely, whether or not a, Hindu temple existed at the site prior to the construction of a mosque there.

In this way the court has tried to keep clear of political controversies of the day.

Judicial Activism

However judicial self restraint is not a rule; it is a case of auto limitation. It necessarily depends,on the temperament, education, training and philosophy of the individual judges. It also depends on the balance of political forces in the other branches of government. In times of political instability, the courts tend to be more activist, reaching more intrusively into daily life of citizens or restricting or directing the legislature and the executive in what they, could do.

Judicial activism can be both negative and positive. Negatively, the court can restrict the legislature and the executive in what they could do. Positively, the court by its rulings could extend the role of what the government could do even when the government did not want to do it. For instance, on March 18, 1985 the Supreme Court asked the Union government to file a statement within two weeks explaining how it proposed to solve the problem of pre-

1964 pensioners and their widows and dependent children in consonance with the principles of social justice.[6]

Activism was advocated as a philosophy of "Practical Idealism" by Rudolf Eucken (1846-1926) and has appeared in diverse forms. In the judicial sphere it has found expression in the U.S.A., India and in many other countries in the form of normative judgements going beyond the public policy of the governntent of the day or pulling up the executive for its lapses, excesses, and failures.

Justice Michael Kirby of Australia says, "The law abhors a vacuum. Into a vacuum left by the failure of the other branches of government to respond to urgent legal and social needs, the courts have sometimes stepped in"[7]

The misuse of powers assigned to different functionaries has, according to senior advocate Shanti Bhushan, necessitated judicial activism.

"As the apathy and indifference of the executive and the officers of the government at various levels denies the underprivileged, disadvantaged and poor sections the benefit of social legislation, Judicial activism is essential for safeguarding, and ensuring that these laws are implemented" concurs senior advocate, K.K. Venugopal. I.K. Gujral regards the phenomenon as "an expression of the failure of the government and the administration to take the timely and right step".[8]

According to Justice Michael Kirby, "the tension between judicial activism and judicial restraint has been present since the foundation of the Republic and the creation of the US Supreme Court".[9]

In the early years of 20th century, the judicial activists of the US Court impeded legislation enacted by the US Congress or state legislation, dealing with social or economic affairs.[10] Thus legislation governing child labour, worker's hours, and worker's rights were consistently struck down as being violations of the commerce clause of the US Constitution or the judicially created doctrine of "liberty of contract" under the due process clause of the US Constitution. A well known example of this kind of judicial activism is the decision of the Supreme Court in *Lochner Vs. New York*[11] where the Supreme Court invalidated legislation regulating the hours that bakers could work. In more recent years it is the judicial activism of the Liberal school which has attracted the ire of Presidents Nixon, ford, and Reagan. Many a political slogan was devised in the USA to attack what was seen as the "adventurism'" of the Supreme Court under Chief Justice Warren. It was the Warren court which took many bold steps in the interpretation of the US. Constitution in matters such as school desegregation, re-apportionment of unequal congressional districts; prohibition of school prayers; aid to parochial schools and restraints on police invasions of individual civil liberties. The period of activism that began with the *Brown* decision in 1954 was followed by far more and far reaching decisions. In 1971the Swann decision legitimated massive busing of children to overcome segregation in a large city.[12] In 1973 the Burger court ruled in *Roe and Doe* that just about all state laws on abortion were unconstitutional and decreed that state laws must treat each third of the pregnancy period according to different standards. In 1975 it applied the limitations of "due process" to the public schools, which now, could not, restrict the constitutional rights of students by suspending or expelling them without at least something resembling a criminal trial.[13] In the same year, it ruled, in the first of a series of important cases on, the rights of mental patients, that harmless persons could not be detained involuntarily in mental hospitals.[14]

Contents of Judicial Activism

Judicial activism denotes that the courts trespass into the roles going beyond the strict function of interpretation of the law, such as—

(1) law making.

(2) laying down of policy.

(3) regulation and control of the executive agencies and bodies.

(4) ensuring compliance with directions and orders given.

Law Making is outside of the court's ambit of jurisdiction. It has the power of interpretation, of law and applying it to the, case in hand, The interpretation of the law may involve expanding its metes and bounds and in this way creation of new rules of law. Judicial legislation is inherent in judicial interpretation Judicial interpretation may even have the effect of amending the Constitution informally. The American Supreme Court arrogated to itself the power of judicial review and vested the Federal government with "implied powers" by a constructive interpretation of the Constitution. These are the earliest instances of judicial activism in the field of Constitutional law. The reason for this unconscious intrusion, of the Judiciary into the realm of law making is that, in practice, it is not possible to separate the interpretation of law from the characteristic beliefs of the class to which the judge belongs. To quote Laski, "The judge is not an automatic and passionless being who, as he does his work, of interpretation, finds a meaning in law which is fixed and invariable. For were the law so fixed and so invariable, men would not go to court; it is the doubt of what the law is that provides the courts with their work. And this means that the judge is, even if incompletely and indirectly, making law no less than merely announcing it".[15]

In this way judicial decisions provide the source of new law, and not merely evidence of the existing one. By this process, judiciary helps to adapt and adjust thc Constitution to the dynamics of socio-economic change. Speaking of the American Supreme Court, one writer has remarked that it has served as the continuous constitutional convention.

According to Cardozo, "a judge is an arbitrator who adjudicates individual causes, an interpreter of the Constitution which gives him an opportunity to canvass the full panoply of his value system, a legislator making law and a pace setter for future action"[16]

Rhode and Spaeth observe that the courts being hiearchically structured, the apex court having a broader jurisdiction is most concerned with policy making.[17]

The courts orders or providirig fresh air to citizens[18] on setting up of an independent authority with wide powers to tackle tanneries pollution[19], its role in sensitising the central investing agencies to discharge their legal obligations in the *Hawala case,* in the *Medical equipment scam* to the tune of over Rs. 5,000 crores[20] and its various judgments ranging from the need for a uniform civil code, preservation of historical monuments, like Taj Mahal, cleaning and keeping the metropolis more hygienic, directing the eviction of unauthorised occupation of government bungalows, interim compensation to rape victims and their *incamera* trial, punishing senior Karnataka IAS officer Vasudevan and former Chairman of the Bar Council of India, V. C. Mishra for contempt, and puncturing the ego of the Chief Election Commissioner, T.N. Shesan, are evidences which prove that the activist role of the judiciary touches upon policy making and even monitoring and supervising the executive agencies in their work of investigation and reporting.[21]

In Rajendra Prasad Vs. U.P. (1979) the Supreme Court observed –

"The activists believe that if the legislative text is too bald to be self-acting, the judge must make the provisions viable by evolution of supplementary principles even if it may appear to possess the flavour of law making".[21]

The court directed the local authorities that "all those who come to see Taj be provided clean water, sanitation and good roads", and a series of orders like "Get back to us if government drags feet in sanctioning prosecution (in Hawala case) ensure safety of chakmas and process their citizenship applications, sort out Cauvery tangle in 48 hcurs", are all instances of the courts trespassing into the legislative, and executive spheres, and this intrusion is called Judicial Activism. It is an expression of the failure of the government, and the administration to take the timely, and right step. There would have been no ground for judicial activism had the executive and legislature not failed. The misuse of powers assigned to different functionaries has, according to Mr. Shanti Bhushan, necessitated judicial activism.

A second element in judicial activism is the widening of the jurisdiction of the court by which the court takes cognizance of and decides matters brought before it. The jurisdiction of the court is carefully defined by the Constitution and the law, but within the parameters of the law and the Constitution the apex court has the power to decide its own jurisdiction and thereby widen its own sphere of activity.

Question of Locus Standi

Traditionally, the locus standi of the petitioner is regarded as a decisive factor in the admission of the case before the court. The strict constructionist court would satisfy itself that, the petitioner, has suffered definite legal injury so that he stands to gain from the decision of the court, before admitting the case. Then alone he can be said to have a locus standi. Unless any of the legal rights of the petitioner is infringed he can not be said to have a locus standi in the case.

In the Bearer Bonds case[23] the Supreme Court was called upon to examine the economic and fiscal policies of the state and to probe into social and ethical morality of fiscal measures. The petitioners in this case were (1) a senior practising Supreme Court Advocate, (2) Editor of a Weekly Magazine and (3) A social worker. None of them could be said to have had a *locus standi* in the case in the strict traditional sense. Their locus standi however, flowed not from any individual personal interest in the case but from the general public interest in the matter. As Justice D.A. Desai said, 'would the citizens of this country deny the court such jurisdiction wherein an economic immorality compounded by the bankruptcy of tax recovery machinery was demonstrably established."[24] The court agreed to admit the petition and to examine the question posed before it.

In another case the Workers Union of Sindri Fertilizers Factory challenged the legality of sale of certain plant and equipment of the factory on the ground *inter alia* that the manner in which the sale was brought about had inflicted a huge loss on public, exchequer. The majority considered it unnecessary to examine, the question of *locus standi*, of the Workers, Union to challenge the sale because in its opinion the sale was not vitiated by any arbitrariness or *mala fide*, but kept the question open, observing that if and when the sale of a public property was found to be vitiated by *mala fide*, it would be necessary to examine the larger question as to who has the right to complain.[25] However Krishna Iyer J in a concurring opinion asked, what, if any, are the fundamental rights of the workman affected by the employer's sale of machinery whose immediate impact may be conversion of permanent employment into precarious service and eventual exit?

The process of Public Interest Litigation (PIL) was initiated by V.R. Krishna lyer J. He observed in the Fertilizer Corporation Kamgar Union Vs. Union of India, "Law is a social auditor and this audit function can be put into action only when someone with real public interest ignites the jurisdiction of the court".[26] The thread was picked up by P.N. Bhagwati J. who is supposed to be the father of this revolutionary concept. He explained the case for the PIL in the celebrated *S.P. Gupta case,* holding that "the court has to innovate new methods, and devise new strategies for the purpose of providing access to justice to large masses of people who are, denied their basic human rights and to whom freedom and liberty have no meaning. The only way in which this can be done is by entertaining writ petitions and even letters from public spirited citizens seeking judicial redress on behalf of those who have suffered a legal wrong or an injury".[27]

The principle of *locus standi* which narrowed the jurisdiction of the court to cases filed by the aggrieved person only and exclusively thus was thrown overboard. The court was now agreeable to admit petitions from public spirited citizens arid bodies thereof on behalf of the suffering person or class of persons provided there was sufficient public interest involved in the case. This was the beginning of the PIL which became a running stream to the higher courts.

However Justice Bhagwati's ruling in favour of the PIL did not disregard any express provision of the Constitution. It was rather derived from the ambiguity of the language used in Art.32 providing for the writ jurisdiction of the Supreme Court. The Article, *inter alia*, says, "The right to move the Supreme Court by appropriate proceedings for the enforcement of the rights conferred, by this part is guaranteed". The article is silent as to who is entitled to initiate the proceedings for the enforcement of the fundamental rights. Similar ambiguity exists in respect of proceedings in the High Courts under Art. 226.

Taking advantage of this ambiguity the activist judiciary in India has allowed and admitted public interest litigation by public spirited lawyers, journalists, researchers, social activists, social scientists, NGO's and even a student of crminology.

The Jain Hawala case which had come to light in March 1991 with the arrest of one Kashmiri militant, Ashfaq Hussain Lone of the Hizbul Mujahideen, was activated only when two journalists, Vineet Narain and Rajinder Puri, on a public interest litigation, moved the apex court to monitor the progress of the CBI investigations into this scandal.[28]

The People's Union for civil liberties (PUCL) has been continually sponsoring the PIL, for instance, the scam relating to the over Rs. 5,000 crore medical equipment import by the Union Health Ministry.[29] The environmentalist lawyer, M.C. Mehta filed a PIL asking, the Supreme Court to direct all "the water polluting industries in Delhi to contribute their share of Rs.40 crore for setting up 28 common effluent treatment plants or face closure of their units.[30] The Vellore citizens forum in another PIL arraigned the tanneries located in five districts of Tamilnadu for causing pollutition.[31] Mr. M.C. Mehta in another P.I. petition brought 7 industries employing children below the age of 13 years in their units before the bar of the Supreme Court.[32] It took cognizance of a newspaper report stating that electroplating industries in Subhash Nagar area of West Delhi were employing child labour on meager daily wages between Rs. 8 to Rs. 10, and directed the Deputy Commissiorier of police and the Labour Commissioner to investigate the report.[33] In one case, the Paschim Vihar Residence Welfare Association filed a PIP and subsequently several other residence welfare associations joined in. They sought enforcement and implementation of the MCD (Municipal Council of Delhi) order banning PVC trade in the Jawalapuri and adjoining areas in West Delhi.[34] In one "unique" case a PIP was filed by the Central Commissioner for Scheduled Castes and Tribes charging the Central government and the state authorities with violating the Constitution and the law so far as they related to the tribals, and denying them the basic right to life.[35] In one case a Judge of the Delhi High Court, Mrs. Usha Mehra, sitting singly, passed an order *suo motto* on October 8, 1996 after reading newspaper reports regarding deaths due to dengue haemmorragic fever, cerebral malaria, hepatitis, malaria and typhoid.[36]

A third year Bachelor of Law Student of Criminology who had visited the VishakapattanamCentral Jail on 16.02.1985 as part of his Degree course was so moved by the conditions of prisoners living in the jail that he filed a petition in H.C. of AndhraPradesh.[37]

Results of the PIL

The PIL enabled the under privileged and the downtrodden to secure access to the courts through the agency of a public spirited person or an organisation acting *bonafide* in the public interest.

It was said in favour of the PIL that if the doors of the court are closed to a person who, though not individually affected, is acting bonafide in bringing cases to the court involving grave injustice resulting from negligence or callousness or inefficiency of public officials, governmental bodies and authorities would be left free to violate the law with impurity. Such a situation would be subversive of the Rule of Law.

Writ Petition: Format and Conveyance

PIL was therefore an expression of judicial activism. An equally revolutionary innovation in the judicial process was the acceptance of letters, telegrams and even post cards, as written petitions. In one case, a letter sent from jail was treated as a writ petition (Sunil Batra's case).

The Andhra High Court treated as writ petition a telegram sent by a village woman, whose son was allegedly detained by the police.[38] The same court, in another case, treated a printed pamphlet as writ petition, a printed pamphlet posted to the court by a domestic servant from Tirupati. The acting Chief Justice, Mr. Justice P. Chenappa Reddy and Mr. Justice A. Seetarama Reddy who accepted the two postal communications as writ petitions directed the state government to file its counter affidavit and also asked the Collector of Chittoor district to file his inquiry report within two weeks.[39]

It was Mr. Hidayatullah who during his tenure as the Chief Justice of the Supreme Court, had made it a law to accept postal communication as a writ petition when he received a postcard from Mungher jail in Bihar from the socialist M.P. Madhu Limaye, challenging his detention.[40]

A UNI report dated 16 July 1985 describes the scene in the Cochin High Court.

"As the usual hustle in the high court dies down in the afternoon, an officer passes a bundle of letters to a judge who scans each one and dictates orders.

"Dealing with letter petitions has settled into a daily routine. The problems scribbled on the letters are diverse: a decrepit school building is about to collapse, a greedy tehsildar is denying a widow her husband's gratuity, a constable is harassing a poor woman.Whatever the complaint, the communication is treated as a writ petition. The result: speedy dispensation of justice.

Kanthimathi Amma's case was a typical example. She was ranked 86th in the list published by the Kerala Public Service Commission for appointment to the lower grade service. In course of time many of those ranked lower got jobs but not Kanthimathi.

Instead of filing a writ petition Kanthimathi posted a letter to the Chief Justice. Treating it as a writ petition under article 226 of the Constitution, the court issued summons to the state and the service commission.

The Commission raised elaborate objections to the conversion of a letter into a writ petition. Mr. Justice P. Subramanian Poti who was the acting Chief Justice then rejected the objection. Rules of procedure, he observed, were not immune from being waived and must necessarily be waived in the interest of justice by a court sitting under article 226 of the Constitution.

His successor, Mr. Justice Bhaskaran received letters from exasperated citizens from all walks of life: Sales girls compelled to work for 14 hours a day, people put to difficulties by failure of civic amenities, families claiming compensation for deaths in road accidents, all have sought and received relief.

Latters pour by the dozen, and are screened before being sent to the judge."[41]

This judicial innovation has thrown open the portals of the court to the poor and the ignorant alike.

Mr. Justice P. N. Bhagwati of the Supreme Court some three years ago on the basis of a letter, took up the case of workers employed in the construction of the Asian games village.[42]

Dismissing the argument that the practice would aggravte the arrears, he observed "no state has a right to tell its citizens that we will not help the poor to come to the courts for seeking justice."[43]

There are instances of the courts acting *suo motto,* simply on seeing newspaper reports. Reference has already been made to Mrs. Usha Mehar of Delhi Hight Court, who, on reading newspaper reports of deaths resulting from the spreading dengue fever, issued notices to the Delhi Administration.[44] Similarly in the case relating to the exploitation of the child labour in electroplating industry in Subhash nagar area of West Delhi, the Delhi High Court issued notice merely on the basis of a newspaper report.[45]

In a landmark judgement delivered on 24, Nov. 2008, the Supreme Court said that courts should not go strictly by the rulebook to deny justice to the deserving litigant as it would lead to miscarriage of justice. The court said, "All the rules of procedure are the handmaids of justice. The language employed by the draftsman on processual law may be liberal or sringent, but the fact remains that the object of prescribing procedure is to advance the cause of justice." It further said that in a adversarial system no party should ordinarily be denied the opportunity of participating in the process of justice dispensation unless compelled by express and specific language of the statute. The court passed the ruling while upholding the appeal filed by Sambhaji who had challenged a judgement of the Bombay High court, refusing to entertain an application moved by him after the mandatory 90 days prescribed under the civil procedure code in a civil dispute with his relatives.

"The mortality of justice at the hands of law troubles a judge's conscience and points an angry interrogation at the law reformers", the court said (H.T. 25.11.08 and The Times of India 26.11.08).

These innovations have revolutionised the whole concept of *locus standi* and are a tribute to judicial activism of the Indian courts. The insistence is no longer on the administration of law. The emphasis has now shifted to the administration of justice. Courts of law are thus being trnsformed into courts of justice.

The Monitoring Role of the Court

Another dimension of judicial activism came to be seen in the Rs. 65 crore Jain Hawala case. In this the apex court not only admitted a PIL seeking the court's intervention in virtually forcing the CBI to emerge from its stupor and start the investigations in right earnest, it took upon itself to monitor the day to day progress in these investigations, saying, at one stage, "get back to us if the government drags its feet in sanctioning prosecution". In this way, after five years of procrastination the CBI on Jan. 16, 1996 filed charge sheets against 7 top politicians.[46] Earlier chargesheets were filed against 8 of the top bureaucrats.

Justice J.S. Verma, who headed the bench that monitored the case said, after his retirement, that investigating agencies had not done a satisfactory job in probing the ease, otherwise it would not have been possible for all the chargesheets to end up in a fiasco. He claimed that the hawala case was one in which the court had granted complete insulation to the investigating agencies from extraneous circumstances. "We even relieved them of the power of supervision by the highest authority in the executive (the Prime Minister) and yet they could not perform."[47]

In Sunil Batra (II) the court asked the District Magistrate to monitor the many directions it made in the case and suggested that a C.B.I. inquiry be instituted.[48]

In B.R. Kapoor, four commissions were appointed by the court to monitor implementation.[49]

Inquiring and Investigating Role of the Court

In the *Bonded Labour case*,[50] Justice Bhagwati on a letter from Swami Agniwesh drawing attention to the miserable plight of the labourers employed in stone quarries in Faridabad Haryana, first appointed two advocates as Commissioners to visit the stone quarries and report on the living condition of these workers. Later he appointed Dr. Patwardhan of the IIT to carry on the socio-legal investigation. He relied on the power of the Supreme Court to "issue directions or orders" or writs whichever may be propriate for the enforcement of any of the rights confered by this part" (Art. 32), to appoint such commissions of enquiry and to consider their report as evidence. Later speaking in an interview with *Frontline,* Justice Bhagwati defended his action and said" we started appointing commissions of enquiry for the purpose of ascertaining material, data, facts, so that the court can come to a right decision". He stated, "we have been appointing district judges, District Magistrates, journalists, social-scientists and many others as Commissioners to visit the particular place and gather facts and later report to the court".[51]

In the *Sheela Barse V. State of Maharashtra*[52], the Supreme Court directed Miss A.R. Desai, Director, College of Social Work, Nirmala Niketan, Bombay, to make a visit to Bombay Central Jail and interview women prisoners there, with a view to ascertaining the charges of custodial violence to women in the police lock up and jail and submit a report.

The inquiring and investigating role of the Supreme Court has given a new dimension to the concept of judicial activism. The court sometimes selected a District Judge, or a Law Professor, or a journalist, or a social activist or an advocate or a public spirited person or a voluntary agency to gather facts and report to the court.

In the *Babubigha case*[53] *(1983)* the Supreme Court appointed an enquiry committee consisting of Additional Sessions Judge Nalanda, Dr. Vasudha Dhagamwar, and Dr. Jose Kananaikil to report on the atrocities committed on helpless men, women and children by a gang of some forty to fifty anti-social elements who let loose a reign of terror on this harijan settlement in retaliation for their refusal to work as bonded labour for their landlords.

In the *Dehradun Lime Stone Quarries case*[54] the apex court appointed a committee (Aug. 11, 1983) consisting of Shri D.N. Bhargava, Controller General Indian Bureau of Mines, Nagpur, M.S. Gahlaut, Director General, Mines Safety and Col. P. Mishra, Head of the Photo Interpretation Institute to report on the ecological effects of lime stone quarrying. In Siddha Raj Dhadda case the Rajasthan High Court affirmed its duty to investigate in a case, even while it could not order the government to constitute a commission of inquiry.

In the Sunil Batra (I) case Justice Krishna Iyer visited Tihar Jail, Delhi and described the jail conditions in a detailed judgement.[55]

In another case, filed by Smriti Acharya (1990) two judges of the Mizoram bench of Guwahati High Court visited the Aizwal Central Jail.

In the sunil Batra (II) *an amicus curiae* counsel was appointed by the Supreme Court to visit the prison, meet the prisoner see the relevant documents and interview witnesses.

The substance of PIL is to secure justice, social, political and economic, within the parameters of existing law. It has so far succeeded in highlighting the following areas of public concern and remedying them –

(1) cases of injustice to the weak, helpless, illiterate and poor, such as the bonded-labour, undertrial prisoners,

child labour, tribals, workers, destitute women, pavement-dwellers, rickshaw- pullers, even convicts;

(2) environmental pollution, deforestation, upkeep of historic monuments like the Taj, supply of pure water, fresh air;

(3) Issues of wider public policy like the bearer bonds public health hazards, pension, appointment and transfer of judges, consumer protection, price control, product-safety;

(4) indifference, negligence, callousness, atrocities of public and police officials and jail authorities.

(5) loopholes in the machinery of government and administration, specially in the investigation of cases involving the high ups and filing cases against them.

(6) high handedness of the government, for example, in the arbitrary transfer of Enforcement Director, Bezbaruah or in not taking suitable action against those held responsible by Srikrishna Commission Report for triggering communal riots in Bombay in the wake of Ayodhya events in December 1992.

Implications of Judicial Activism

PIL has vastly expanded the ambit of judicial function. It is a multidimensional expansion. The judiciary has as a result trespassed into the jurisdiction of the legislative and the executive branches of the government.

The judiciary has taken on the role of policy-making, which is strictly speaking the domain of the legislature and the executive. Referring to the decision in the pension case, Justice Bhagwati acknowledged the policy making role of the Supreme Court. He said, "Now, in a way, it was policy making because the government wanted to give it to only one class of persons. The court said, it must be given to all"[56]

Secondly, the judiciary has taken over many of the functions of the executive, such as-directing, superintending and controlling the activities of the governmental agencies and departments.

It has been devising its own methods to collect facts and data, appointing commissions of enquiry for the purpose. Bhagwati J explained this in an Interview :

"Now, when a social action group or a public spirited individual comes, how are we going to gather material, data, facts bearing upon issues arising in that litigation? ......we started appointing commissions of enquiry for the purpose of ascertaining material, data, facts, so that the court can come to a right decision. We have been appointing District Judges, District Magistrates, journalists, social-scientists and many others as commissioriers to visit that particular place and gather facts and later report to the court"[51]

The courts have monitored the investigations into the alleged crimes, directing at one stage in the Jain Hawala case, that the CBI shall directly report to the court and take instructions from it and not from the PMO. They have been issuing directions for the conduct of the cases, pulling up the police for delay in filing charge sheet, in completing investigations.

Through the PIL the judiciary has moved on from adversarial adjudication to arbitration between public causes and the government. As Justice Bhagwati explained in his interview with the Frontline.

".......we felt that adversarial system of justice can not work. The adversarial system is evolved to deal with private right-duty pattern, the pattern of private law where one individual seeks relief against another individual but not where, because of what I would call the massification phenomenon, rights of classes of people are involved".[58]

In most of the PIL cases the judiciary has been giving directions to the administration to initiate affirmative action.

Initiating Affirmative Action

The giving of directions to the executive to initiate affirmative ameliorative action may unconsciously slip into policy-making. In any case, these directions are no part of the traditional judicial function; they are rather in the nature of rule-making by the judiciary.

Not only rule making, the court also wants to hold the executive accountable to itself for carrying out its directions. Whatever the cause pursued in PIL, whether it be the rights and interests of bonded labourers, undertrial prisoners, convicts, pavement dwellers, rickshaw pullers, workers, the court has been eager to issue detailed directions in an endeavour to do complete justice and plug all possible loopholes. The number and range of such directions is in many a case baffling for the executive.

In the Bandhua Mukti Morcha case[59] the Supreme Court gave as many as 21 directions, spelling out a programme of affirmative action. It included rehabilitation of bonded labour, ensuring the payment of minimum wages, provision of pure drinking water and medical facilities. The Central Board of Worker's Education was directed to organise periodic camps near stone quarries and stone crushers to make workers aware of their rights and entitlements.

The apex court evolved a humane, new jail jurisprudence through its directions in the PIL cases. It insisted on the residuary rights of prisoners, their release on parole, payment ofwages to prisoners for work done by them, speedy trial, reasonable procedure, even their psychological treatment including transcendental meditation and *yoga* exercises. Compensation was granted to Rudal Shah for illegal detention after acquittal by the court[60], directions were given to provide loans to rickshawpullers to enable them to buy rickshaws[61], instructions were given to the state of Kerala to increase seats in medical colleges,[62] mandates were issued to bring about necessary changes in rules so that poor may not have to pay court fee in automobile accident cases,[63] directions were given for the protection of the Taj Mahal from air pollution,[64] and of the rivers Yamuna and Ganga from industriai pollutants[65]. In the Bihar Blinding case the Supreme Court suggested a series of relief measures. It suggested that the blinded prisoners be kept in Blind Relief Association, New Delhi and failing it, other relief centres be found for them and the Bihar state must incur all expenses in their treatment.[66]

Petitions filed on behalf of the individuals were treated as though they were filed on behalf of the class to which the petitioners belonged. Likewise relief granted to individual was extended to the class in so far as these reliefs were general in character. This was stretching the judicial process to extreme lengths. In this manner the court laid down the public policy for juvenile delinquents. It directed that child under trials and convicts should not be kept in jails. The number of children's Remand Homes must be increased. The court suggested that the Union government should initiate legislation on the subject "so that there is complete uniformity in regard to various provisions relating to children in the entire country". The Central Act should also contain provisions for social, economic and psychological rehabilitation of children. In the Agra *Protective Home for Women case,* the court issued a ten point direction to the U.P. Government with regard to the upkeep of the building and, its approach road.[67] In the *Delhi Nari Niketan case,* the Supreme Court directed that sanitary napkins be provided to the women inmates. In the former case the court laid down a detailed programme of rehabilitation for the women inmates.

In several cases the Supreme Court gave specific directions for providing legal assistance to prisoners and women prisoners. It issued detailed directions to the administration on how to handle cases of women prisoners and convicts.

On a petition filed by two Municipal Corporators of theVaranasi Nagar Nigam, the Allahabad High Court stayed the implementation of the Ganga Action Plan, launched in 1985.[68] It ordered a thorough reassessment of the entire project by an expert group. The court said, "it is almost clear that on account of ailure of the scheme, everywhere and in Varanasi in particular, pollution instead of controlled, had multiplied". It further said, "It has become' necessary to stop work till the entire project is carefully examined and scrutinised by a group of environmental experts". The court directed—

(1) A team of seven officers, headed by Mr. Samir Gupta, a retired official of the C & AG Office should do audit of Rs. 500 crore spent on the GAP so far.

(2) This team should have full powers to check the accounts of all the departments, including the departments of the Central government as also the local bodies, apart from the state government departments wherever they find that money had been sanctioned for GAP.

(3) The team should have the authority to requisition services of experts to assess whether the work undertaken by agencies had been performed properly and efficiently as per technical specifications set originally.

(4) The projects under the GAP could be taken up for implementation only after getting clearance from the committee, to be set up by the Environment Ministry.

(5) The GAP should be implemented by involving local bodies who should be authorised to construct, maintain and operate the treatment plants and undertake the river conservation work at their own level with the help of the government.

(6) There should be total transparency regarding the action to be taken and an effort made to educate the people on keeping the river free of pollution.

(7) The U.P. Pollution Control Board and Varanasi Nagar Nigam should take water samples from the bathing ghats for daily analysis and display the pollution level to alert the public if it does not meet the pollution control standards.

These are just illustrations to show how the court in PIL cases has tended to deviate from its judicial function and unwittingly stray into the executive jurisdiction. Its motive, no doubt, has been to prescribe guidelines and provide administrative details so as to secure work efficiency, honesty, economy and justice.

Criticism of P.I.L.

Public Interest Litigation has been criticised mainly on the ground that it has blurred the traditional division of governmental functions and encouraged the judiciary to trespass into legislative and executive spheres. This makes the judiciary the dominant branch of government, holding the executive accountable to itself, exercising the power of direction, superintendence and control over it.

This is not what the Constitution intends or prescribes. This is to disturb the constitutional scheme of division of powers and functions. Under the Constitution the Ministers are collectively responsible to the Parliament. They are accountable to the Parliament even for day to day working. They must formulate and finalise governmental policy with approval of the Parliament.

PIL has to some extent made the judiciary supplant the Parliament in the exercise of these functions.

The courts have thus come to combine the role of policy making, prosecution, and adjudication, all rolled into one. This is contrary to the basic tenets of political development or modernisation. In the Result –

1. The courts are being overloaded with excessive work, not only on the judicial side, but with fresh responsibilities of direction', superintendence and control over the executive. The mounting arrears of cases in the Supreme Court and the High Courts on both the civil and the Criminal sides are already a cause of growing public concern.[69]

It seems indefensible and illogical that the court should add to its own work and responsibilities.

Inaugurating the silver jubilee celebrations of the Maharashtra Bar Council, Mr. R.S. Pathak, ex-Chief Justice of India, warned that "the courts should not overstep the limits of their powers nor trespass into the territory which the Constitution has properly assigned to the others organs of the state"[70]

He continued, "perhaps few would object to the concept of the movement which was a new chapter in court jurisdiction, for it would serve an appreciable section of people, who would otherwise have no opportunity for redress from courts. But there were obvious limitations which should be observed and guidelines drawn to strengthen the content of this jurisdiction". He stressed the need to define the concept of PIL more clearly and said it was time to evaluate court's work in this area and lay down the procedures.

2. Judicial encroachment into the executive sphere has in some quarters been criticised as an attempt to governing through courts or governance by the judiciary.

The superintendence, direction and control of the executive by the courts is an extra constitutional growth. It subordinates elective representative government to the whims and caprice of individual judges. It is an individualist personal response to an equally individualist and personal initiative. As such PIL must necessarily rise and fall with individuals in the Bar and on the Bench.

3. The encroachment of the judiciary into the sphere of policy making and governance is subversive of faith in the democratic process and constitutional government. The apex court is hardly equipped to supervise the running of a vast, populous, developing state. The court is not equipped to go into such complex issues as telecom licensing, Cauvery tangle, rehabilitation of chakma refugees, and the like. In issuing directions in matters which are purely administrative and about which the court does not possess the requisite expertise and experience, it is overstepping its areas of operation. Such decisions often put the administrative machinery in an awkward situation and make it bear the brunt of its decisions. Mr. Justice Kuldip Singh's directive to the Union government for enacting a uniform civil code, one of the Directive principles of state policy, is a case in point. Commenting on apex court's order on safety and citizenship applications of Chakmas, a core committee headed by Arunachal Chief Minister, Georg Apang regrets that "the identity and culture of our state and its protection were not appreciated in the judgement

of the Supreme Court and the direction given therein to provide continued protection and status to the refugees have affected its interests and hopes.[71]

On the apex court's order to the Prime Minister to sort out the Cauvery tangle in 48 hours; former Irrigation Secretary Ramaswamy Iyer's comment was: "one wishes that the Supreme Court had passed an order that would have strengthened the hands of the Tribunal and reaffirmed the supremacy of the Constitution and the rule of law."[72]

Justice Kuldip Singh has himself often admitted that the Supreme Court should not have embarked on the decade old effort to rehabilitate the Rohtas Industries to save the jobs of thousands of workers as it has resulted in colossal losses to the government of India and the government of Bihar.[73]

It is no function of the courts to assume such onerous responsibilities. The court can not be a vanguard of social and economic reforms. Nor can it afford to be an organ of regulation and control over the executive. That will, as justice Khanna remarked in a recent article, result in judicial oligarchy dethroning democratic set up. It will strike at the very root of our democratic polity and pave the way for judicial despotism.

4. The judiciary is set above the executive in the sphere of day to day administration. It can not be said that the court is infallible and do no wrong. If the court were to err in its dieectives, where is the executive or citizen to go for redressal? The displacement of thousands of people and of shops, restaurants, hotels, offices, and other commercial establishments in and around the Taj Mahal complex, the demolition of unauthorised constructions on road-sides and lanes in cities, the cancellation of allotments of petrol pumps, plots, houses, LPG dealership, are not simple, legal, non technical questions but involve sociological and

humane considerations which may be beyond law and logic.[74]

The Supreme Court has acquired the final say in all matters relating to the governance of the country. For instance, it can now ask for the records based on which the President and the Governors may have reached their subjective satisfaction with regard to say, imposition of President's rule in a state. This means that these issues are no longer non justiciable, and can be challenged on various ground like the malafides, unreasonableness etc.

Many other provisions of the Constitution relying on the pleasure of the President have been brought under judicial control through creative interpretation of Articles 14, 19 and 21 of the Constitution.

One columnist remarks, "when the other wings of state overstep their limits, the aggrieved party can always approach the courts for redress. But when the courts are themselves guilty of such transgression, to which forum would the aggrieved turn for justice?[75]

Chief Justice Harlanin *U.S. Vs.* Butler wrote, ".......While unconstitutional exercise of power by the executive and legislative branches of government is subject to judicial restraint, the only check upon our own exercise of power is our own self-restraint".[76]

5. The judiciary has to depend on the executive for giving effect to its directives. Art. 142 authorises that the Supreme Court "in the exercise of its jurisdiction may pass such decree or make such order as is necessary for doing complete justice in any cause or matter pending before it, and any decree so passed, or order so made shall be enforceable throughout the territory of India, in such manner as may be presćribed by law made by Parliament and, until provision in that behalf is so made, in such manner as the President may by order prescribe".

Further, Art. 144 enjoins– "All authorities, civil and judicial, in the territory of India shall act in aid of the Supreme Court"

In practice, the compliance with the Supreme Court directives has been very slow, uncentain and unsatisfactory. The court can do very little to secure faithful compliance of its directives by the executive.

In many cases the court's directives end up as *much ado about nothing,* In many cases the directives are unrelated to ground reality and there is no option for the executive but to avoid, evade or ignore them.

In a recent judgement Patna High Court expressed its resentment over non-compliance of its orders on removal of illegal constructions by the state government.[77]

There is no follow up on compliance. It is not certain how far the directives issued to various agencies in the Bandhua Mukti Morcha case or in the various environmental cases have been caried out. In some cases, as for instance in the case relating to protecting the Taj from polluting industries and air pollution, the court's directives, may be dragged into endless litigation. The executive may indeed devise ways and means to frustrate the court's directives.

The judicial activism has come under heavy attack from the political quarters as more and more of PIL has sought to expose political corruption and implicate the politicians, Ministers, MPs, party leaders and even the Prime Minister.[78] In October 1966 several Congress MPs came out with sharp criticism of judicial activism. They demanded that a special session of Parliament be summoned to discuss the issue and pass the necessary constitutional amendment to set limits on judicial activism. Even the former Lok Sabha Speaker, P.A. Sangma, in a symposium of presiding, officers of legislatures fired a bombshell against judicial activism.

The politicians adopted a two pronged strategy to escape the judicial dragnet. One was to disclaim that they were "Public Servants" within the meaning of Prevention of Corruption Act. The other was to curb PIL through legislation.[79] A hastily drafted bill to this effect proposed to make it mandatory for a petitioner to deposit Rs. 1 lakh for filing a PIL petition in the Supreme Court and Rs. 50,000 in the High Court. If the petitions were found to be frivolous the amount would be forfeited.

According to a note appended to the proposed bill, the new legislation had become necessary as

(1) the judiciary has digressed from its traditional duties and functions as an interpreter of the Constitution and the laws,

(2) has failed to recognise that it, cannot be substitute for the failure or the irresponsibility of other branches of the government.

(3) and, has been delivering increasingly legislative or administrative judgements.

Besides, abuse of PIL for personal or political gains and considerable increase in the workload of courts because of such cases were other reasons cited to justify the proposed measure.

There was such a widespread outcry against the proposed bill that it was quietly dropped.

In Defence of Judicial Activism

Much of the criticism of PIL is misconceived. The outcry against it in the political circles is clearly malicious and motivated.

As for the allegation that PIL was the main reason for the huge pendency of cases before the apex court and the High Courts, Mr. Shanti Bhushan, a former Law Minister (1977-1979) said'[80]

"I totally disagree with this view. It is not the judicial activism or public interest litigation but the paucity of judges and courts in the country which is responsible for the serious problem of backlog facing the judiciary. Present Judge-ratio in our country considering its population, is the lowest in the world. It was for this reason that the eleventh Law Commission had recommended five fold increase in the present judge strength to clear the huge backlog of pending cases. But nothing has been done so far".

Presiding over a symposium in Delhi, Justice Kuldip Singh denied the charge of "judicial activism" He said, "What we are doing today is a part of our duty........... judges only perform their constitutional duty to safeguard people's right when there is no one to administer or execute social justice legislation". He asked how could one call it "judicial trespass or judicial terrorism,when the court intervened to investigate innocent people being killed by the law enforcing agencies, or when the government was asked to have a treatment plant for the Yamuna where 75 per cent of Delhi's sewage was being dumped, causing serious health hazards"[81]

Justice Kuldip Singh returned to this theme in his 12th Bir Memorial Lecture on "Human Rights and Judiciary". He said, the Supreme Court was duty bound to step in whenever the government failed to enforce basic human rights and it was a misnomer to call it judicial activism. It is in the very purview of the judiciary to see that the government agencies were performing in the people's interest"[82]

Chief Justice A.M. Ahmadi said in defence of judicial activism that the role of the judiciary in a developing country is not "static or status quoits". He added "when new litigations came up before the judiciary, it had to act on them. As such the pattern of litigation and the judicial response to it was changing".[83]

The President of the Bar Association of India, M.R F.S. Nariman says that when the bureaucracy shows a callous indifference and insensitiveness to its mandatory duties, the judiciary can not procrastinate. It must respond. In such circumstances, the judiciary cannot be accused of exceeding its jurisdiction as long as the exercise of judicial power by it is for bonafide purposes and in good faith.[84] Can it be said that the Supreme Court over stepped its constitutional limits if it mandates the executive to carry out its constitutional obligations and pulls up the law enforcing agencies for violations of human rights of citizens? Asks Mr. Nariman. He further asks, if the executive abdicates its responsibilities which could be the forum to be approached by the people barring the judiciary to ventilate their grievances and what options would be left for the common man today? Defending the new role of the Supreme Court, Mr. Ram Jethmalani says that in a democratic society like India, the courts have to play an active role if law is to keep pace with social needs. In his words, "when more than 80 per cent of the people are socially suppressed, economically depressed and educationally backward, when the executive and legislature are apathetic and fail to discharge their constitutional duties, the apex court has no other choice but to step in and direct these functionaries to discharge their obligations"[85]

It must be emphasised that the exercise of judicial power is not for vainglory or aggrandisement but in discharge of its constitutional obligations. For otherwise, the canstitutional government will be paralysed. In his 12th Bir Memorial Lecture Justice Kuldip Singh noted that same of the apex court's judgements were not being enforced. "We, therefore, invented methods of monitoring anti reporting, we cannot wait for the government agencies to perform", he added.[86]

Judicial Activism does not mean government by the judges, as is alleged by vested interests. It only means dispensing with legal, procedural technicalities and adapting a pro-ative and goal-oriented approach in the interest of "the weaker sections community.........such as undertrial prisoners languishing in jails without a trial, inmates of the protective home in Agra or Harijan workers engaging in road construction in Ajmer district, who are living in poverty and destitution, who are barely eking aut a miserable existence with their sweat and toil, who are helpless victims of an exploitative society and who do not have any access to justice"[87]

The court was thus able to expose, among other things, the brutality of Bhagalpur blinding, the state callousness towards pavement dwellers, pathetic plight of children in juvenile homes, of destitute women in protective homes, the merciless exploitation of bonded labour, adivasis, the dalits, the workers. The apex court's rulings in some cases provided prompt relief to victims of injustice, resulted the conviction of guilty policemen, government officials, and led to the enforcement of labour laws relating to minimum wages, and elimination of bonded labour. The court sensitized the central investigating agencies to discharge their legal abligations in the Jain hawala case and its judgements ranging from the need for a uniform civil code, pollution control, preservation of historical monuments like Taj Mahal, cleaning and keeping the metropilis more hyginic, directing the eviction of unauthorised occupants of government bungalows, interim compensation to rape victims and their incamera trial, puncturing the ego of T.N. Shesan, Chief Election Commissioner, are evidence of the court's endeavour to re-define justice in terms of public interest. The executive has exhibited little concern, keenness or competence for pratecting the rights and freedoms of the people. In many cases it itself has been responsible for their infringement or disregard. In such circumstances judicial activism has served to contain the resulting rising revolution of public frustrations. It has served to sustain peaple's faith in democracy and constitutional government. It is a tribute to the vigilance, vision and wisdom of the court that it evolved its jurisdiction with courage, creativity and circumstances. Judicial Activism is but reflection of that creativity and pragmatism.

References

1. Osborne Vs. Bank of United States, 8 Wheat, 738, 866.
2. Harold J. Laski, *Parliamentary Government in England,* Allen & Unwin, London, 1952, p. 360.
3. In re Berubari Union (1960) 3 S.C.R. 250; A.I.R. 1960 SC 845.
4. In re Special Court's Bill, 1978, AIR 1979 SC 478.
5. *Ismail Faruqi V. Union of India* (1994) 6 S.C.C. 360.
6. *Times of India,* 20 March 1985.
7. *Pioneer,* 10 January, 1997.
8. *Pioneer,* Lucknow, 13 Nov. 1995.
9. *Pioneer,* 10 January, 1997.
10. Glazer and Kristol. *The American Commonwealth,* 1976, New York, p. 108.
11. *Lochnr Vs. New York,* 198, US. 45 (1905).
12. Nathan Glazer and Irving Kristol, *The American Commonwealth,* New York, 1976, Towards an Imperial Judiciany?' pp. 106-108.
13. Glazer and Kristol, *The American Commonwealth,* p. 107.
14. *Ibid.*
15. Laski, *Parliamentary Government in England,* p. 362.
16. B. Cardozo, The Nature of the Judicial Process, Yale University Press, New Heaven, 1921, p. 168.
17. Quoted in Justice Desai's Inaugural address to the All India Lawyers Seminar, dated 10.4.1982.
18. Times of India, 24 March 1996.
19. Pioneer, 29 Aug. 1996.
20. *Ibid.*

21. The Hindustan Times, 8 July 1996, Limits of judicial activism, by Bal Krishna.
22. AIR 1979 SC 916 (924).
23. Bearer Bonds Case (1981) *4 SCR 675:* R. K. Garg Vs. Union of India known a Bearer Bonds case, AIR, 1981.
24. (1981) SCC 1675 at pp. 713-714.
25. Inaugural address of Justice D.A. Desai to the All India Seminar of Indian Society of Lawyers, dated *10.4.1982.* Also see Fertilizer Corporation Kamgar Union Vs. Union of india: AIR 1981 SC 344.
26. *Fertilizer Corporation Kamgar Union Vs. Union of India,* AIR 1981 SC 344.
27. *S.P. Gupta and others Vs. Union of India,* AIR 1982, Supreme Court, p. 149.
28. After five years of procrastination, the CBI on Jan. 16, 1996 filed charge sheets against 7 politicians, namely, L.K. Advani, Devi Lal, Arjun Singh, Arif Mohammad Khan, Kalpnath Rai, Yashwant Sinha, and Devilal's grand nephew, Pradeep Kumar, and sought permission from the President of India to proceed against- three central Ministers, Madhavrao Scindia, Balram Jakhar and V.C. Shukla.
29. Pioneer, 29.8.1996.
30. *M.C. Mehta Vs. Union of India,* AIR, 1987, SC 1086.
31. Hindustan Times, New Delhi, 12 April, 1996.
32. *Pioneer,* 29.8.1996.
33. *Hindustan Times*, 11 April, 1985.
34. *Times of India,* 24.3.1996.
35. *Hindustan Times,* 16.12.1996.
36. *Pioneer*, 30 Oct. 1996.
37. Poola Bhaskara Vijaya Kumar Vs . State of Andhra Pradesh A.I.R. 1988, A.P. 295.
38. In a telegram, a village woman Konikammna sought the court's help in getting her son, Mirampal, freed from the Konda village police station in Prakasam district. The

Additional Advocate General received the court notice on the government's behalf. See *The Times of India, July 17, 1985.*

39. The court had received a pamphlet from Shanti of Kamataka who alleged that she was employed without any payment as a domestic servant and washer woman by a flour mill owner in Tirupati. The court called for a report from the Chittor Collector. The Times of'India, 17 July 1985.
40. *Ibid.*
41. *Ibid.*
42. Asiad PUDR Vs. Union of India AlR, 1982 SC 1473.
43. *Ibid*
44. *The Pioneer,* 30 Oct. 1996.
45. *The Hindustan Times*, 11 April 1985.
46. 'These were L.K. Advani. Deve Lal, his grand nephew Pradeep Kumar, Arjun Singh, Arif Mohammad Khan, Kalpnath Rai and Yashwant Sinha.
47. *The Pioneer,* 29 August 1998.
48. Sunil Batra (II) New Delhi Administration (1980) 3 SCC 488.
49. B.R. Kapoor Vs. Union of India AIR 1990 SC 752.
50. Bandhua Mukti Morcha Vs. State of Haryana, AIR 1984, SC 828.
51. *Frontline,* 3 (1) Jan. 11-24, 1986, p. 10.
52. AIR 1983 SC 378.
53. See P.D. Mathew, "Babubigha scheduled caste people show the way", Struggle for Justice Series, Indian Socila lnstitute, New Delhi, 1986.
54. *Rural Litigation and Entitlement Kendra Dehradun versus State of U.P.* AIR 1985 SC 1259, AIR 1987 SC 359 and AIR 1987 SC 359 and AIR 1987 SC 2426.
55. (1978), 4. SCC, 494).
56. *See Fronline,* Justice Bhagwati's Interview under the caption, "The Supreme Court and the People" Jan, *11-24-1986, pp. 11-12.*
57. *Ibid.*

58. *Ibid p. 10.*
59. AIR 1984 SC 837.
60. *Rudal Shah Vs. State of Bihar,* AIR 1983, SC 1086.
61. *Azad Rickshaw Puller's Union case,* AIR 1981, SC. 15.
62. *State of Keral Vs. T.P. Roshana,* AIR 1979, SC 766.
63. *State of Haryana Vs. Darshana Devi,* AIR 1979, SC 766.
64. *See The Hindustan Times,* New Delhi, 11 April 1996.
65. *See The Hindustan Times,* Lucknow, 6 August, 12 August 1996, and 19 August, 1998. Also see Shri Ram Fertilizer case, AIR 1986, SC 955.
66. *Khatri Vs. State of Bihar,* AIR 1981, SC 930.
67. *Upendra Baxi Vs. State of U.P.,* AIR 1987, SC 195.
68. *See:* The Hindustan Times, Lucknow, 19 October, 1998.
69. The Union Law Minister, Mr. Rama Kant Khalap told the Rajya Sabha in July 1996, that there was a backlog of about 25 million cases before various courts in the country. Allahabad High Court had arrears of 8 lakhs, Madras 3.20 lakhs, and Kolkata 2.55 lakhs. The total number of cases pending inthe District and subordinate courts in Delhi was 5,72,903.

    See *The Pioneer,* Lucknow, 20 October 1996.
    In judgement delivered in the case *Siddhartha Kumar Vs. Upper Civil Judge,* the Allahabad High Court noted that there were 9.25 lakh civil cases pending in the courts of U.P. out of these abut 3 lakh are one to 3 lakh old, about 2.5 lakh are three to 10 years old, about 60,000 cases are over 10 years old, possibly including those embroiling succeeding generations in litigation started by ancestors. Clogged Courts: cases backlog can be cleared. See *The Times of India,* New Delhi, 12 August 1988, p. 13.
70. *Times of India,* dated 8 February 1998.
71. B. B. Iyer, The Court Rules, *Pioneer* Lucknow, 23 January 1996.
72. *Ibid.*
73. *Ibid.*

74. 'Senior Advocate K.K. Venugopal emphasises, "The court has to be more cautious where it seeks to take affirmative action in areas not covered by statute or express constitutional provisions repuiring a particular thing to be done or action to be taken". In his view, this implies that the court "would be taking upon itself the function of laying down policy. It would also encroach upon the legislative powers of parliament or the state legislatures". *See* The Pioneer, Lucknow, November 13, 1995.

75. The former Chief Justice of the Supreme Court, Justice Venkataramaiah's ovservations express this same concern. He said, "if the legislature exceeds its power, this court steps in. If the executive exceeds its power then also this court steps in. If this court itself exceeds its powers what can people do? Should they be driven to seek an amendment of the law on every such occasion. The only proper solution is the observance of restraint by this court in its pronouncements so that they do not go beyond its own legitimate sphere". *The pioneer,* Lucknow, 4 Sep. 1996.

76. 297 U.S. 1 (1936) quoted in William Quirk, Judicial Dictatorship, Society, Jan. - Feb. 1994.

77. *The Hindustan Times, Lucknow, 17* October 1998.

78. The former Prime Ministery P.V. Narsimha Rao (1991-1996) has been accused of forgery (St. Kitts case), fraud (Urea Scandal), Cheating (Lakhoobhai Pathak case), and bribery (JMM MPs case) in various cases.

79. The sudden provocation for the PIL bill was the spate of Judgements by the apex court in the allotment of petrol pumps case Jain hawala cases, housing scam and others of the ilk dealing with corruption in high places. See R.D. Sharma, Justice for *All, The Pioneer,* Lucknow, 2.4.1997.

80. Senior Advocate of the Supreme Court, Mr. Shanti Bhushan, in an Interview with the pioneer. See *The Pioneer,* Lucknow, 28 November, 1995.

81. *The Pioneer,* Lucknow, 23 January 1996.

82. *The Pioneer,* Lucknow, 14 October, 1996.

83. *The Pioneer,* Lucknow.
84. *The Hindustan Times,* New Delhi, 8 July 1996.
85. *The Hindustan Times,* New Delhi, 8 July 1996.
Chief Justice Ahmadi inaugurating a Seminar at Pune on judicial process - social legitimacy and institutional validity said that there are situations in which people wait for some action from the executive but when nothing emerges they move the court. He is therefore appreciative of the Supreme Court's in ovative approach. See B.B. Iyer, "The Court Rules", The Pioneer Lucknow, 23.1.1996.
86. *The Pioneer,* Lucknow, 14 October, 1996.
87. S.P. Gupta Vs. Union of India, AIR 1981, SC 149.

PART-II

4

Judicial Activism in Action: Police, Prisoners and Under Trials

The broad purpose of judicial activism is Social Justice. Social Justice is not merely upliftment of the weaker sections of the society It's sweep is much wider than that. It extends to every nook and corner of society where ever there is suffering, deprivation or neglect.

Judicial Activism which is implicit in judicial review is made explicit in the hands of an activist court. It's aim is Social Justice, not merely enforcement of law. It permits the court to project the personal views of its members on questions of public policy, without manifestly violating the provisions of law, but often deviating from precedents and standard practice. According to Justice V.R. Krishna Iyer, Judicial activism is "legally tuned affirmative action, activist justicing and benign interpretation within the parameters of *Corpus Juris*".

Black's Law Dictionary defines judicial activism as "The Philosophy which motivates judges to depart from strict adherence to judicial precedent in favour of progressive and new social policies, which are not always Consistent with the restraint expected of appellate judges. It is commonly marked by decisions calling for social engineering and occasionally these decisions represent intrusions in the legislative and executive matters".

The impact of judicial activism in protecting and promoting social interest can be seen in almost every area of governance, notably, the following:

(*a*) Police, prisoners and undertrials,

(*b*) Women and children,

(*c*) Poor, indigent an homeless persons,

(*d*) Urban development, health and hygiene,

(*e*) Upliftment of weaker sections of society,

(*f*) Environment and pollution.

This chapter deals only with cases relating to police, prisoners and undertrials.

Police, Prisoners and Undertrials

Judicial Activism first splashed the radar of national Media in the reports regarding the blinding of more than 30 notorious criminals in police custody during the period Oct. 1979-Nov. 1980. Presumably with the knowledge, consent or corinivance of the administration.[1]

Bihar Blinding Case

Writ petitions filed in the Supreme Court during the period 1980-81 disclosed a series of lapses on the part of Police, Distnct Administration and even Judicial Officers. These lapses were serious violations of the Constitutional guarantees held out in Articles 20 to 22.

It was apparent that the prisoners were subjected, to inhuman treatment in police custody: The police had them even blinded and reported that, that was the result of injuries sustained by the accused.

The Judicial Magistrate did not bother to enquire as to how these injuries were caused.

No legal service was provided to the blinded prisoners. The Magistrate did not care to tell them that they had a right to free legal service.

The accused were not presented before a Magistrate within 24 hours of their arrest, as required under Art. 22.

The court painfully noted the state of affairs in Bihar Jails and ordered that the blinded undertrials be shifted to Delhi and the cost of their stay there should be borne by the state of Bihar.[2]

Since no medical or surgical treatment could restore eyesight to those prisoners, the Blind Relief Association, New Delhi should house those people and the expenses should be borne by the state of Bihar.

The Association showing inability to take them, the court suggested in its order[3] dated Jan. 14, 1981 that other relief centers be found for them.

The court directed the state to ensure treatment of these prisoners, who had been bailed out, in the AIIMS, at the cost of the state of Bihar, The court in its order dated 14.01.81 directed that investigation into blinding of prisoners should be completed and charge sheets, if any, were to be filed with in three months. The respondent state was directed to take responsibility for the lodging, board and vocational training of those prisoners, and was ordered to provide them with warm clothing. The state was directed to ascertain the method and mariner in which prisoners were blinded.[4]

These directions show the concern of the Supreme Court at the failure of the local administration and the judiciary to work within the framework of law and at the violations of constitutional provisions. It is doubtful if they can be treated as judicial intrusions into the executive sphere. Even if they are, are they not necessary to keep the executive within the bounds of law and to ensure justice?

In the Guntaben Gang Rape case, the Supreme Court appointed its own commission of inquiry with a senior police officer from outside the state (Gugarat), K.V. Joseph and Ela Pathak, a social worker, as commissioners. The report of C.B.I. investigation having not been received inspite of two extensions the court directed the report to be produced, within ten days.

The court on receiving the report described the attitude of the state governtnent in not taking action against the six policemen named as responsible for the rape and its subsequent cover up as disclosing "a pathetic state of affairs."

The court noted that nearly two years after the incident had taken place and despite two investigation commissions identifying the culprits, the state government had failed to take any action.

It further ordered the Gujarat government to bring all original records of the case to the court and to have submitted to the Supreme Court any charge sheets issued to the policemen held responsible.

The SC pressure resulted in departmental inquires being commenced against various officers and compensation of Rs. 50,000/- directed to be paid to Guntaben.[5]

In the Kokrajar village Gang Rape Case, involving rape of women from Bode-tribe by policemen, the state government, soon after receiving the court notice appointed a judicial commission, and a day earlier to the final hearing, arrested eight of the policemen.[6]

Rudal Shan Vs. State of Bihar

As Chief Justice V.Y. Chandrachud pointed out in his judgement, this case discloses a sordid and disturbing state of affairs in the prisons of Bihar. It brings to light the case of one Rudal Shah, who inspite of his acquittal by the Sessions Court on June 3, 1968 lingered on in the jail for fourteen years. The court noted that the records did not explain why he was detained and who was responsible for his illegal detention for such a long time. It was contended by the respondent state that the petitioner was insane at the time of the acquittal, and was, therefore, detained further. The court did, not believe this story and thought that it was an after thought, and the jailer was made a escapegoat.

It burst heavily on the administration and said, "we hope (and pray) that the higher officials of the state will find time to devote their personal attention to the breakdown of prison administration in, the State and rectify the grave injustice which is being perpetrated on helpless persons."[7]

The Supreme Court (asked the High Court of Patna to examine this matter and call for statistical data from the Home Department of the government of Bihar and then release those who had been unlawfully detained.

Affirmative Action

The court also ordered the state of Bihar to pay Rs. 30,000/- as an interim payment as a token compensation. This amount was in addition to the Rs. 5,000 – already, payed by the state as exemplary costs. The court added that its award would not prevent the petitioner from bringing a suit for damages against the state and its erring officials.

The action of the court in awarding token compensation to Rudal Shah was obviously an extension of judicial power resting on no provision of constitution, but simply the discretion of the court.

This discretion was seen in two other cases, **Deoki Nandan Prasad Vs. Stae of Bihar**[8] and Sebastian M. Hangrey Vs. Union of India.[9]

In the first case, Supreme Court awarded a compensation of Rs. 25,000/- to the petitioner who was not payed his pension for twelve years despite the *Mandamus* issued by the Supreme Court.

In the second case the Supreme Court awarded Rs. One lakh each to the wives of two persons as compensation for mental torture and harassment. Their husbands had been arrested by the Army in Manipur and the state had failed to produce them before the Supreme Court inspite of a *Habeas Corpus* writ on Nov. 24,1983.

Clearly the award of compensation in such circumstances was an executive decision which the court had taken upon itself in discharge of its duty to uphold fundamental rights.

In another case, **Paschim Banga Khet Majdoor** Samity.[10] The court awarded compensation, while acknowledging that its order may have wide-reaching financial implications.

Another aspect of affirmative action is the court's intrusion into the legislative sphere. **In Sunil Batra (II)** **case** the court pointed out the need to amend the Prisons Act and the need to overhaul the Prison Mannual.

In Kishore Singh Ravinder Dev the Supreme Court stated that the rules governing prisons were incongruous with the Constitution.

In Gurdev Singh Vs. Himachal Pradesh[11] the court held that the state government should undertake comprehensive jail reforms within a year by appointing a high powered committee comprising men from the jail administration, social workers and criminologists to advise the state government in the field. The court itself appointed a committee to look into the possibilities of starting open air institutions, with provisions of adequate work and different correctional institutions for young prisoners and hardened criminals, and education and vocational training for prisoners and the provision for after-release guidance and help.

Taking cue from the activist judiciary the National Human Rights Commission directed the Delhi Government to pay Rs. 3 lakh as compensation to the family of Pappan, an undertrial prisoner who had died following an attack by fellow inmates in Central Jail at Tihar on May 4, 2003. The commission found that the deceased was not only a victim of assault in jail but also of doctor's negligence in treatment for the injury sustained by him due to assault. (*The Hindu, 22.01.2009*).

Prisoner Welfare Measures

It was held that prisoners have a right to society (family etc.) but it is subject to search and other security criteria. The District Magistrates were directed to visit prisons in their jurisdiction personally or through surrogates, so that prisoners could relate their grievances. Grievance deposit boxes were to be maintained for prisoners and opened as frequently as deemed fit. A wall paper was to be put up for the prisoners to write upon, to reduce stress.

The state was directed to take steps to keep up to the standard minimum rules for the treatment of prisoners as recommended by the U.N., specially those relating to work and wages, treatment with dignity, community contact and correction strategies.

In Hussainara Khatoon case based on a habeaus corpus petiton by an advocate on the basis of news reports in the Indian Express on 8-9/2/79 the court held that all undertrials must be informed of their entitlement to bail and that they must be released if they had been undertrials for longer than the maximum possible sentence.

The court held that each accused person who cannot engage a lawyer on account of poverty, indigence or incommunicado situation has a constitutional right to free legal services provided by the state.

The court directed the jail authorities and social welfare department to make suitable arrangements for the care of women and children released on personal bond. The state government was directed to immediately release women held in "protective custody" and put them in welfare centres to be opened by the state.[12]

Activist Measures

The Supreme Court played an active role in highlighting the conditions prevailing in the prisons and the plight of their inmates. It noted the lack of adequate basic amenities such as water and clothing in the prisons and found that the majority of inmates belonged to economically and socially disadvantaged sections of society, to scheduled castes and scheduled tribes, vulnerable to intimidation and harassment by officials.

(a) Delay in Trial:

It noticed delays in trials and stated that speedy justice is a fundamental right and that the rights of undertrial were violated by delays and procedural difficulties.

Anyone charged of the multiple offences who had been in prison for more than the total maximum period possible for all the offences was to be released. Where the period in prison was less than the total maximum period possible but more than the maximum if the sentences were to run concurrently, such undertrials were to be released on a personal bond of Rs. 50/- without surety.[13]

In one case, it was alleged that almost 73% of entire jail population was found to be that of undertrials.[14]

In this context Mr. Joginder Singh, former Director C.B.I., records, "The most disturbing aspect of Indian prisons is the presence of undertrials. They constitute, 75 per cent of the country's prison, population. In many jails, they constitue about 90 per cent of the prison population."[15]

In state of Punjab Vs. Ajaib Singh,[16] a need to increase strength to clear backlog or devise some mechanism for early disposal of criminal appeals was stressed upon.

Recently Prime Minster Manmohan Singh expressed anguish at the plight of undertrials and said, "many such undertrlals have been in jail for periods longer than they would have served had they been sentenced. This is indeed very disturbing" (*The Times of India, 17.08.09*).

On January 26, 2010, the Law Minister M. Veerappa Moily announced an ambitious plan to decongest the country's prisons within six months. True to his announcement the government by July end had ensured the release of more than 2 lakh undertrial prisoners. "We found that majority of undertrials suffered in jails for years after being arrested for petty offences and were kept in confinement during the entire period of their trials", Moily said.

"In many cases the undertrials had already served the maximum sentence that would have been imposed on them had they been convicted by the courts, "the Minister added.

Moily said that the initiative would provide relief to more than a million (10 lakh) people. "Every family, on an average has five members. With the release of two lakh prisoners, we have ended the agony of more than a million people" he said. (H.T. 26.07.2010).

On 31 August 2010, taking serious note of detaining of a prisoner in excess of the sentence awarded to him, the Allahabad High Court directed the State Government to immediately release him. It also directed the state government to take immediate steps to identify all such convicts who have undergone their full sentence but are still languishing in jail and take immediate steps for their release.

Passing the above directive, Justice B.K. Narayana also directed the state government to consider about compensation to the appellant. (Hindustan Time Lucknow, 01.09.2010)

(b) Torture of Prisoners:

The court held that the prisoners could not be held in fetters or tortured.

In Kadra Phadiya and others Vs. State of Bihar[17] four boys aged 18 to 22 years were allegedly kept in leg irons in the Pakud sub-jail in the Santhal Parganas, Bihar. At the time of their arrest they were no more than 9 to 11 years old, but because of the delays in the sessions court they had not been tried.

The court directed the removal of leg irons from the boys and ordered the state to begin the trial immediately and provide legal assistance to the accused.

The court directed the superintendent of Tihar jail to ensure that no more corporal punishment or physical violence was meted out to Sunil Batra.

In Prem Shankar Shukla Vs. Delhi Administration a telegram sent by an undertrial prisoner of Tihar jail said that despite court orders in Sunil Batra (II), handcuffs were forced on him and other prisoners. The court noted that general advice had been issued by the Delhi administration to the effect that ordinary Indian undertrials shall be routinely handcuffed during transit between jail and court but the better class of prisoners shall be so confined only if reasonably apprehended to be violent. The court said, "we lay down as necessarily implicit in Articles 14 and 19 that when there is no compulsive need to fetter a person's limbs, it is sadistic, capricious, despotic and demoralizing to humble a man by manacling him."

The court held that even a detainee is entitled to minimum freedom under Art. 19, and no class differentia was permissible.

On the question of handcuffing the court directed the Union of India to frame rules[18], or guidelines within three months.

In Sept. 2008, the Punjab and Haryana High Court issued directions to the Police authorities in Punjab, Haryana and Chandigarh that no undertrial is handcuffed without prior permission of the court. The court also directed all the magistrates of Punjab, Haryana and Chandigarh to verify from every undertrial produced before them if they were handcuffed by the police.[19]

In Sunil Batra (II), Anil Yadav and Khatri the court acknowledged the need to punish the officials responsible for the torture, but did not record any punishment. Of course the police, officers concerned were arrested but those who disclosed the facts were victimized and the Superintendent of the jail who admitted that the torture had been meted out was suspended.

The Supreme Count has from time to time expressed concern over the increasing number of custodial deaths, custodial violence, torture and abuse of police power. It has noted that torture in custody violates both the Declaration of Human Rights 1948 (Art. 5) and Art. 21 of the Indian constitution. Art. 5 of the Universal Declaration stipulates, "no one shall be subjected to torture or to cruel, inhuman or degrading treatment or punishment.

In the case filed by Indu Jain, wife of R.K. Jain, Dy. Commissioner, commercial Taxes, Bhopal, incriminating five police office working under the Madhya Pradesh Lok Ayukata, the Supreme Court held that if an asthmatic is confined by policeman to a dusty room with cobweds resulting in his/her death, it would amount to custodial death and the officers could be punished for culpable homicide not amounting to murder under section 304 (The Hindu, 10.12.08).

In another case the court said, "Torture in custody flouts the basic rights of citizens recognized by the Indian constitution and is an affront to human dignity. Police excesses and the maltreatment of detainees / undertrials prisoners or suspects tarnishes the image of any civilized nation and encouraged the men in "Khaki" to consider themselves to be above the law and some times even to become law unto themselves" (The Hindu, 08.02.09)

A report released by the Asian Centre for Human Rights (ACHR) reveals that for eight years since 2000, a 54.02 per cent increase has been recorded in prison deaths, while deaths in police custody have gone up by 19.88 per cent.

Deaths in Police custody during 1999-2009

Highest		**Lowest**			
Maharashtra	–	246	Pondichery	–	3
Uttar Pradesh	–	165	Mizoram	–	1
Gujarat	–	139	Sikkim	–	1
West Bengal	–	112	Dadra & Nagar Haveli	–	1
Andhra Pradesh	–	97	Andaman & Nicobar	–	1

The government is currently pushing for an anti torture law. The Cabinet in the last week of April 2010 approved the Prevention of Torture bill 13 years after the country signed an international treaty against torture. The numbers of deaths in Judicial custody Jail between 2000 and 2008 were 10,721 while 1,345 people died in police custody says the Report based on figures released by the National Human Rights Commission.

A.C.H.R. director Suhas Chakma demanded the scrapping of the law requiring sancion to prosecute police and other government officials and implementation of the Law Commissions report on "custodial crimes" that calls for shifting the burden of proof on the police in custodial death case (H.T. 14.4.2010).

(c) The Right of a Prisoner not to be put in Solitary Confinement Unnecessarily (Sunil Batra) (II):

In Kishore Singh, Ravinder Dev etc. Vs. Rajasthan, (3.10.80) prisoners had been kept in solitary confinement in fetters for more than eight months.

The court held solitary confinement to be justified in extreme cases only and that the infliction of physical torture violated Art. 21.

(d) Overcrowding in the Jails

In a letter written by A.K. Chakraborty to the Deputy Registrar of Patna High Court (Sept. 1988) in Ranchi it was stated that while the jail (Ranchi) capacity was for 325 prisoners, it contained over 1,100 prisoners. There were only 12 wards for all the inmates, 70 unlashed lavatories.

Confirming over crowding in jails, the former Director of C.B.I Mr. Joginder Singh writes, "Bihar has a total of 54 jails including the six central prisons, which house over 42,000 prisoners against the total capacity of 19,000.

In Beur jail, Patna alone there are over 2,600 prisoners against a capacity of 1,400..... In Meerut, NHRC found that against the authorized capacity of 650 prisoners there were 3,000 prisoners and 90 per cent of them were undertrials."[20]

It was reported that in the Lakhimpur Kheri district Jail there were nearly 1,800 prisoners including about 1,650 under trials, while the jail has the capacity to accommodate only 500 prisoners. The jail authorities have limited beds as well as limited budget to attend to the ailments of the jail inmates.[21] The overcrowded jails are posing health hazardsto inmates.

Expressing concern over the overcrowding and shabby conditions in the jail, the Allahabad High court in a recent order held that the court should modulate their policies of sentencing accordingly and it is time they look around for other punishments besides imprisonment in prison, like community service and other assignments of similar nature." It is the time the state considers the feasibility of providing such punishments in the statute", the court added.[22]

Justifying this suggestion Justice Barkat Ali Zaidi said, "The other perspective which the courts have to keep in mind is that our jails are over populated, and the prisoners are being maintained in jails, without necessary facilities. It has already been pronounced by the Supreme Court that a prisoner does not loose a right to basic necessities of decent living. While undergoing sentence in jail. It is not, a secret that conditions in our jails are shabby and shoddy."

(e) Bail Procedures:

Bail procedures were relaxed for the poor and helpless. The bail system was described as oppressive and discriminatory against the poor, so the court held that the background of the accused should be examined and lower courts should not insist on bail with sureties.

In the **Hussainara Khattoon** the court held that Art. 21 incorporated the right to speedy trial and again in this case, as in others like Khatri, the right to free legal aid was stressed.

(f) Free Legal Service :

Over the years Indian laws and its interpretation by the Supreme Court as well as the High Courts are emphatic that an accused charged with committing heinous offences would have to be provided legal aid, irrespective of the fact whether he asks for it or not." Free legal assistance at state cost is a fundamental right of a person accused of an offence which may involve jeopardy to his life or personal liberty", said a three judge bench of the Supreme Court in a landmark judgement of 1986 in Sukhdas vs. Union territory of Arunachal Pradesh.

The legal circles have argued for providing legal aid to a terrorist such as Mohammad Ajmal Amir Kasab, the lone militant captured alive in the 26/11 Mumbai terror attacks. Such is the weak ridiculous and pathetic situation arising from the liberal democracy.

It has been held that the right to free legal srvice is implicit in Art. 21 and without it the procedure in courts cannot be said to be "reasonable, fair and just".

The court recommended that the Central and State government should introduce a comprehensive legal aid programme.

In a special interview granted to The Hindu in New Delhi on 8 January 2009, the Chief Justice of India spoke on wide range of issues relating to the Judiciary. Asked for his views on the debate on providing legal aid to Ajmal Kasab K.G. Balkrishnan, C.J.I. said, "under our system the accused should be provided the aid of counsel. If not, the court has to engage counsel at the expense of the state. Fairness demands that whatever may be the heinous crime he has committed, whether he is a Pakistani or a foreigner, he is entitled to get legal aid" (The Hindu, 10.01.2009).

(g) Physical exploitation in the form of Begar:

In judgements from the High Courts the applicability of Art. 23 of the constitution to prison labour (Begar) was considerd. The exploitation of prison labour was first referred to by the Supreme Court in Sunil Batra (II). In two separate cases the High Court of Keral and Shimla held that Art. 23 of the constitution prohibiting forced labour or Begar was applicable to prisoners.[23]

(h) Labour Wages:

Some letters were sent to the court by prisoners in various jails while others, deposited in the grievance deposit boxes maintained in the jails, had been forwarded by the High Court to the government. These letters asked that the wages of prisoners be enhanced.

The court had appointed a committee to look into these matters, to which the government had responeded by nominally revising the minimum rate of wages to 50 paise and the maximum to Rs. 1.60. Another committee was then appointed by the court, which in its report, asked the government to adopt a reasonable wage structure.

The consequence is that to deny a prisoner reasonable wages in return for his work will be to violate the mandate in Article 23 (1) of the Constitution. Consequently the state could be directed not to deny such reasonable wages to the prisoners from whom the state takes work inthe prisons.

Delay in Disposal of Mercy Petitions

The Supreme Court has asked the Central Government to get moving on mercy petitions pending with it. 'It warned that mercy petitions of death row prisoners should not be used for political ends. Presently the government continues to sit on the mercy pleas of more than 50 prisoners on death row. A bench headed by Justice H.S. Bedi said (sometime in October 2009), "We must.... say with the greatest emphasis that human beings are not chattels (slaves) and should not be used as pawns in furthering some larger political (goal) or government policy."

The court reminded the government that delaying decision on mercy petitions violated the condemned prisoners' right to live with dignity. It observed that in some cases the court had awarded the sentence more than a decade ago, but no decision was taken on account of the mercy petitions before the President (H.T. 11, May 2010).

Conclusions

This bird's eye view of important criminal cases in the Supreme Court and in the High Courts shows that the judiciary was called upon to redress wrongs and suggest suitable remedies in almost every aspect of criminology.

The court not only relieved the sufferings of the victims but also provided the necessary and valuable check to executive excesses and injustices. It helped to ensure that the executive and the subordinate judiciary worked within the framework of law and where existing law was found wanting, it did not hesitate to suggest suitable amendments and reforms. All in all, it can be said that the judiciary by its intervention has enlarged the area of justice.

The anomaly is that our police establishment is based on a piece of legislation enacted in 1861. The Indian Police Act, 1861 was in fact a tool in the hands of the colonial power to suit their imperial interests.

Mr. Prakash singh a retired high ranking police officer filed a Public Intetrest litigation petition in 1996 seeking directions to reform the police administration. The court found merit in his petition and in a judgement delivered in 2006 made these observation : "The commitment, devotion and accountability of the police has only to be to the rule of law. The supervision and control has to be such that it ensures that the police serves the people without any regard whatsoever to the status and position of any person while investigating a crime or taking preventive measures. It's approach has to be service odented, its role has to be defined so that in appropriate cases, where on account of acts of omission and commission of (the) police, the rule of law becomes a casualty the guilty police officers are brought to book and appropriate action is taken without delay.

The Supreme Court also observed that there was a convergence in the views of almost all the panels, that is, the National Police Commission, the Law Commission, the Riberio Commission, the Padmanabhiah Committee, the Soli Sorabjee Committee and the Malimath Committee, setup to look into issues of police reforms.

These deferent panels have uniformly recommended (a) the establishment of the State Security Commission at the state level. (b) a transparent procedure for the appointment of the police chief with a fixed tenure, (c) the separation of investigation work from law and order and (d) the enactment of a new Police Act which should reflect the democratic ethos of the society.[24]

It is notable that the criminal procedure court was amended (effective from 19.01.2009) to take care of many of the above recommendations. The following changes in the Cr.PC are notable:

1. It restrains the police from arresting a person for any noncognisable offence for which the maximum sentence is upto seven years,[25] in imprisonment, except under a warrant or order of a Magistrate. However, arrest can be made without a warrant, after recording the

reasons in writing, if the police officer is satisfied that it is necessary for proper probe, or to prevent the person from committing any further offence or making any inducement, threat or promise to anyone acquainted withthe facts of the case.

The amended law says a police officer who is making an arrest will have to bear his identification badge or tag. Besides a memorandum of arrest shall be prepared, witnessed and countersigned. The person arrested shall be told that he/ she has the right to inform a relative or friend.

It mandates the state government to establish police control rooms at the district and state levels and display on notice boards kept outside the control rooms the names and addresses of the persons arrested and the names and designations of the police officers who made the arrests. The law provides for payment of compensation to victims for illegal arrest and police harassment.

References

1. See: Sunday, Dee. 21, 1980 pp. 20.27.
2. Khatri and others Vs. State of Bihar and others, Order dated 3/12/80 reported in (1981) 1 SCC 623.
3. *Ibid*, 635.
4. (1981) 1 SCC 635.
5. P. Rethinam Vs. Union of India, 1993 (2) Scale - (Supreme Court Almanac) 126 (631).
6. (1988) 1Guwa LR (489).
7. Rudal Shah Vs. State of Bihar AIR 1983 SC 1086.
8. AIR, 1983, SC 1134.
9. AIR, 1984, SC 1026.
10. Sangeeta Ahuja, People, Law and Justice, Vol. 1, Orient-Longman, 1997 p. 25.
11. AIR 1992 H.P. 76.

12. Hussainara Khatoon and Others vs. Home Secretary, State of Bihar (1980) 1 SSC 81, 93, 98, 108, 115.
13. Order dated 4/5/79 by Bhagwati and Chinnappa Reddy Reported (1980) SCC 115.
14. R.D. UpadhyayVs. State of A.P. (2000) 10, SCC 255.
15. "Jail Breaks, Riots and Escapes", South Asia Politics, Feb. 2008, Vol. 6, No.10.
16. (1995) 2 SCC 486.
17. AIR 1981 sc 939.
18. 1988, 4 SCC. 54, Aeltemash Rein Vs. Union.
19. *The Hinndu* 30, Sep. 2008.
20. Joginder Singh, Opcit pp. 37-45.
21. Hindustan Times, 12 Oct., 2008.
22. *Hindustan Times;* 11 Oct. 2008·
23. In the matter of prison reforms, enhancement of wages of prisoners etc., AIR 1983, Ker, 261.
24. The Hindu, 24th Septemlier, 2008, N.L. Rajah, "Anti terrorism laws and some imperatives."
25. The IPC provides for punishment up to seven years for offences including attempt to commit culpable homicide, robbery, attempt to suicide, kidnapping, voluntarily causing grievous hunt, cheating, outraging a woman's modesty and death caused, by negligence and dowry harassment.

5

Women and Children

Another area in which Judicial activism has been operative is the issues relating to women and children, specially child labour and Juvenile delinquents.

Women

In case after case the Supreme Court has been confronted with women subjected to injustices, indignitics and exploitation in the prison or in protective homes or at work place.

However domestic violence has so far not been a subject of Public Interest Litigation (PIL) So, till now, it is largely outside of the purview of Judicial Activism.

Women, Police and Prison

The first recorded Public Interest Litigation order by the Supreme Court came in Hussainara Khatoon vs. Home Secretary, State of Bihar. It was a *habeas corpus case* flied by an advocate on the basis of news report in the Indian Express on 8-9/2/79. It was a departure from the procedural rule that a *habeas-corpus* petition can be filed only with a power of attorney or by a close relative. Hitherto only letters were treated as *habeas corpus* petitions but after Hussainara case letter petitions began to be admitted for all kinds of relief.

In the beginning the PIL's were in the form of letters from convicts and undertrials. Soon the letter petition becamc thc mcdium to gaining excess to the court and for seeking relief for a whole class, be they prisoners or undertrials. Moreover the PIL petition could be filed by any public spirited citizen or group or organisation.

The Hussainara case is notable in that it emphasised that:

1. A speedy trial is the essence of criminal justice, delay in a trial constitutes a denial of justice.
2. Courts should not necessarily insist on bail with sureties and the background of the accused should be examined in granting bail.
4. The jail authorities and social welfare department were directed to make suitable arrangements for the care of women and children released on personal bond.
5. The state government was directed to immediately release women held in "protective custody" and put them in welfare centres to be opened by the state.[1]

It is women's groups who have been active in filing PIL cases before the court so as to activate the judiciary and use the law to get specific reliefs.

In one case women volunteers demonstrating in Central Delhi in support of the Bharat Bandh, police made a lathicharge on the women led by Birnda Karat, the secretary of Janwadi Mahila Samiti.

The Supreme Court in an order said that the state should formulate proper rules for the conduct of members of the police force in conjunction with women's organisations.

In the Anjalakshmi Vs. State of Tamil Nadu, the court ordered the release of Ayyanar, who had been detained by the police as a suspect terrorist, for his marriage ceremony. The court ordered Ayyanar to be released for his marriage and for two nights thereafter, even though there was no record of request for parole.

The court stated "though it is settled law that power of parole should normally be exercised only by the state government and courts very rarely step in, in this area, we are inclined to approach the request made in this petition in a humanitarian way, for a marriage fixed should not be allowed to be thwarted. Orders passed in this petition shall stand restricted to the facts of the instant case alone and it can not be treated as a precedent.

The Judicial Activism in this case is also seen in the fact that a special bench was constituted to decide this case. This bench sat at 5.45 pm (26.03.93) while the usual time for the court business to end was 4.30 p.m.[2]

In Sheela Barse vs. Union of India permission to interview female prisoners lodged in the Bombay, Pune and Kolhapur Jails and tape record such interviews was granted as a right flowing from right to life. The court held that the meaning given to the term "life" will cover the living conditions prevailing in jails.

Therefore, citizens have the right to visit jails for collection of information but access has got to be controlled and regulated. As and when factual interview is conducted the same should be cross checked with authorities so that a wrong picture is not given. Moreover access to a prisoner can be with the permission of the prescribed authority.

With the intervention of courts there has been a substantial improvement in the conditions prevailing in jails. The provisions of jail manuals have undergone change and the jail authorities have changed their approach to administration and method of control.[3]

In Sheela Barse vs. State of Maharashtra there were disclosures of recurrent custodial violence done to women in Bombay central jail. The court proceedings in fact turned into a meaningful and fruitful discussion as to the steps which should be taken to protect women prisoners from custodial violence.

The state of Maharashtra, through its advocate, extended full cooperation in formulating the guidelines and also accepted most of the suggestions made by the court.[4]

The court directed its attention to the urgent need of legal assistance to all prisoners and especially to women prisoners. It laid down specific directions for providing legal assistance to prisoners and women prisoners. For want of such assistance to women prisoners, one German and the other Thai, were relieved of their jewellary and cash in the jail by a lawyer on the promise of legal assistance in return.

The court also issued detailed directions to the administration on how to handle cases of women prisoners and convicts.

(*i*) Four or Five lock-ups should be earmarked for female suspects in good localities.

(*ii*) The lock-ups should be guarded by women constables.

(*iii*) Women prisoners should be interrogated in presence of women police officers or constables.

(*iv*) Maharashtra Board of Legal Aid and Advice was directed to bring out a pamphlet in Marathi, Hindi and English, spelling out the legal rights of an arrested person.

(*v*) The police was directed to inform the nearest legal aid committee when they make any arrest and the committee was to provide legal assistance to such person.

(*vi*) A Session Judge, preferably a lady judge, should make surprise visit to police lock-ups and jails.

(*vii*) The police was directed that after arresting a person his nearest relative must be informed of the news of the arrest.

(*viii*) The Magistrate was directed to find out from the arrested person, when produced before him,whether he was subjected to torture.

Women Protective Homes

The Supreme Court has concerned itself with women welfare are in the protective homes like the Nari Niketan in Delhi and the Agra Protective Home for women. The Nari Niketan, Delhi is a rescue home for fallen women. The conditions in the home were horrifying. Even the basic amenities including sanitary napkins were denied to women. Justice P.N. Bhagwati, who received the letter from a social worker was so shocked to learn of these deplorable conditions that he immediately ordered that sanitary napkins be provided to women during their period, by the Delhi Administration Nandita Haksar, advocate, supreme court, pointed out that, "The next day many lawyers were heard asking whether it was the job of Supreme Court to supply sanitary napkins"[5]

Another notable case on this topic relates to the maintenance of the Government Protective Home at Agra where the conditions were equally horrifying.

On the petition of Delhi University law professor and Ex-Vice chancellor, Upendra Baxi, the Supreme Court asked the District Judge to make periodic inspection of the Protective Home. The court passed orders on the basis of the reports received from the District Judge. As a result of these orders the conditions improved and became agreeable for the women living in the protective Home.[6]

But these efforts to improve the living condition of women in the Agra Protective Home received a set back when the government shifted the Home to another building in which sanitation and living conditions were worse.

The Supreme Court was approached again and the court started, the process all over again and commenced giving directions for improving the living conditions in the new building. These directions prescribed the affirmative action to be taken by the administration.

(*i*) The approach road to the new building was to be made pucca or semi-pucca within three months.

(*ii*) Proper cross ventilation was to be provided for fresh air and the District Judge shall determine the number of windows necessary for the purpose. Exhaust fans were to be fitted.

(*iii*) The state government was to provide 24 hour police protection.

(*iv*) Mosquito nets were to be provided to the inmates of the protective Home.

(*v*) Conveyance was to be provided to carry inmates to the court and back home.

(*vi*) Telephone was to be installed at the Protective Home immediately.

(*vii*) The state government was to provide cooking gas to the home.

(*viii*) Detailed directions regarding fitting of electricity were given.

(*ix*) The court outlined a detailed programme of rehabilitation of the inmates and suggested that they should be given vocational training and guidance.

(*x*) It even went to the extent of suggesting that the state should find out suitable bridegrooms for their marriage. In this way the court assumed the role of the super executive and the welfare state.[7]

Women at Work Place

Three cases are given here to illustrate the role of the court in protecting the rights and interests of women at workplace. These are Brij Bala Vs. State of H.P.[8] and others, Sanjit Rao vs. State of Rajasthan[9] and Vishaka vs. state of Rajasthan.[10]

Brij Bala Vs. State of H.P. and Others

In this case a letter was sent by a scheduled caste woman, Brij Bala to the Chief Justice of Himachal Pradesh High court complaining that she was being denied the opportunity of recruitment as a patwari on the ground that "the field duties of a Patwari are not congenial to girls." In reply an affidavit on behalf of respondent stated that the contention regarding the suitability of women for the post of Patwari was only a personal opinion of the Director of Land Records. It further stated that the rules do not provide any bar for the recruitment of girls. It promised that in case of a vacancy of Patwari arising in the future there would be no bar to her selection on merits for the post.

Sanjit Rao vs. State of Rajasthan

Sanjit Rao vs. State of Rajasthan underlines the court's concern with labourers in general and with women workers in particular. The workers engaged in constructing Madanganj Harmara Road were not being paid the agreed minimum wages for a worker, that is Rs. 7/- per day. Instead the workers were being paid less than the minimum wage on the ground that the quantity of their work was less than the minimum expected and in case of women worker they were paid even less than the male workers. There were differential payments to various bands (a band consisted of 20 workers) and to different workers of the same band.

The Supreme Court termed these inequities and the infringement of the minimum wages Act as unconstitutional. The court directed.

1. That the difference between the minimum wage and the wage actually paid shall be paid by the P.W.D. of Rajasthan within two months from the date of judgement.
2. The state would thereafter pay to every worker engaged in any work (including famine relief work the minimum wage for his or her labour.
3. No deduction should be made on the ground that the work did not conform to the norm laid down by the P.W.D.
4. A norm on minimum work, in order to be valid, must be spelt in a notification.
5. Rajasthan Famine Relief Work Employees (exemptions from abour laws) Act 1964, was no longer valid.

This decision is evidence of the intrusion of the judiciary into the legislative sphere in as much as it not only annulled a State Act but also laid down new norms for wage payment to workers.

Vishaka Vs. State of Rajasthan

This case is the most glaring example of judicial legislation. It is a case of the judiciary making the law where none existed.

In this case the Supreme Court held that the sexual harassment of working women at workplace amounts to violation of right of gender equality and right to life and personal liberty. By inference, it amounts to be violation of right to "practice any profession, occupation or trade".

In the absence of any law on the subject, the Supreme Court proceeded to lay down certain guidelines to be observed at all workplaces or other institutions which would be binding and enforceable in law, until suitable legislation enacted for the purpose. The said guidelines which were tantamount to law declared by the Supreme Court under Art. 141, are as follows:

1. It shall be the duty of the employer or other responsible persons in workplaces or other institutions to prevent or deter the commission of acts of sexual harassment.
2. For this purpose sexual harassment includes such unwelcome sexually determined behaviour (whether directly or by implication) as—
   (*a*) Physical contact and advances.
   (*b*) A demand or request for sexual favours;
   (*c*) Showing pornography;
   (*d*) Any other unwelcome physical, verbal or non verbal conduct of sexual nature.
   where any of these acts is committed in circumstances whereunder the victim of such conduct has a reasonable apprehension that in relation to the victim's employment or work such conduct can be humiliating and may constitute a health and safety problem.
3. All employers or persons in charge of workplace whether in public or private sector should take appropriate steps to prevent sexual harassment. A few steps to be taken by them have been mentioned in the guidelines.
4. Where such conduct amounts to a specific offence under Indian Penal code or under any other law, the employer shall initiate appropriate action in accordance with law by making a compliant with the appropriate authority.

5. Where such conduct amounts to misconduct in employment as defined by the relevant service rules, appropriate disciplinary action should be initiated by the employer in accordance with those rules.
6. Whether or not such conduct constitutes an offence under law or a breach of the service rules, an appropriate complaint mechanism should be created in the employer's organisation for redress of the complaint made by victim. Such complaint, mechanism should ensure time bound treatment of complaint.
7. Employees should be allowed to raise issues of sexual harassment at workers meetings and in other other appropriate forums and it should be affirmatively discussed in employer-employee meetings.
8. Where sexual harassment occurs as a result of an act or omission by any third party or outsider, the employer and person in charge will take all steps necessary and reasonable to assist the affected person in terms of support and preventive action.
9. The Central/State government, are requested to consider adopting suitable measures including to legislation to ensure that the guidelines laid down by this order are also observed by the employer in private sector.

Children

The Judicial intrusion into the realm of children hit national news media with the reporting of the Delhi High Court decision stopping interviewing children, for admissions in nursery schools. A public debate was triggered by a division bench of the Supreme Court comprising A.K. Mathur and Markandey Katju, J.J. Making scathing observations on the tendency of the High Court on admitting writ petitions like nursery admission, unauthorised, schools, criteria for free seats in school which, the bench said, "were matters pertaining exclusively to the executive or legislative domain."

The bench cursorily discussed one of the cases, the PIL, challenging the practice of interviewing children for admissions in nursery schools. It faulted the Delhi High Court for stopping such interviews as there was no statute or statutory rule prohibiting them. The bench said, "hence the Delhi High court has by a judicial order just created a law (which was wholly beyond its jurisdiction) and has then sought to enforce it. This is clearly illegal for judges cannot legislate."[11]

Apart from these trivial issues, judicial activism has been to the great relief and rescue of the child, as a juvenile delinquent, as a child labour and the like.

The PIL cases have focused on the non implementation of statutory and constitutional provisions for children. It was the judicial pressure that in 1986 juvenile justice issues were codified in a central enactment, the Juvenile Justice Act. This Act deals with issues like – (1) the illegal confinement of children in jail for long periods. (2) The treatment of mentally and physically handicapped children and (3) The conditions prevalent in jails.

The court in case after case has ordered inquires and monitored the progress of the case and the implementation of its orders. The court has also monitored the implementation of the existing statutory framework.

In Munna and others[12], the Supreme Court directed that the Children's Act be implemented and in the Sheela Barse case[13] on prisons, the implementation of the Juvenile Justice Act 1986 was ordered.

The court orders in various cases also resulted in the setting up of statutory institutions under the Juvenile Justice Act.

In Munna vs. State of U.P. the SC directed that, "no person apparently under the age of 16 years is sent to jail but is detained in a children's home or other suitable place of safety set-up by the government", and added that this direction will apply to the Magistrates not only in U.P. but in the other parts of the country where the Children's Act is in force.[14]

In Sanjay Suri and another vs. Delhi Administration the court directed that every warrant of detention should specify the age of the person to be detained and this warrant should be used to determine whether the prisoner should be lodged at the Tihar jail or Juvenile jail. The prison warders were directed that aVisitors Board be constituted with social activist, media people, jurist and the executive, as members.[15]

In Kamala Devi Chattopadhyay Vs. Punjab children together with women rounded up in an army action in the Golden Temple, along with devotees and pilgrims were ordered to be released as no reason for their detention had been given.[16]

In Sheela Barse vs. Union of India[17] the petition was filed on behalf of all the children below 16 years languishing in jails all over the country. In its judgement the Supreme Court ordered.

(1) That the state take care of the mentally and physically handicapped children by providing them with medical treatment, vocational training and moving them to places of safe custody.

(2) If there were not enough places for these children in homes then social service organisations were to be entrusted with the task of rehabilitating them.

(3) The social welfare board was ordered to provide a list of non-governmental, governmental and semigovernmental organisations offering their services in this regard.

(4) Children's Acts should be brought into force without delay.

(5) A central legislation be passed to replace the State Acts.

(6) Children must not be imprisoned but kept in Remand Homes set up by the state. There should be Juvenile courts with a specialised cadre of magistrates in every district.

(7) Lastly, the court stressed the importance of the National Policy Declaration for the welfare of children, 1974 in this context.

In one case, Supreme Court directed that rules under Juvenile Justice Act, 1986 be framed by each state government and placed before the Supreme Court for review. It further stated that Juvenile, and Observation Homes should be set up to deal with delinquent juveniles. It further directed that Advisory Boards should be set up at state level under the scheme.[18]

Child Labour

The judiciary has been equally protective of the rights and interests of the child labour, especially the children engaged in hazardous work such as Beedi and Cigar manufacturing, glass bangles, making matchsticks, carpet weaving etc. In many cases it has ensured that the constitutional provisions contained in Articles 23 and 24 are observed in good faith.

The court issued several directions for rescue and rehabilitation of child prostitutes and children of fallen women. It suggested several measures to retrieve such women from prostitution and rehabilitate them to lead a life of dignity through self-employment by provision of avenues in this behalf. The court criticised the customary initiation of women in the practice of Devadasis (Andhra Pradesh), Jogins (Karnataka) and Venkatasin (Maharashtra) which have no legal sanction and are violative of the law and Constitution.[19]

The Supreme Court favoured the progressive (not total) banning of child labour, starting from children below the age of 14 years, and from most hazardous and intolerable activities.

In M.C. Mehta vs. Tamil Nadu[20] the court held that children can be employed in the process of packing but not in the process of manufacturing and final production of match-sticks or fireworks. It insisted that the minimum wages for child labbur should be fixed and special facilities as required under the Factories Act for improving the quality of life of children should be provided. This would require facilities for education, recreation and medical attention.

These directions of the court were reiterated in Bandhua Mukti Morcha vs. Union of India.[21] In this case directions were given for evolving principles for progressive elimination of child labour in all employments, consistent with the scheme to provide—

(*i*) Compulsory education to all children either by industries or in coordination with government.

(*ii*) Periodical health check up.

(*iii*) Nutrient food.

In a PIL case in Dec., 1996 the Supreme Court directed setting up of a child labour-rehabilitation worker fund in which employers were asked to make contribution of Rs. 25,000/- per child worker.

Miscellaneous Cases

In another case the Delhi High Court fixed the freeship quota for the students belonging to the economically weaker sections at 15 per cent.

Yet in another case in July 2004 the court warned against

the charging of capitation fees by private self financing educational institutions. In 2007 the Delhi HC directed the UPSC to make public the scaling system and cutoff marks for the Civil Services (Preliminary) Examination.

The Supreme Court barred Medical Colleges form admitting students to post-graduate courses once the session starts, felt if there are vacancies.

Conclusion

These cases are instances of the judicial incursion into the executive sphere. They exhibit judicial activism in exercising control over the Executive. They also show the passivity and indifference of the Executive to the problems of governance and its insensitiveness to human suffering and want. However, judicial activism should not be seen as a substitute for the Executive or for the Legislature. In a way judicial activism supplements the legislature in exercising, control over the Executive. It also provides the safety valve to the institutions of liberal democracy which may otherwise be blown off by popular anger and frustration.

References

1. Hussainara Khatoon vs. State of Bihar, (1980) ISCC 81, 93, 98, 108, 115.
2. Sangeeta Ahuja, "People, Law and Justice" Vol. I. Orient Longman, 1997, p. 227.
3. Sheela Barse vs. Union of India, (1987) 3 SCJ 543.
4. Sheela barse vs. State of Maharashtra (1983), 2 SCC 96; AIR 1993 SC 378.
5. See Nandita Haksar "Justice for the CommonMan", "Public Interest Law Reporter", Vol. I, No.1, July-September, 1983 p. 7.
6. Upendra Baxi vs. State of U.P. (1983) 2 SCC 308.
7. Upendra Baxi vs. State of U.P. AIR 1987, SC 191.

8. Brij Bala vs. State of H.P. and others (1984) 2 SLR 408 (Service Law Reporter).
9. Sanjit Roy vs. State of Rajasthan, AIR 1983, SC 328.
10. (1997) 6 SCC 241: AIR 1997 SC 3011.
11. The Times of India, Allahabad Dec. 13, 2007
12. Munna and Others vs. State of U.P. (1982), I SCC 545.
13. Sheela Barse vs. Union of India AIR 1988, SC 2211.
14. Munna vs. State of U.P. (1982), I SCC 545.
15. Sanjay Suri and another vs. Delhi Administration (1987) (2) SCALE 276 (Supreme Court Almanac).
16. Kamala Devi vs. State of Punjab AIR 1984, se 1895.
17. Sheela Barse vs. Union of India, AIR 1986, SC 1773; (1986) SCC 596.
18. Supreme Court Legal Aid Committee vs.Union of India (1989) 2 SCC 325; AIR 1989, SC 1278.
19. Gaurav Jain vs. Union of India (1997), 8 SCC 114; AIR 1997, SC 3021.
20. Workers Union vs. State of Tamil Nadu, (1992) 1 SCC 221 (1991) 1SCC 293.
21. (1997), 10 SCC 549.

6

Labour, Poor, Helpless Indigent Denizens

The rule of law is gradually being transformed into the regime of justice by the process of judicial activism.

Judicial activism is virtually taking on the role of the welfare executive. This is nowhere more evident than in the attention paid by the judicary to the problems of labourers, poor, helpless, indigent denizens. This is particularly significant in the present era of liberalization, Privatisation and Globilization (L.P.G.).

In one case[1] Bhagwati J. delivering what appears almost to be a professorial lecture said, "The rule of law does not mean that the protection of the law must be available only to a fortunate few or that the law should be allowed to be prostituted by the vested interests for protecting and upholding the status quo under the guise of enforcement of their civil and political rights. The poor, too, have civil and political rights and the Rule of Law is meant for them also, though today it exists only on paper and not in reality."

He further said, "Public Interest Litigation is an effort.. ..... to secure observance of the constitutional or legal rights, benefits and priviliges conferred upon the vulnerable sections of the community and to reach Social Justice to them............ The State........ should, infact, welcome it, as it would give it an opportunity to right a wrong or to redress an injustice done, to the poor and weaker sections of the community whose welfare is and must be the prime concern of the state or the public authority."

Bonded Labour

In a large number of cases Public Interest Litigation focussed on the survival of Bonded Labour despite its abolition by the Act of 1976. PIL cases poured in from Haryana, Chhatisgarh, Maharastra, Tamil Nadu, Bihar and Karnataka.

In one case the Supreme Court entertained a matter concerning release of Bonded Labourers of stone quarry workers in Haryana. The State contended that there were no bonded labourers. Bhagwati J. said, "The government need not be shy of admitting, that there were bonded labourers but it should be ready to take steps to implement the Act...... (and) to free bonded labourers and rehabilitate them."[2]

The Issue of bonded labour was raised again in Salal Hydroelectric Project Vs. State of Jammu and Kashmir[3] and in Neeraja Choudhary Vs. State of M.P.[4] It was held that "whenever it is found that any workman is forced to private labour for no remuneration or nominal remuneration, the presumption would be that he is bonded labourer."

In Mukesh Advani V. State of M.P.[5] there were allegations of bonded labourers working in the stone quarries at Raisen in M.P. The court appointed the District Judge of Bhopal to inquire into the matter. The District Judge reported that the bonded labourers had been released by the time the court commission made its investigation.

In T. Chakkalackal, the administration refused to testify to the existence of Bonded Labourers despite its earlier declaration.

In all these cases the appointment of Commissions of inquiry, issuing of directions and monitoring them have been common features. In Neeraja Choudhary the court also agreed to monitor the rehabilitation of labourers freed.

The court ordered the establishment of an administrative machinery in the form of vigilance committees to oversee implementation of the Act.

In Bandhua Mukti Morcha Case it was alleged that bonded labourers were migrants from M.P., Rajasthan and U.P. These workers were not paid even the minimum wages and Labour Laws were being flouted.

The court issued twenty one directions which are tantamount to Judicial Legislation. These included that the government of Haryana was.

(1) to constitute a vigilance committee under the 1976 Act, within six weeks.

(2) draw a scheme within three months for the rehabilitation of freed bonded labourers.

(3) take all necessary steps to ensure that minimum wages were paid to the workers of the stone quaries and crushers, within six weeks.

The court directed the Joint secretary, Ministry of Labour, Government of India to ascertain whether any of the labourers working in the stone quarries and crushers in Faridabad Distt. were bonded labourers and if so what was their number.[7]

In Hav. P. Sivaswamy, social action groups were used to monitor the implemention of the court's order and given a place on the vigilance committees.

The governments have been slack in identifying, releasing and formulating programmes for rehabilitation of freed bonded labourers.

In Neeraja Choudhary Vs. State of M.P. the court noted, "It is imperative that neither the government nor the court should be content with securing identification and release of bonded labourers but every effort must be made by them to see that the freed bonded labourers are properly and suitably rehabilitated after their identification and release."[8]

As a result of the judicial pressure hundreds of bonded laburers were released in various States, 135 in M.P., 292 in Maharashtra, 86 in Odisha 1417 in Andhra Pradesh and so on.

Labour Laws

The PIL petitions brought to the court a stream of cases involving labour laws violations and labour related issues such as payment of minimum wages, equal pay for equal work for both men and women, working condition of labour, and the like. The Supreme Court, was relentless in ordering investigation, appointing commission and issuing directions and monitoring their implementation in case after case.

The major laws which were reportedly in breach were—

(*i*) Minimum Wages Act, 1948.

(*ii*) Contract Labour (Regulation and Abolition) Act, 1970.

(*iii*) The Bonded Labour System (Abolition) Act, 1976.

(*iv*) Inter-State Migrant workmen (Regulation of Employment and conditions of service) Act, 1979.

(*v*) Industrial Disputes Act, 1947.

(*vi*) Equal Remuneration Act, 1976.

(*vii*) Employment of children Act, 1938.

The constitutional provisions allegedly in breach were the Directive Principles such as 39 (d) that, there is equal pay for equal work for both men and women.

(*viii*) that the health and strength of workers, men and women, and the tender age of children are not abused.

(*ix*) that children are given opportunities and facilities to develop in a healthy manner and in conditions of freedom and dignity and that childhood and youth are protected against exploitation.

Art. 42 – the state shall make provision for securing just and humane conditions of work and for maternity relief.

Art. 43 – The state shall endevour to secure to all workers...... a living wage, conditions of work ensuring a decent standard of life........

Art. 43 (a) – The State shall take steps .....to secure the participation of workers....... in the management of undertakings....... engaged in any industry.

The Supreme Court has been very alert and active in responding to petitions raising issues of violations of these laws and constitutional provisions, and in safeguarding the rights and interests of workers.

Sindri Fertilizer Corporation Case

In the Sindri Fertilizer Corporation Kamgar Union case, petition was dismissed on the facts of the case, but the court conceded that the workers had a stake in the closure of the factory and in the sale of its plants and equipment.[9]

Rohtas Industries

In another case it was held that in the event of the closure of plants (of Rohtas industries, Dalmia Nagar) the salary dues of the workers upto the date of the closure should be paid by the sale proceeds of goods lying in stock and that payment of salaries and wages due to the workers will have priority over payment to creditors like the banks and financial institutions. The court also held that the viable units of the industry should be revived and allowed to resume Production.[10]

Sanjit Roy Case— In Sanjit Roy, Vs. Rajasthan[11] the court indicted the P.W.D. of not paying the minimum wages to labourers and instead making arbitarary deductions resulting in differential payments to workers and to women workers. It stated that the payment of less than the minimum wages could not be justified even on the ground of serving a public cause like famine relief.

Asiad Case – In the case known as the Asiad Case[12] the court directed the Delhi Development Authority to carry out weekly inspections of the various Asiad construction projects and to ensure the payment of minimum wages and implementation of other Labour Laws.

It went so far as to appoint two independent institutions to act as Ombudsmen for protecting the interests of the workers and ensuring observance of the contract Labour Act, Minimum Wages Act, Employment of children Act and the Inter State Migrant workmen Act, by the contractors.

The Court expanded the definition of "forced Labour" to include in it the compulsion of economic circumstances or through a legal provision for imprisonment or fine in case the employee fails to provide labour or service.

The court directed the public sector Corporations to ensure that Labour Laws were being observed without waiting for a complaint and that periodic inspections should be carried out to ensure implementation of the laws. The court has given effect to the Directive Principle requiring equal payment for equal work, to both men and women, in various case.

In the Dhirendra Chamoli, Vs U.P.[13] the court held that equal pay for equal work was implicit in the equality guaranteed under Art. 14. The workers whether regular or casual, must receive the same salary and conditions of service.

Dhirendra Chamoli decision was followed in Surinder Singh Vs. Engineer in chief, P.W.D.[14]

As a result, 20,000 employees working on daily wages in C.P.W.D. demanded enhancement of dally wage paid to them and went on complete strike demanding full compliance with Surinder Singh decision. Thus judicial activism promoted a social drive to force the executive to implement the principle of equal pay for equal work.

Salal Hydro Electric Project Case

In the Salal Hydro Electric Project Case[15] the court directed that the Central Government or the contractor should provide schooling facilities to children of construction workers living at or near the project site.

In the M.K. Sharma V. Bharat Electronic Ltd (BEL) the court directed bi-annual checks for safety and insurance cover for the employees, who were exposed to the ill-effects of radiation. The court also recorded BEL's promise to pay compensation to its workers, if and when any ill effects were found.[16]

Poor, Helpless, Indigent Denizens

The Judiciary did not have much legal substantial ground to stand on, in cases of eviction of slum dwellers and pavement dwellers or in cases involving hawkers and vendors and rickshaw pullers. However when approached by Social activists it was able to extend relief on humanitarian grounds and on the principles of natural justice.

Rickshaw Pullers

In the Azad Rickshaw Pullers case while upholding the ban on the pulling of hired rickshaws, the Supreme Court made arrangements for loans from Punjab National Bank for enabling rickshaw pullers to buy their own rickshaws. It set out a detailed scheme for amelioration of the professional conditions of the rickshaw pullers.[17]

Pavements Dwellers and Slum Dwellers

The Maharashtra government had announced a massive programme of "Pavement Clearance" and to deport about one lakh pavement dwellers outside city limits. The Olga Tellis case[18] was filed in reaction to horrific evictions of pavement dwellers and the defencelessness of the evictees in the fate of seizure of their belongings by the Municipal employee and lack of alternative accommodation. The Supreme Court upheld the right of the government of Maharashtra to evict the pavment dwellers but negatived the assumption that they were criminal or anti socials.

The Court said that it is impermissible to characterize these "poor and helpless specimen of humanity" as "trespassers" because their occupation of pavements arises from economic compulsion. The court insisted that they must be treated humanely and the force used to evict them must be reasonable and appropriate. They must be given adequate time to vacate on their own. It directed that—

(1) no evictions were to take place until one month after the end of the current Monsoon season.

(2) Steps may be taken to offer alternative premises to the pavement dwellers though it was not a condition precedent to the removal of the encroachments.

(3) The slums in existence for more than 20 years were to be-left intact, unless the land was required for a public purpose.

(4) For such slums alternative accommodation was to be provided under the Low Income Scheme Shelter Programme. Meanwhile the slum up gradation Programme was to be implemented without delay.

The directions as to alternative accommodation and evictions only in case the land was required for a public purpose were reiterated in the K. Chandru V. Tamil Nadu[19] and in several other cases.

Slum Dwellers

The slum dwellers in all major towns faced more or less the same predicament as the pavement dwellers due to demolition of their hutments, their forcible eviction and consequent dispossession of their belongings.

The State is absolved of even minimal obligations in respect of demolition of unauthorisied slums or where land is required for a public purpose.

The courts have been unable to provide any lasting relief to slum dwellers, but all the petitions filed on Municipal services (drainage, Sanitation etc.), and recreational land have been allowed and directions issued. The court became involved in monitoring the formulation of schemes and urging the Municipal bodies into action, as in Foot Path, Dukandar, New Lajpat Rai Market Patri Union case.[20]

In a Madras case (1990),[21] the court held that the authorities should not evict slum dwellers without providing them an alternative site.

In Bombay Hawker's Union Case[22], the court seemed to place the prevention of public nuissance on public streets above poverty on the list of its priorities. It was held that any slum could be removed if the land occupied was needed for a public purpose.

Modifying its stance in the Olga Tellis, the court held that slum dwellers have a right to be heard before demolition.[23]

In the case of slum dwellers of Slamagar, the Supreme Court held that slum dwellers were to be moved to sites located at reasonable distance from the place of employment of its residents.

Hawkers and Vendors

In a sense pavement dwellers, slum dwellers and hawkers and vendors are in the same boat in as much as they occupy public space in contravention of Municipal laws and regulations. The courts have tended to place the prevention of public nuissance on public streets higher on its list of priorities than the right to carry on trade or business (Art. 19 (g). It has subjected this right to the imperative of avoiding nuissance, annoyance or inconvenience to the general public.

In the Bombay Hawkers Union Case the court accepted the need for creating special hawkers zones and for framing a scheme to regulate the grant of licences to hawkers. The court insisted that the scheme must accommodate all interests.

In another case the Supreme Court ordered that the vendors selling vegetables in Manek Chowk (Ahmedabad) for generations be not deemed to be "encroachers" into traffic space. The court ordered that certificates be issued that would serve as temporary licences until alternative accomodation was given to enable the vendors and hawkers to ply their trade. It was held that members of Self Employed Women's Association (SEWA.) were entitled to carryon vending vegetables at the place where they had been doing so.[24]

In a case reported in the News media on April 20, 2007 it was alleged that women vendors always get pushed out of the hawking areas by local goons who run extortion rackets in connivance with police and M.C.D. officials. The petition Pleaded with the court to pay a little more attention to the demand for hawking zones exclusively for women and said that one was being built near New Delhi Railway Station.[25]

In the same year (2007) the Supreme Court directed the Municipal Authorities to free roads, footh-paths and public streets in the national capital from unauthorised hawkers and squatters and to formulate a policy for them keeping the welfare of general public in view.

It also approved the civic body's urban street vendor schemes which banned road side cooking.

Infact the encroaching vendors are a problem common to every urban civic body. In Lucknow it is estimated that there are around 1.5 lakh vendors in the city.

A National Vending Policy has been formulated but not followed in practice. The Lucknow Bench of the High court (September 4, 2008) asked the Lucknow Municipal Corporation as to why the rules regarding Vending Zones, have not been followed and why the vending committees have not been formed. The High Court also asked the LMC the reason for not complying with the terms of the National Policy on Urban Street Vendors.

The Times of India (17.01.2009)

Action Required

What needs to be done under the National Vending Policy.

- *Formation of vending committee comprising mayor, Municipal commissioner, DM, SSP and vendors' association.*
- *Zonal identification of vending zones with the help of corporators.*
- *Issuance of ID cards to vendors.*
- *The ID card would be valid for 3 years for a payment of Rs. 300.*
- *The vendor would pay a fee of Rs. 300 per month to the municipal body.*

HC's Orders

A bench comprising Justice Pradeep Kant and Justice Ved Pal on September 4, 2008, had asked the LMC as to why the rules of 2007 (viz-a-viz vending zones) have not been followed and why the committee has not been constituted. The high court had also asked the LMC the reason for not complying with the terms of the national policy of urban street vendors.

Where can the vending zones be set up

Vendors Suggest

- *Zonal identification of land.*
- *Master plan allocates 1 per cent space of the total development area as vending zones.*
- *Space below flyovers and railway over bridges can be used as a vending zone.*
- *Open space and grounds which are not used often – Ram Lila maidan is one such area.*

LMC's Excuse

- *A large chunk of land near Mohan Market in Aminabad.*
- *No systematic approach for vendors.*
- *Over 1,500 vending associations claiming for their rights.*
- *LMC claims of having a humanitarian approach in allowing the vendors to operate—But that is until smooth flow of traffic is not affected.*

The Times of India (17.01.2009)

In 2009 the Housing and Urban Poverty Alleviation Ministry drafted a Model Street Vendors (protection of Livelihood Regulation of Street Vending) Bill, 2009.

The Supreme Court on October 19, 2010 directed the government to take steps to translate the bill into law by June, 30, 2011 to regulate hawkers rights which often come into conflict with consumers rights to road and streets. Declaring hawking a fundamental right the court acknowledged that a hawker's fundamental right to do business on a puublic street is subject to reasonable restrictions under Article 19 (6) of the Constitution. "These two apparently conflicting rights must be harmonized and regulated." The Supreme Court was acting on petitions filed by Delhi hawkers challenging various aspects of vending schemes framed by the capital's civic agencies – the MCD and N.D.M.C. – on its directions. Commenting on the often repeated argument that the rural poor migrate to cities and choke their roads, it said: "there is a section that due to its ever increasing wealth, is buying any number of cars, scooters.....no restriction has apparently been imposed by law on such purchase."

But the court made it clear that till a law is enacted, hawkers must go by the schemes framed by the Municipal bodies and approved by the Supreme Court (H.T. Lucknow, 20.10.2010).

It is notable that the Union Cabinet approved a resolution for grant of cashless health insurance scheme for roadside cooking vendors on 20.10.2010. This will form part of National Health Insuranc Scheme (R.S.B.Y.). The scheme so far was applicable only to B.P.L. families. According to the 2001 census there are about 42 lakh such vendors in the country. The government has decided to being all of them under the National Health Insurance Scheme (R.S.B.Y.) by 2013- 2,014. These families, will be entitled to free treatment in government hospitals while the expenses will be borne by the government.

Conclusion– These various cases relating to the marginalised sections of society show the role of the Supreme Court in maximising the area of justice within the parameters of the bourgeois, liberal, democratic frame work. This tendency is described as Judicial activism. It is the judicial activism which has sustained the dwindling faith of the common man in the judicial system which otherwise is plagued with the mind boggling demands of the laywers and the endless delays in rendering decisions, besides, the harassment and hardship which the litigant has to face in having to move from court to the lawyers chamber and may be to the police station.

References

1. People's Union for Democratic Rights vs. Union of India (1982) 3 SCC 235: AIR 1982 SC 1473.

   Also See: Lok Adhikar Sangh Vs. State of Gujarat, Sangeeta Ahuja; People, Law and Justice, Vol. I. Orient Longman, 1997, pp. 287-291.
2. Bandhua Mukti Morcha Vs. Union of India, (1984) SCC 161; AIR 1984 SC 802.
3. (1984) 3 SCC 538; AIR 1984 SC 177.
4. (1984) SCC 243; AIR 1984 SC 1099.
5. (1985) 3 SCC 162; AIR 1985 SC 1368.
6. T. Chakkalackal Vs State of Bihar JT 1992 (1) SC 106.
7. 1986 (SUPP) SCCS 41.
8. AIR 1984, SC 1099.
9. Fertilizer Corporation Kamgar Vs. Union of India, AIR 1981 SC 344.
10. Workers of Rohtas Industries Vs. Rohtas Industries Ltd. (1987) 2 SCC 588, AIR 1990 SC 481.
11. AIR 1983 SC 328.
12. People Union For Democratic Rights (PUDR) Vs. Union of India, AIR 1982, SC 1473.
13. (1986) 1 SCC 637.
14. (1986) 1 SCC 637.
15. (1983) 2 SCC 181; (1984) 3 SCC 53.
16. (1987) 3 SCC 231.
17. Azad Rickshaw Pullers Union, Amritsar Vs. State of Punjab, AIR 1981, SC 15.

18. Olga Tellis Vs. Bombay Municipal Corporation, 1985 SCC 545; AIR 1986 SC 180.
19. K. Chandru Vs. Tamil Nadu, 1985 (2) SCALE 3 (31).
20. Footpath Dukandar New Lajpat Rai Market Patri Union and others Vs. MCD and others, 1986 (2) SCALE 169 (711).
21. Madras Citizens Progressive Council Vs. the Secretary to Government of Tamil Nadu, AIR 1991, Mad, 390.
22. Bombay Hawker's Union Vs. Bombay Municipal Corporation, AIR 1985 SC 1206; (1985) 3 SCC 528.
23. Scheduled Caste and Weaker Section Welfare Association and another Vs. State of Karnataka and other (1991) 2 SCC 604.
24. Self Employed Women's Association Vs. Municipal corporation of Ahmedabad, 1986 (2) SCALE 291 (1254).
25. *The Times of India,* Lucknow, April, 20, 2007.

7

Judicial Activism, Power Politics and Social Justice

There is an area of Public Policy – reservation policy – where activism of party politics had to be countered by judicial activism. While the former was keen on promoting the sectorial interests even beyond the Constitution, (as it originally was in 1950) the Supreme Court was called upon to safeguard the fundamental rights of the people as constitutionally guaranteed.

Reservation policy is the main plank of the movement for social justice but the reservation policy has been overtaken by power politics. Therefore the people in general and the students in particular were forced to knock at the doors of the judiciary to seek enforcement of a balance between the fundamental right to equality and the social interest in uplift of the weaker sections of society.

Champakam Dorairajan Vs. State of Madras

The first clash between fundamental rights and the demands of social justice for backward classes occurred in Madras, soon after the promulgation of the new Constitution.

For many years before the commencement of the Constitution seats in Medical and Engineering colleges of the State, four each, were apportioned between four groups of Districts to be filled up community wise in proportions set forth in a Communal G.O.

Even after the commencement of the Constitution, the admission to these colleges continued on communal basis set forth in the G.O.

In view of the reservation of seats on a communal basis the prospects of admission for students of each community were limited to the seats allocated to that community.

This reservation on communal basis was challenged as unconstitutional in the state of Madras Vs. Champakam Durairajan.[1] The petition complained of the breach of the fundamental right to get admission into educational institutions maintained by the State as but for the reservation on communal basis the applicant, "would not have been denied admission if selections had been made on merit alone."

The court agreed that the classification in the communal G.O. proceeds on the basis of religion, race and caste and said, "in our view, classification made in the communal G.O. is opposed to the Constitution and constitutes a clear violation of the fundamental rightes guaranteed to the citizens under Art. 29 (2)."

In this way the Supreme Court annulled the Communal G.O. fixing proportionate seats for different communities in engineering and medical colleges of the State of Madras. It thus upheld the principle of equality of opportunities for all sections of society without discrimination on the basis of religion or caste.

The Indian society and politics were not prepared to go that far on the road to equality. The society was split into castes and sects and classes which were unequal in social and economic status and also in educational levels. There were the scheduled castes, the scheduled Tribes and other Backward Classes, besides women, who were not at par with the rest of the society. Equal treatment of unequals could only accentuate inequalities, and not promote Equality. Therefore, politically, it was thought necessary that the State should take affirmative action and be empowered to make special provision for the advancement of these weaker sections of society.

It was with this sociological imperative in mind that an amendment was made, the First Amendment (1951) which permitted the State to make special provisions for the advancement of the weaker sections of society. The newly added clause 4 to Art. 15 provided as follows –

Art. 15 (4) – "Nothing in this article or in clause (2) of article 29 shall prevent the State from making any special provision for the advancement of any socially and educationally backward class of citizens or for the scheduled castes and the scheduled Tribes."

The state has translated this power into the Reservation policy, reserving seats in educational institutions and posts in State services for members of the Scheduled Castes, Scheduled Tribes and Other Backward classes.

Since the backward classes were not an identifiable category, the provision of reservation at the Central level remained confined to the SCs and STs' only. It was in August 1989 that the Prime Minister V.P. Singh made a public announcement of the governments resolve to implement the, Report of the Backward Classes Commission, recommending 27 per cent OBC quota in seats and posts.

The doors was thus opened for reservation for OBC's besides SC's and ST's, in government service at the Union level. But there was so far no legal provision for OBC's reservations in educational Institutions. Under pressure from political parties and the OBC lobbies the government was impelled to push through Parliament the Central Educational Institutions (Reservation in Admission) Act,

2006, providing for 27per cent OBC quota, and the 83rd Constitution Amendment under which the legislation was enacted. The said amendment added clause (5) to Art. 15 providing as follows—

Art. 15 (5) - "Nothing in this article or in sub-clause, (g) of clause (1) of article 19 shall prevent the state from making any special provision, by law, for the advancement of any socially and educationally backward classes of citizens or for the scheduled castes or the scheduled Tribes in so far as such special provisions relate to their admission to educational institutions, whether aided or unaided by the state, other than the minority educational institutions referred to in clause (1) of article 30."

In this way the constitutive and legislative power of the state has been employed to promote the cause of social justice. But the political parties and power politics have been ever eager to hijack the state power for their own sectional and partisan interests. It is on such narrow political partisan interests that the judiciary has endeavoured in one case after another, to apply a constructive check. It is these checks which constitute the core of judicial activism vis-a-vis power politics.

Ceiling on Reservations

The first and foremost check applied by the Supreme Court in the Reservation policy is on the quantum of reservations. The upper limit of reserved seats or posts is determined by legislation and the legislation may set any limit which is practically expedient and not necessarily rational or reasonable. Dr. Ambedkar conceded in the Constituent Assembly that while there should be equality of opportunity, the backward classes also must have an opportunity of getting into the public services. While there should be reservation of posts for the backward communities the principle of equality should not be completely destroyed. He gave an illustration "Supposing, for instance, reservations were made for a community or a collection of communities, the total of which came to something like 70 per cent of the total posts under the state and only 30 per cent are retained as the unreserved. Could anybody say that the reservation of 30 per cent as open to general competition would be satisfactory from the point of view of giving effect to the first principle, namely, that there shall be equality of opportunity? It cannot be, in my judgement. Therefore the seats to be reserved, must be confined to a minority of seats.[2]

It is notable that while Sheduled Castes and Tribes are Statutory categories of persons and classes, "Socially and educationally backward classes of citizens" are not so ascertainable and their enumeration or specification has been left to the discretion, necessarily, polltical decisions, of the state government. The Constitution itself is silent as to the critenon for determining backwardness. The result is that State Governments have felt free in designating classes as "backward", according to their whim and caprice and not based on any scientific data empirically collected and tested. It may be recalled that in Mysore (Karnataka State) in an order dated the 16 July 1958 the State had directed that all communities excepting the Brahmins fell within the designation of socially and educationally backward classes, besides the Schduled Castes and Tribes, reserving for them 75 per cent of the seats in the state's educational institutions. Even communities whose ratio of student population was very near or almost equal to and even above the state average, for instance, the Lingayats of Ganigas or the Muslims, had been statutorily treated as socially and educationally backward classes. This aspect of the matter attracted the attention of the Supreme Court in the famous Balaji Case (1963)[3] and the Court found such reservation bad in law.

There is no criterion or limit prescribed in the Constitution as to the extent of reservation. In the Balaji case, the impugned order of the state government had paved for reservation of 68 per cent of the seats in the State medical and engineering colleges for backward classes of students and only 32 per cent are left in the merit pool. This tendency was constantly on the increase until a halt to it was called by the Supreme Court Judgement in the Balaji case. The Supreme Court ruled that in no case should the proportion of reservation be in excess of 50 per cent of the totality of seats in any educational institution, but how much less will depend upon the circumstances of the case. It said that the constitutional provisions regarding special measures for backward classes could not be so interpreted as to ignore completely the fundamental rights of the rest of the citizens. To quota from the judgement," it would be against the national interest to exclude from the portals of' India's Universities students on the ground that all seats in the Universities were reserved for weaker elements in society. It would cause grave prejudice to the national interest if consideration of merit was completely excluded by wholesale reservation of seats in all technical medical and engineering colleges."

Even the balaji decision has been, applied by State governments in letter the not in spirit. The State governments have taken the 50 per cent limit as the permissible limit of reservation though the intent behind the judgement was that the quantum of reservation should be fixed in each case after scientific investigation and collection of relevant data, upto a maximum limit of 50 per cent.

Even so judicial insistence on 50 prt cent ceiling on reservations means that only 27 per cent the seats and posts are left for the OBC Quota because 15 per cent seats are reserved for scheduled castes and 7 $^{1}/_{2}$ per cent for Scheduled Tribes that leaves only 27 per cent for the OBC in the reservation pool.

Nevertheless many States continued to flout this limit. The Tamilnadu government sought constitutional protection for its law providing for 69% reservation in services and colleges of the State and the 76th Constitutional amendment placing the Tamilnadu measure in the IXth schedule was enacted by the Parliament in the year 1994. In the Karnataka Assembly, a bill providing for 80 per cent eservation for SC, ST and OBC was introduced on 7.9.1994 amidst stiff opposition from the opposition members. The same day the Parliament passed the 76th Amendment, Andhra government passed an order to add the Kapu, the Muslim and 12 other communities to the list of backward classes providing them reservation in educational institutions and government jobs, in addition to castes and communities already included in the list. Even the Andhra Pradesh Backward classes welfare association has contested in a writ petition before the state High court the legality of this step. They contended that the G.O. was illegal and was issued solely with an eye on the coming Assembly polls."

It may be mentioned that the Andhra High Court had on an earlier occasion stayed similar attempts by the State government to extend of the benefit of reservation to the Kapus. The Muslims as a whole cannot be branded as backward nor can reservation be validly based on religion. The Chief Minister declared that the State will approach the Centre to obtain constitutional protection for the measure on the Tamil Nadu lines. Sitaram Kesari the then Union welfare minister publicly declared that the Union goverment was honour bound to Cansider such request favourably.

I.R. Coelho Vs. Tamil Nadu

In the judgement delivered on 17.01.2007 in the above case the Supreme Court has ruled that "Amendments made to the Constitution after 24th April 1973, by which 9th scheduled is amended by inclusion of various laws therein, shall have to be tested on the touchstone of the basic or essential features of the constitution ...... to put it differently, even though an Act is put in the 9th schedule by a constitutional amendment, its provisions would be open to attack on the ground that they destroy or damage the basic structure."

In view of this ruling of the Supreme Court the validity of the 76th constitutional amendment and the Tamil Nadu law on 69 per cent reservation have fallen into Jeopardy.

The Supreme Court on 13 July 2010, directed the governments of Karnataka and Tamil Nadu to place their laws providing reservation quota over and above 50 per cent AP, before the Backward Classes Commission along with quantifiable data about OBC population, to justify quotas exceeding the 50 per cent ceiling. If the Commission wanted to exceed the 50 per cent ceiling while refixing the quota, it could take into consideration the parameters laid down by the supreme Court in the Indira Sawhney case: compelling circumstances based on local conditions

The State maintained that the 50 per cent cap would not apply to Tamil Nadu as in the Mandal case judgement itself an exception had been provided for peculiar facts and circumstances. "Prescribing a rigid 50 per cent ceiling in the matter of reservation would be contrary to the very spirit of the Constitution and the objectives sought to be achieved by the Constitution".

The Tamil Nadu government had passed legislation providing for reservation upto 69 per cent Karnataka government passed a law in 1994 providing upto 73 per cent reservation.

The order is interpreted to suggest that the Court could consider relaxing the 50 per cent ceiling prescribed by it if the states were to support their demand by evidence of the size of the OBC population and their "social and educational backwardness".

Both state laws providing for quota in excess of 50 per cent cap were challenged before the Supreme Court by an NGO – Voice represented by senior advocate K.M. Vijayan. Disposing of the petition without expressing any opinion on the merits of the case, the Bench said the question raised in it was whether the 1993 quota law was valid in the light of the judgement in I.R. Coelho case and in the Mandal case and other subsequent cases. The Bench while extending the continuance of the Tamil Nadu and Karnataka laws for one more year, directed the States to place before the Backward Commission the quantifiable data on the Backward Communities for a fresh determination of the quota. Until the exercise was completed the interim order protecting the existing limit of quota would continue for one year. (*The Hindu* 14.07.2010, *Time of India* 15.7.2010).

Once agan judicial activism has sought to curb vote bank politics.

Carry Forward of the Backlog

The Supreme Court has held fast to its ruling that 50 per cent ceiling on reservation should not be breached on any ground. In the Devadasan case[5] it was held that reservation of posts by addition of unfilled posts of the previous year or years to the vacancies of the current year will render the guarantee of equality of opportunity (Art.16 (1) illusory.

In the Indira Sawhney case (1992) the court clarified that the ceiling of 50 per cent to be applied not with reference to the total strength of the entire cadre or service but with reference to the vacancies existing and advertised at any time.

Setting aside the decision in Devadasan Case that the carryover rule was impermissible, the Supreme Court in Indira Sawhney Case said, "carry forward rule of unfilled reserved vacancies is not per se unconstitutional but such rule should not result in breach of the 50 per cent."[6]

The vested interests and party politics were not prepared to take these rulings laying down and to let the backlog of reserved seats go by the board. Under these circumstances a constitutional amendment was the only wayout. The result was the 81st Amendment (2000) which added clause (4B) to Art. 16, providing inter alia, as follows:—

(4B) Nothing in this article shall prevent the State from considering any unfilled vacancies of a year which are reserved for being filled up in that year in accordance with any provision for reservation made under clause (4) or clause (4A) as a separate class of vacancies to be filled up in any succeeding year or years and such class of vacancies shall not be considered together with the vacancies of the year in which they are being filled up for determining the ceiling of fifty per cent reservation on total number of vacancies of that year.

The political will thus overruled the judicial wisdom. It was the triumph of political activism over judicial findings.

Promotion

Another area in which the Supreme Court tried to restrict the scope of reservation was in respect of promotions of employees. Setting aside the decision in *General Manager*

V. Rangachari,[7] it ruled that reservation in promotions is not a requirement of social justice.

Among the reasons for denying reservation in promotions the following three are notable:

(1) Reservation in promotion is constitutionally impermissible as once the advantaged and the disadvantaged are made equal and are brought in one class or group then any further benefit extended for promotion would be treating equals unequally. It would not be eradicating efforts of caste discrimination but perpetuating it.

(2) At the initial stage of recruitment reservation can be made in favour of backward class of citizens but once they enter the service, efficiency of administration demands that these members compete with others and earn promotion like all others; no further distinction can be made thereafter with reference to their "birth mark".

(3) Reservation in promotion means that the members of reserved categories need not have to compete with others but only among themselves. There would be no will to work, compete and excel among them. Whether they work or not, they tend to think their promotion is assured. This in turn is bound to generate a feeling of despondence and heart burning among open competition members.

In the Indira Sawhney case the Supreme Court said that reservation of posts can be only at the stage of initial recruitment, not at the stage of promotion.

But party politics got the better of judicial activism. The 77th constitutional amendment (1995), adding clause 4 (a) to Art. 16-empowers the state to make a provision for reservation in matters of promotion to any class or classes of posts in the services under the State in favour of the

Scheduled Castes and the Scheduled Tribes which in the opinion of the state are not adequately represented in the services under the state, not with standing anything contrary contained in Article 16.

Creamy Layer

By the time of appointment of the Second Backward Classes Commission (BCC), headed by B.P. Mandal, the feeling in political circles was widespread that while backwardness may be defined in terms of caste and community, the uppermost segment within that community, the rich, land owning and powerful must be separated from the rest and excluded from the privilege of reservation. The argument was that if some segments or members among the backward classes are able to advance economically, and, may be educationally as a result of reservation benefits or otherwise and, acquire positions of power and status, they can no longer be said to be in need of reservation. The Supreme Court said in the Indira Sawhney case, "the connecting thread between them and the rest snaps. They would be excluded from the benefit of reservation Such exclusion benefits the truly backward."

In Chhotelal vs. Court U.P. (1979)[8] had said, "the object of reservation will be defeated if on the inclusion of a class in a list of backward classes, the class is treated as backward for all time to come.

In order to limit reservation benefit to the truly backward, most political parties favour a "Means Test" applicable within a backward class to measure backwardness. In others words, they hold that the caste should be moderated by the economic criterion to decide who shall be eligible for reservation.

The pattern of reservation introduced by Karpoori Thakur government in Bihar in 1978 adopted the economic criterion for grant of reservation for certain backward classes. It provided for reservation without the "Means Test" for the most backward classes only.

The Congress Working Committee (C.W.C) meeting on 30th August 1990 adopted a resolution sponsored by Rajiv Gandhi which barred affluent and the well to do among the backward classes from the purview of reservation.[9] "The relevant C.W.C. resolution recalls:

"The equity and fairplay demanded that job reservations and other special measures for the backward classes as a whole be not pre-empted by the richer or more privileged segments of backward classes."[10]

In this way a national consensus was emerging soon after the announcement on implementation of the Mandal Commission Report:

(1) On the need to keep out the more affluent and well to do among the backwards from the purview of reservation scheme.

(2) On the need to evolve some economic criterion or the means test or the income ceiling for this purpose.

(3) Not to treat caste as the sole basis of social backwardness.

It was however the Indira Sawhney decision (1992) which clinched the issue of exclusion of what the Court called creamy layer of the backward class from the benefit of reservation. Kuldip Singh J. suggested the Means Test to skim off the, affluent section of the backward classes for the purpose of job reservation.

The Government of India issued Office Memorandum dated September 8, 1993 specifying the categories of persons excluded for availing reservation. These were more or less the same as were suggested in the Rajiv Gandhi formula. These include sons and wards of serving as well as former

Presidents Vice-Presidents Prime Ministers, Ministers, Chief-Ministers, Judges of the Supreme Court and High Courts, Bureaucrats Professionals and commissioned Military Officers. The Office Memo, specified upper income limit of Rs. 1 Lakh per annum for the purpose of identifying the creamy layer in a backward class. This limit was raised to Rs. 2.50 lacs in 2004 and to 4.5 lacs in October 2008. Now this limit has been raised to Rs. 9 lacs in Nov. 2011.

(The Times of India, 13-11-2012)

Admission to Higher Eductional Institutions

The order for 27 per cent reservation of posts for backward classes was issued soon after the Prime Minister's announcement of acceptance of the Mandal Commission Report. But there was no provision for reservation of seats in Central Educational Institutions for the backward classes. This lacuna was removed by the adoption of the 93rd constitutional amendment (2006) which empowers the State to make any "special provision by law for the advancement of any socially and educationally backward classes of citizens or for the Scheduled Castes or the Scheduled Tribes in so far as such special provisions relate to their admission to educational Institutions..........."

In pursuance of this provision Parliament enacted the Central Educational Institutions (Admission) Act, 2006.

The validity of the above Amendment as well as the Act has been upheld by the Supreme Court in their judgement delivered on 10, April 2008.

However the Supreme Court has ruled that reservation for the SC, ST and Backward Classes will not extend to "creamy layer" in anyone of these castes or communities.

The Court pointed out that in the existing OBC list there may be an affluent section which cannot be included in the list of Socially and Educationally Backward classes (SEBCs). Writing the main judgement, Chief Justice K.G. Balakrishnan wrote, "They are excluded because unless this segment of caste is exclude from that caste group, there cannot be proper identification of the backward class."

The Chief Justice further stated that, "by excluding those who have already attained economic well being or educational advancement, the special benefits cannot be extended to them and, if done so, it would be unreasonable, discriminatory or arbitrary resulting in reverse discrimination."[11]

The Court said that the parameters for identification of creamy layer given in the Office Memorandum dated September 8, 1993, may be applied. The Chief Justice said, "OBC should be deemed to mean SEBC after exclusion of creamy layers."

This is a clear illustration of judicial activitism in the cause of social justice. However power politics threatens to jeopardize this gain. Several political parties protested vehemently the decision to keep creamy layer out of OBC reservation. These included the JD(U), the CPI, the Lok Jan Shakti Party and the Pattali Makkal Katchi (PMK), the latter two being constituents of the ruling UPA. Union Health Minister and PMK leader, Anbumani Ramodoss told journalists that the likeminded parties in the UPA and Cabinet would meet and discuss the possibility of filling a review petition against the exclusion of creamy layer.[12]

The National Commission for Backward Classes has already been pressed by the State units to recommend to the Central government doubling up of the income limit for identifying the creamy layer within a class. This will render the very concept of creamy layer utterly meaningless.

However the judicial ruling on exclusion of "creamy layer" and the consequential political divisions may lead to splits within the castes and communities. They may be divided between the few, the 'haves', opposing, the exclusion of creamy layer ana the many, the 'haves' not, favouring such exclusion.

There is already a parallel development in respect of the SC quota. The Usha Mehra Commission Report (May 1, 2008) has recommended sub-quotas within the SC quota on the ground that very few castes have cornered all the benefits of the SC quota. A number of castes included in the sc category – like the Valmikis, the caste of scavangers and Safai Karmacharis – have been demanding sub-quota. They argue that some "advanced" Dalit communities, like the Jatavs in U.P. Mahars in Maharashtra and Malas in Andhra Pradesh have walked away with most of the reserved posts.[13]

Identifying Backward Classes

In Indian sociology, castes denote their social status, economic position and educational level of their members Social inferiority, economic misery and little or no education are the hallmarks of hackwardness. So a backward class is identical with a backward, caste. In the recent 27 per cent OBC quota case, (2007). Chief Justice K.G. Balakrishnan, speaking for himself and for P.K. Thakker, said that caste skimmed off its creamy layer is a valid unit of a backward class.

He said, "OBC should be deemed to be SEBC after exclusion of creamy layer."

The first pre-requisite of a national policy on reservation for backward classes is the identification of such castes as would qualify for reservation. In India no scientific investigation and collection of data on casts has ever been done. The first Backward Classes Commission headed by Kaka Kalelkar (1955) identified 2,379 backward castes, while the second Backward Classes Commission headed by B.P. Mandal (1979), put the number at 3,743 but in both cases the base data was the census figures of 1931. Census after 1931 omitted the caste column from the bio-data altogether.

Reservation was prevalent in southern India even prior to Independence but no scientific investigation was ever made to identify the backward classes and the factors taken into account in such identification. Therefore the lists drawn were subjective and arbitrary and not free from bias either. The lists were not revised so that once a caste was declared backward, it remained backward and vice versa. This led to heart burning, dispute and agitation.

In the OBC quota case, the petitioners questioned the relevance of the 1931 Census for drawing up the OBC lists and argued that implementation of the quota law should be held up till fresh identification.

They further argued that the impugned Act was unconstitutional for the reason that a wholly arbitrary power was delegated to the Centre without any guideline laid down for identifying the socially and educationally backward classes, and no machinery was provided for this purpose. They further argued that historical maltreatment and misbehaviour with certain classes was not by itself a factor for determining the beneficiaries under the 27 per cent OBC Quota law.

In P. Sagar vs State of Andhra Pradesh[14], the Supreme Court said, "proper inquiry or investigation should be conducted by the state government before listing certain castes as socially and educationally backward."

In their judgement in the OBC Quota case (10, April, 2008) Justice Arijit Pasayat, for himself and Justice C.K. Thakker stated that for "determination of backward classes ..... a notification should be issued by the Union of India after exclusion of the creamy layer for which necessary data must be obtained by the Central and state governments." He further said, "for identifying backward classes the Commission set up pursuant to the directions of this Court (in the Mandal case judgement) has to work more effectively and not merely decide applications for inclusion or exclusion of castes."

Revision of Backward Classes Lists: The Supreme Court in the interest of Social Justice, has consistently insisted that the backward classes lists should not be static but should be reviewed and revised periodically to keep abreast of the sociological movements. However such (revisions) whenever undertaken in the past, for example, in Gujarat, Karnataka, Andhra Pradesh, have met with stiff resistance and violent protests from the vested interests and their supporting parties.

As early as 1968, in Chhotelal Vs. U.P.[15] the Allahabad High Court had said, "The object of reservation will be defeated if on the inclusion of a class in a list of backward classes, the class is treated as backward for all times to come." It therefore advised the State government to keep under constant periodical review the list of backward classes and the quantum of the reservation of seats for the classes determined to be backward at any point of time.

Although no wholesale revision of OBC lists has been made based on scientific studies, the Commission set up pursuant to the directions of the Supreme Court in the Mandal case judgement has been at work, deciding applications for inclusion or exclusion of castes.

In response to a query from the court, in the OBC Quota case, as to how long the quota law could continue and whether there could be any time limit for reservation for the OBCS, the Centre made it clear that conceptually there could not be any time limit for the policy of reservation in admissions to educational institutions or in employment.

The argument was, "the policy of reservation flows from the mandate of equality and till the time the constitutional objective of real equality is achieved, there is a constitutional mandate on the State to have special provisions in the nature of reservation, for the uplift of backward classes."[16]

In their judgement in the above case the Supreme Court directed that a review of the lists of backward classes be made every five years.[17]

Conclusion

In his way, we find that the political activism on reservation policy at every stage had to be moderated by an activist judiciary so as to save it from being hijacked into power politics and keep it within the bounds of social Justice.

But in the end, the political will, if unified, strong and determined, prevailed over the judicial decisions as the constitutional amendments in regard to carry forward of unfilled seats and posts, on promotion, and the modified G.O. on the upper limit for creamy layer amply demonstrate. So it is a question of political and parliamentary will. The judiciary can provide a halt to political activism, but can not thwart it forever.

References

1. State of Madras vs Champakam Dorairajan, AIR, 1951, SC 226.
2. Constituent Assembly Debates, 30. November 1948, pp. 701-702.
3. M.R. Balaji vs. The State of Mysore, AIR 1963, SC 649.
4. I.R. Coelho vs. Tamil Nadu, (2007) 2 SSC I, AIR 2007 SC 861.
5. Devadasan vs. Union of India, AIR 1976, SC 490.

6. Indira Sawhney vs. Nion of India, AIR, 1993, pp, 447-762.
7. AIR 1962, SC 36 (p. 41)
8. Chhotelal vs. U.P. AIR 1979 Allahabad 135.
9. For details of Karpoori Thakur formula and Rajiv Gandhi formula see: Nilanjana Jain, The problem of Justice in Political theory and State Practice, Anamika, New Delhi pp. 173-175.
10. *Hindustan Times,* 31 August 1990.
11. *The Hindu* (Delhi) 11, April 2008, pp. 12.
12. *The Hindu,* dated June 13, 2008, p. 3.
13. *Hindustan Times,* Lucknow, 03.06.2008, See *Hindustan Times* 10 April 2008 for details of the Usha Mehra Commission findings.
14. P. Sagar vs. State of Andhra Pradesh, AIR, 1968, SC 1379.
15. Chhotelal vs. U.P. AIR 1979, Allahabad 135.
16. *The Hindu,* New Delhi, 2. Nov. 2007.
17. Extracts of Supreme Court Judgement in the 27 per cent, OBC quota case delivered on 10th April 2008 are based onthe Report in *The Hindu* dated Firday April 11, 2008.

8

Urban Development, Health, Hygiene and Sanitation

Justice is the coordination of law, liberty and equality in the life of the individual and of the society. Life requires appropriate and pollution free environment which should ensure health, hygiene and sanitation. Without them life of safety, decency and dignity are inconceivable.

The Supreme Court has therefore widened from time to time the sweep and scope of the right to life (Art. 21) so as to cover all these aspects of urban life.

Land Acquisition

Land Acquisition by the government or its agencies, under the Land Acquisition Act. may be:

(A) Either for individual, private, industrial undertakings, such as the POSCO steel plant in Odisha,Gas Based Power Project in Dadri (Ghaziabad, U.P.), Tata Motor Car Project in Singur, in West Bengal.

OR

(B) For the setting up of Special Economic Zone, (SEZ) in the state for the purpose of encouraging the establishment of private industrial units such as 25,000 acre SEZ in Nandigram (West Bengal).

In either case land acquisition is resisted by the land owners for loss of their land and means of their livelihood.

In several writ petitions the Supreme Court has been approached to stay land acquisition from farmers for industrial projects. The Central Government has embarked upon the policy of establishing Special Economic Zones (SEZ) in every state and in many cases acquisition of land has led to violent conflicts between the local residents and farmers and the government. In West Bengal, in Nandigram and Singur, the leftist government led by Buddhadeb Bhattacharjee had to face stiff opposition from the local land owners. Due to the Mayhem created in the wake of establishment of SEZ, the proposed chemical unit was shifted from Nandigram to Navachar.

In U.P. the Gas based Power Project to be established in Dadri (Ghaziabad) by Reliance Group has been in difficulties owing to several writ petitions challenging the acquisition of land for the project[1] filed in the Allahabad High Court. One such petition (PIL) was filed by the former Prime-Minister, V.P. Singh.

Under intense pressure from various quarters the Central government had to announce some policy decisions to appease the agriculturists and their supporters, such as:

(*i*) no land will be acquired forcibly from any land owner.

(*ii*) Corporate houses will be asked to deal directly with land holders to acquire land.

(*iii*) As far as possible Special Economic Zones (SEZs) will be established avoiding fertile cultivable land.

In the year 2007 the government announced the National Rehabilitation and Resettlement Policy and made it effective from 31, Oct. 2007.

In consonance with the policy, following amendments are proposed in the Land Acquisition Act 1894—

(*a*) Provision for acquisition of land for Companies to be deleted.

(*b*) Government shall acquire land for private companies only when private requiring bodies acquire atleast 70 per cent of the land requirements through direct purchase then only government will acquire remaining 30 per cent area.

(*c*) Compensation of the land is to be calculated at the market rate.

(*d*) Provision of solatium to be enhanced from the existing 30 per cent of the market value to 60 per cent of market rate in case of normal acquisition and 75 per cent in case of urgent acquisition.

(*e*) Compensation to be given within definite timeframe before actual displacement.

(*f*) In case of transfer of acquired land, 80 per cent of the net unearned profit would be shared with the original land owners or their legal heirs[2],.

Land acquisition has become a sensitive and political issue in the wake of the controversy kicked up by the Special Economic Zones where the land requirement can be 1,000 or 2,000 acres or even more. A whole lot of foreign developers have floated ventures in different States for the development of such SEZs.

But after the controversy generated by the Nandigram and Singur projects in West Bengal and the national political debate that they sparked, state governments have become wary of acquiring huge tracts of land, or even getting involved in facilitating this exercise by private investors. Government agencies now ask the developers to deal directly with the land owners.

Illegal Construction

The High Courts have been regularly approached to check illegal constructions and order their demolition and to prevent encroachments on public roads and to ensure their removal. In Allahabad the High Court ordered the demolition of the Leelakunj apartments in the year 2007 and the Supreme Court has refused to stay such operations.

Similar demolitions of unauthorized structures and encroachments by shopkeepers on public streets have been carried out under the orders of the High Court.

The Supreme Court itself, during 2006, issued directives for demolition of unauthorized constructions. It issued orders staying of ongoing construction of some premiere Malls near Vasant Kunj in the South-West Delhi, for want of environmental clearance.

During 2006, the Delhi High Court on the petition of Residents Welfare Association directed the Delhi Municipal Corporation (DMC) to identify and demolish illegal constructions. This resulted in the dismissal of several Engineers of the DMC on charges of corruption. As many as 80,000 constructions were identified and the court appointed Observers and a Commissioner to supervise the demolition of these illegal constructions. This led to violent riots in Seelampur area of North-East Delhi. The Delhi government proceeded to cover up these constructions by issuing new regulations and notifications, but the Supreme Court held these notifications to be questionable.

On 16 February 2006, the Supreme Court ordered the sealing of the commercial units operating in the residential colonies. The Delhi Administration adopted adhoc measures to give relief to the affected people but the Supreme Court did not yield and the sealing of commercial units commenced again. In this way the judiciary and the executive were at pains to nullify each other's action. On September 7, 2006 Urban Development Ministry made amendments to the Master Plan of Delhi to notify mixed use and commercial use streets areas.

On 27 June 2008, the Union minister of state for Urban Development and Delhi Chief Minister jointly, announced that government had decided to soon initiate the process of issuing Provisional Regularisation Certificates to 1,639 unauthorized colonies that came up before March 31, 2002, including 149 unauthorised colonies which came up as extension to village abadi and 85 left-out portions of already regularized unauthorized colonies.[3]

In the Palani Hill Conservation Council vs Tamil Nadu the petition challenging the unauthorized construction of a hotel in violation of rules, having serious environmental repercussions, depletion of ground water level and encroachment" on government land, the High Court directed that no construction be carried out.

Public Health

The Supreme Court in case after case has held that the right to life in Art. 21, included protection of health and just humane conditions.

In one case the Supreme Court directed the State Government to set up a monitoring committee headed by the Commissioner of Agra to look into effective functioning of public authorities responsible for supply of drinking water, disposal of solid waste and providing proper system of sewerage.[5]

In another case the Supreme Court directed the Central Pollution Control Board to adopt measures that will prevent the possibility of contamination/ pollution of drinking water. This direction as made on a PIL petition alleging that dairy owners stored cow/ buffalo dung and waste of dairy products near main drinking water pipeline supplying water to Jabalpur city.[6]

In Lok Adhikar Sangh vs. State of Gujarat[7] the court directed the authorities not to grant No Objection, Certificates to Cinema Halls, Factories and high rising buildings unless sufficient fire safety system was unstalled in these buildings.

In the interest of public health and safety the court—

(a) Prohibited the sale of arrack in polythene sachets[8],

(b) Ordered annual checks of workers and employees of the Bharat Electronics Limited[9] engaged in assembling transmitters, exposing them to the baneful effects of X-ray radiation, and to pay them compensation whenever the ill effect of such exposure were manifested.

(c) To strictly follow its own as well as World Health Organisation guidelines for manufacture and procurement of Oral Polio Vaccine (OPV) and to adhere to the internationally accepted standards and norms for Polio eradication.[10]

(d) Directed the Chief Secretary, State of Bihar to suspend the Superintendent of T.B. hospital in Bihar where utter mismanagement in water supply and supply of standard diet and drugs was noticed and insanitary conditions prevailed.[11]

(e) Directed the establishment of a National Council of Blood Transfusion and state councils, and a separate legislation for regulating collection, storage, distribution and transportation of blood and operation of blood banks.[12]

(f) Held that the employer is obliged to provide protective measures to workmen in Asbestos Industries and is bound by ILO directions, and to maintain health record of workmen during service, and after retirement and compulsorily insure their health coverage.[13]

(g) Directed the Chief Secretary, State of Bihar to put forth a definite scheme for improving the conditions in the mental hospital at Konke near Ranchi (Bihar) where a State of near anarchy prevailed.[14]

(h) directed the MCD (Municipal Corporation of Delhi) and the NDMC to be alert in performing their duties relating to sanitation, public health and prohibition of accumulation of garbage and wastes and neither non-availability of funds nor inadequacy of staff can be pleaded as grounds for non-performance of their statutory obligations, directions were issued to MCD, NDMC, to AIIMS, Central Pollution Control Board and even to Doordarshan telling it to telecast programmes on civic education.[15]

(i) directed the Ministry of Environment, Govt. of India to appoint a Central Ground Water Board for regulation and control of ground Water Board for regulation and control of ground water management and for regulating indiscriminate boring and pumping out of underground water.[16]

Open Airy Space

In Bangalore Medical Trust Vs. Mudappa, the Karnataka High Court as well as the Supreme Court held that the conversion of a public park into a private nursing home was illegal. The Supreme Court said that a private nursing horne is not a necessary improvement over a public park.[17]

In another case the Allahabad High Court ruled that a writ petition under Art. 226 of the Constitution for the preservation of fresh (air and for the protection of environment can be filed by the environment activists living in the Same locality or otherwise. The petition prayed that an open space called Adupark should be used only for a public park and not for any other purpose.

The Court directed that a blueprint be laid down for the park and the park to be fully developed, as a priority within one year. The Court directed that no other construction be allowed except in relation to the maintenance of the park.[18]

In Ram Sahai Verma vs. State of M.P. the Court looked askance at the action on Municipal authorities placing arbitrary and illegal restrictions of movement on a road leading to the courts and educational institutions. This had resulted in hardship and inconvenience particularly to students and lawyers and to people from all walks of life. The alternative routes were described as inconvenient and the restrictions as not being in the interest of public safety and convenience. The Court allowed the petition.[19]

In another case the court stayed the construction and erection of arches and cutouts on the pavements of the city of Madras which obstructed the road and impeded the smooth flow of traffic.

Sanitation

Art. 47 lays down as a Directive Principle of state policy that "the state shall regard..... the improvement of Pubic health as among its primary duties."

The Supreme Court has in case after case insisted upon the discharge of statutory duties by the municipal bodies in protecting public health by providing salutary drainage and sanitary system.

In Municipal Council Ratlam vs. Vardhichand, the petitioners asked for specific directions to the Ratlam Municipal Council to improve the drainage system and prevent the drains from being polluted. The Supreme Court virtually reprimanded the municipal council and, its executive officers for not devoting any attention to cleaning up the streets and construction of the drains. It ordered that—

(i) drains be constructed so that the flow of water did not stagnate.

(ii) The big pits and earthen drains near the college were to be closed and filth removed.

(iii) The big drain was to be covered and the Malaria department was to sprinkle D.D.T and work towards the eradication of mosquitoes.

(iv) The Municipal Council and Town Improvement Trust to do whatever necessary to prevent dirty water from the alcohol factory flowing into the drain.

The court added that the implementation of these directions would be watch dogged by the court and desired that the state government will make available by way of loans or grants sufficient financial aid to the Ratlam Municipality to fulfill its obligations.[20]

The Ratlam decision was followed by the high courts in various cases. L.K. Koolwal vs. state of Rajasthan[21] raised the issue of sanitation in Jaipur city. In this case the court held that it is the primary duty of the Municipal Council to remove filth, rubbish, nightsoil, odour or any other noxious or offensive matter. The court stated that there could not be any plea regarding the availability of funds or staff. It allowed six months to municipal council to clean the entire city of Jaipur.

Similarly in Aparna Kashyap vs. Himachal Pradesh the court directed the Municipal Corporation to provide necessary civic amenities to the Totu village, a suburb of Shimla. It directed the Municipal Corporation to provide an adequate water supply, to improve sanitary conditions, to provide for a drainage and sewerage system, to improve existing roads and pathways and to construct public latrines and urinals.

In M.C. Mehta vs. Orissa-[23] the court directed the state government to take steps to protect the water of Taladanda Canal from pollution resulting from mass bathing in Mahanadi during Kartik Purnima. It directed the State Government, "to maintain the wholesomeness of water which is supplied for human consumption, ways and means to prevent entry of sewage water and effluents to the rivers Mahanadi and Kathajadi and Taladanda canal to be worked out. If there is a necessity and desireability of having a sewage treatment plantor plants, the same to be set up without further delay."

Detailed steps were directed to be taken within one year of the order.

Conclusion

The cases discussed above mark the judicial trend in expanding the scope of Right to life (Art. 21) to those basic civic amenities which makes life meaningful and to link it to the policy principle directing the state to regard the improvement of public health as among its primary duties (Art. 47). The affirmative action by the judiciary consists in its directing the municipal bodies to perform their Statutory duties to the community, and, in permitting the citizens to initiate legal action against the defaulting bodies. As Justice V.R. Krishna Iyer said in the Ratlam case, "The key question we have to answer is whether by affirmative action a court can compel a statutory body to carry out its duty to the community by constructing sanitation facilities at great cost and on a time bound basis. At issue is the coming of age of that branch of public law bearing on community actions and the court's power to force public bodies under public duties to implement specific plans in response to public grievances."[24]

The court's response to this dilemma is one more illustration of judicial activism in the cause of justice.

References

1. *Hindustan Times*, February 16, 2008, March 1, 2008.
2. *The Hindu*, 28.06.2008, p. 7.
3. *Ibid.*
4. See Sangeeta Ahuja, People, Law and Justice, Vol. I, Orient Longman 1997, p. 399.
5. D. K. Joshi Vs. Chief Secretary; State of U.P. (1999) 9 SCC 578.

6. Ramji Patel Vs. Nagrik Upbhokta Marg Darshak Manch, (2000) 3 SCC 29.
7. AIR 2000, Guj 28.
8. George Mampilly (Dr) Vs. State of Kerala, AIR 1985 Ker. 24.
9. M.K. Sharma vs. Bharat Electronics Ltd., (1987) 3 SCC 231.
10. Sahil Society for welfare of the Aged, Poor and Homeless vs. Union of India, AIR, 1999 All. 87.
11. S. Lal vs. State of Bihar, (1994) SCC 506.
12. Common Cause Vs. Union of India, (1996) 1 SCC 753.
13. Consumer Education and Research Centre Vs. Union of lndia, (1995) 3 SCC 42.
14. Rakesh Chandra vs. State of Bihar, AIR 1989 SC 348.
15. B. L. Wadehra vs. Union of India (1996) 2 SCC 594 and Almitra H. Patel vs. Union of India (2000) 2 SCC 679.
16. M.C. Mehta vs. Union of India (1997) 11 SSC 312.
17. AIR 1991 SC 1902.
18. D.D. Vyas vs. Ghaziabad Development Authority, AIR 1993 All 57.
19. Ram Sahai Verma vs. State of M.P. AIR 1989, AP 334.
20. Municipal Council Ratlam vs. Vardhichand, AIR 1980.
21. See Sangeeta Ahuja, People, Law and Justice, Vol. I, Orient Longman 1997, p. 404.
22. *Ibid.*, p. 404.
23. AIR 1992 Ori 225.
24. Municipal Council Ratlam Vs. Vaidhichand, AIR, 1980 p. 1623.

9

Environment and Pollution

Clean environment is the basic necessity of life. So a pollution free environment is implicit in the right to life and the court has held that every person has the right not to be slowly poisoned by environment pollution.

Environment denotes water, air and earth. The Supreme Court has held that every person is entitled to fresh air, potable water and healthy sanitary conditions. Since the Stockholm Conference (1972) the environment pollution, and the resulting climate change is continuously on the international agend and in India also appropriate legislation has been enacted and an administrative machinery put in place to protect environment.[1]

Constitutional Provisions

The Constitution (42nd amendment) Act., 1976 added in Art. 48A, a Directive Principle of State Policy that "the State shall endeavour to protect and improve the environment and to safeguard the forests and wildlife of the country."

It also included among the fundamental duties of the citizens (Art. 51 A) the duty to "Protect and improve the natural environment including forests, lakes, rivers and wildlife and to have compassion for living creatures.

To implement the constitutional mandate environmental jurisprudence is expanding in order to prevent, control and abate various forms of environmental pollution.

As Professor Gurdip Singh notes, "Even the fundamental principles of international environmental law are not enforced through legislative measures. The judiciary in India has demonstrated exemplary activism in plugging the legislative gaps in the environmental legislations."[2]

Judicial Activism and Environment

The Supreme Court has, in cases relating to environment, given juristic recognition to the doctrine of sustainable development. This doctrine has been the running theme at all international conferences relating to environment and climate change, from Stockholm (1972) to Johannesburg (2002), It has now been recognized as a part of customary international law. Sustainable development is a balancing concept between environment and growth. It rests on the foundation of equity. According to Gurdip Singh, "Sustainable development is structured on two forms of equity, namely intra generational equity, and intergenerational equity."[3]

The Supreme Court has held that the two essential features of sustainable development are –

(i) Precautionary Principle.

(ii) Polluter Pays Principle.

The precautionary principle means:

(i) environmental measures by the state government and statutory authorities must anticipate, prevent attack the causes of environmental degradation.

(ii) Where there are threats of serious or irreversible damage, lack of scientific, certainty should not be used as a reason for postponing measures to prevent environmental degradation;

(iii) The onus of proof is on the actor or the developer industrialist to show that his action is environmentally benign.

Precautionary Principle requires that the development activity must be stopped and prevented if it causes serious and irreversible environmental damage. Therefore it determines whether development process is sustainable or not.

The 'Polluter Pays Principle as interpreted by the Supreme Court means that the absolute liability for harm to the environment extends not only to compensate the victims of pollution, but also the cost of restoring the environmental degradation.[4]

The Supreme Court has held that these two principles have been accepted as a part of the environnrental law of the country.

The courts have applied these principles in deciding cases related to environmental pollution. In one case the High Court of Kerala issued a stay order against the functioning of the Bijili Rubber Company producing rubber cream latex in a factory near the Y.W.C.A in Pattanapurum, Quilon district in Kerala. It was contended that the ammonium and other toxic gases emitted pollute fresh water supply, spread diseases and kill the fish in the river.

In another case it was contended that building of shopping plazas or commercial complexes built on reclaimed wetlands in Calcutta would damage the ecosystem, the wild life of the area, the soil, the water, and the reservoir area for the city waste.

The Court agreed that "the issue of environmental degradation can not but be termed to be a social problem...... and Law Courts should rise up to the occasion to deal with the situation."

It further said that wetland should be preserved and no interference or reclamation should be permitted. The Court prohibited the issuing of permission for reclamation of wetland areas and any change in the land use.[5]

In M.C. Mehta vs. Union of India the court issued directions to Delhi Development Authority, and Municipal Corporation of Delhi and Central Pollution Control Board to stop mechanical stone crushing activities in and around Delhi, Faridabad and Ballabhgarh areas and for the establishment of a stone crushing zone to rehabilitate the existing stone crushers whose operations were stopped by the Court.[6]

Earlier in 1983 mining of lime stone quarries in the Mussoorie - Dehradun belt which was affecting the ecological balance in the valley and posing a hazard to the environment was questioned in a case before the Supreme Court. The Court decided to close a number of these quarries and to allow others to continue operating under detailed conditions. The Supreme Court appointed a Committee, the Bhargava Committee, to study the effect of these mining operations on environment. The committee reported that certain stone quarrres were unsuitable for mining and recommended their closure. The court then passed an interim order by which the mining operations carried out through blasting were stopped in those quarries which had adverse impact on safety and health of the people of this hill area.[7]

Mining and Quarrying operations carried out under lease have been the subject of writ petitions in several cases before the state high courts and the Supreme Court. The Quarrying operations in the Doon valley and in the Sirmaur district of Himachal Pradesh[8] where hills were ruthlessly blasted for extracting lime stone, are two examples.

In Andhra Pradesh[9] and in Maharashtra also such petitions have been filed. In Maharashtra[10] the case related to the Commercial quarrying of sand from Yeral river bed. In Rajasthan[11] 400 mining leases were awarded in the core and buffer zones of Sariska Tiger Park which have been declared a "game reserve", to excavate lime and dolomite.

In all these cases it was contended that mining by blasts was hazardous to the surroundings ecology and environment.

In the Rajasthan case, the court directed that no mining operation shall be carried on within the protected area. In other cases it balanced the need to protect the environment and the commercial requirements.

In M.C. Mehta vs. Union of India[12] the issue of pollution caused by the stone crushers, pulverisers and mine operators in the Faridabad Ballabhgarh area was raised. These operations were affecting adversely the tourist resorts of Badkal Lake and Surajkund in the state of Haryana.

The court directed Haryana Pollution Control Board to inspect and ascertain the impact of mining operations on the ecology of these tourist resorts. On the basis of the report the court ordered that the mining operations within the three kms radius of the Badkal Lake and Surajkund areas be stopped.

Construction Activity

Construction Activity may occupy space allocated for parks recreational grounds. Such activities may also have the effect of upsetting the ecology of the area or cause environmental degradation. In one case the land allocated by the development plan for recreational parks was proposed to be used as residential area by the LIC and Income Tax Department. The Andhra Pradesh High Court held that the attempt to build houses on land reserved for parks would disturb environmental balance and ordered the Municipal Corporation of Hyderabad to prohibit such modification in the plan.[13]

The decision was based on the premise that environmental pollution is a violation of the right to lifeunder Art. 21 of the Constitution.

In M.C. Mehta vs Kamal Nath,[14] a motel belonging to Span Motels Private Limited carried out various constructions on the river bed and the banks of river beds and was discharging untreated effluents into the river.

The Supreme Court held that any disturbance of the basic environmental elements namely air, water and, soil, which are necessary for life, would be hazardous to 'Life' within the meaning of Article 21 of the Constitution. The Supreme Court further held that in cases of violation of the right to life guaranteed under Article 21, damages can be awarded not only for restoration of the ecological balance but also to compensate the victims who have suffered due to the disturbance of any of the basic environmental elements.[15]

Industries

Industrialisation is the main tool of development and development requires exploitation of natural resources. Therefore industrialization affects ecology and environment. It is the main cause of emission of Green House Gases which produce Global warming and climate change.

Therefore industrialization has in recent years attracted the notice and concern of environmentalists. They have knocked at the doors of the courts to seek moderation of impact of industrialization on environment, in accordance with international conventions and national laws.

Judicial activism can thus be seen in prohibiting activities which damage the ecological balance and awarding damages not only for the restoration of the ecological balance but also for the victims who have suffered due to that disturbance.

In order to protect environment – air, water and soil – from pollution the court has ordered the banning of industries causing pollution in the environment. Thus in M.C. Mehta Vs. Union of India[16] as many as 168 hazardous/ noxious / heavy / large industries in Delhi were directed to stop functioning / operating in the city of Delhi and to relocate / shift themselves to any other industrial estate in N.C.R. for which purpose National Capital Region Planning Board was required to render all assistance. The court ordered that the workmen employed in these industries should be protected in respect of their rights and benefits.

The process of identification of more of such industries for relocation was to continue.

In Dec. 1985, there was a leakage of Oleum gas from one of the units of Shriram Foods and Fertilizers industries,[17] affecting several persons and killing one advocate in Delhi. A petition was moved in the Supreme Court praying for orders against reopening of certain plants of Shriram Industry manufacturing hazardous and lethal chemicals and gases on the ground that they pose danger to health and life of workmen and people living in the neighbourhood.[18]

The court applying the 'Polluter Pays Principle and the 'Precautionary Principle regarding safety measures, permitted the power plant but not the industrial plant to restart temporarily subject to strict observance of the eleven conditions laid down by the court. The court left it to the government to evolve a national policy for the location of toxic or hazardous industries with a view to ensure that there were no defects or deficiencies in the design or structure or quality of the plants and equipments and the necessary safety devices and instruments were installed and were in operation.

On the queation of compensation for the injured people the court held in a PIL case that compensation can be awarded. It said," where an enterprise is engaged in a hazardous or inherently dangerous activity and harm results to anyone on account of an accident in the operation of such hazardous and inherently dangerous activity, resulting, for example, in the escape of toxic gas the enterprise is strictly and absolutely liable to compensate all those who are affected by the accident.

Industries discharging untreated effluents and causing pollution of soil and water have been the subject of PIL and the Supreme Court has held them liable to bear the financial costs of remedying and preventing the damage caused by pollution.

In Bichhri village in Udaipur district in Rajasthan factories of an industrial complex manufacturing chemicals like Oleum, acids and fertilizers were discharging highly toxic untreated effluents - iron based and gypsum based sludge - (there was no equipment to treat these effluents).

Since the toxic wastes were flowing freely and the untreated sludge was thrown in the open in and around the complex, the toxic substances percolated deep into the bowels of the earth polluting the aquifers and the subterranean supply of water, rendering it unfit for human consumption, unfit for irrigation and cultivation. It spread diseases, death and disaster in the village and surrounding areas.

The Supreme Court upheld the liability of the polluter to remove the sludge and defray costs of remedial measures and directed the Central Government to determine the amount required for remedial measures.[19]

In A.P. Pollution Control Board vs. M.V. Nayudu[20] it was held that oil processing plants within 10 km radius of

Osman Sagar and Himayat sagar should not have been sanctioned by authorities as these plants were discharging vegetable oils including solvent extracted oils which were listed among the hazardous industries.

Tanneries

In Vellore Citizens Welfare Forum Vs. Union of India[21] it was alleged that a number of tanneries in Tamil Nadu were discharging untreated effluents into agricultural fields, road sides, waterways and open lands which finally found their way into the river which was the main source of water supply to the residents.

A similar petition was moved by M.C. Mehta in respect of the Calcutta tanneries,[22] which were alleged to be discharging untreated, noxious effluents into the Ganges, polluting land and river alike.

Earlier Mehta had moved the Supreme Court towards the nuisance caused to the people of Kanpur[23] by the pollution of the Ganges due, among other causes, to the various tanneries discharging their effluents directly into the river.

In all these cases the court called upon the Central Government realize its statutory duty to protect the degrading environment of the country.

In Vellore Citizens Welfare Forum Vs. Union of India, the court stated that if the conditions in the five districts of Tamil Nadu where the tanneries were operating, were permitted to continue, then in the near future all rivers/canals would be polluted, underground water, contaminated, agricultural lands turned barren and the residents of the area exposed to serious diseases. Therefore, the court directed the central government to take immediate action under the provisions of the Environment (protection) Act. The Supreme

Court inter alia passed the following directions to the Central Government:

(i) The Central Government shall constitute an authority as required under section 3 (3) of the Act. and confer on the said authority all the powers necessary to deal with the situation created by the tanneries and other polluting industries in the state of Tamil Nadu. The said authority shall have powers to issue directions to appropriate authorities.

(ii) The authority so constituted by the central government shall implement the, Precautionary Principle and the 'Polluter Pay Principle'. The authority shall, with the help of expert opinion and after giving opportunity to the concerned polluters assess the loss to the ecology / environment in the affected areas and shall also identify the individuals / families who have suffered because of the pollution and shall asses the compensation to be paid to the said individuals / families.

(iii) The authority shall compute the compensation under two heads, namely for reversing the ecology and for payment to individuals.

(iv) The authority shall direct the closure of the industry owned / managed by a polluter in case he evades or refuses to pay the compensation awarded against him.

(v) The authority in consultation with expert bodies like National Environmental Engineering Research Institute (NEERI), Central Board shall frame scheme/ schemes for reversing the damage caused to the ecology and environment by pollution in the state of Tamil Nadu. The scheme / schemes so framed shall be executed by the state government under the supervision of the Central Government.

In Tirupur Dyeing Factory Owners Association Vs. Noyyal River A. Protection Association, decided on 06.10.09 the Supreme Court held that while industries and power projects are necessary to improve employment opportunities and generation of revenue, the damage to environment cannot be ignored and if the degradation of environment continues and reaches a stage of no return, the court may consider the closure of industrial activities. in areas where there is such a risk.

Tirupur in state of Tamil Nadu is an industrial hub providing employment to 5 lakh persons. A large number of industries had indulged in dyeing and bleaching works at Tirupur area. Undoubtedly, there had been unabated pollution of Noyyal River by discharging the industrial effluents into the rivers. The Supreme Court held that such responsibilities to meet out the expenses of reversing the ecology. They are held bound to meet the expenses of removing the sludge of the river and also for cleaning the dam : (Lawyers update, Delhi, Vol. XV, Part II Nov., 09, p. 53).

Judicial activism in environmental cases has resulted in closure of hundreds of individual units or their relocation or adoption by them of requisite safety devices.

Industrial / Mathura Refinery Emissions, brick kilns, Vehicular traffic and generator sets polluted the ambient air around the Taj Trapezium Zone (T.T.Z.) and had damaging affect on the Taj and on people living around the T.T.Z.

The Supreme Court in M.C. Mehta Vs. Union of India[24] ordered a total of 292 industries to change over from coke/ coal to natural gas as industrial fuel and ordered stoppage of functioning or relocation of those industries which were not in a position to obtain gas connection for any reasons.

As a result of the environmentalist pressure and PIL....

(i) the latest pollution control equipment was installed in Mathura Refinery.

(ii) The coal yard in Agra was shifted and the Thermal Power Station was closed down.

(iii) The polluting industries situated on the banks of the river Yamuna were required to install air and, water pollution control devices to check further pollution.

Pollution of River Ganga

Similarly the Supreme Court in another case was approached in the matter of the pollution of river Ganga at Kanpur. The holy river was increasingly being polluted by sewage, textile waste, power plant waste, tannery effluents, the dung and fodder waste discharged by dairies. Its water was no longer fit to be used by the people either for drinking or for bathing.

The Supreme Court noted[25] that the Ganga Action Plan to improve the sewage system and prevent pollution of Ganga was going on at at a "snail's pace". It issued the following directions.

(*i*) The Kanpur Nagar Mahapalika may either direct the dairies to be shifted, outside the city so that the waste accumulated at the dairies does not ultimately reach Ganga or it may arrange for removal of such waste.

(*ii*) Immediate action should be taken by Kanpur Nagar Mahapalika to construct sufficient latrines urinals for the poor people.

(*iii*) Steps should be taken to ensure that dead or half burnt bodies are not thrown into the river.

(*iv*) Applications for licences to establish industries should be refused unless adequate provisions have been made for treatment of effluents from factories.

(*v*) Educating People and creating awareness through various programmes regarding pollution.

Under orders passed by Allahabad High Court a high powered committee headed by the Chief Secretaries of U.P. and Uttarakhand was constituted.

Hearing a PIL regarding pollution in the Ganga, the High Court asked the state authorities to file an affidavit detailing the steps taken by the committee in this matter. (August 27, 2008)

It also asked the Chief standing counsel of the state to indicate the manner in which the grant by the Central Government in the matter of Ganga pollution was being utilized.

The court also directed the D.M. Kanpur to give details of the action taken against the tanneries whose functioning had been stopped on account of the violation of directions issued by the court from time to time.[26]

Vehicular Pollution

One of the several indices of development is the growth of transport and communication facilities, both public and private, leading to enormous rise in fuel consumption and environmental pollution. Therefore Vehicular pollution is a matter of growing public concern and has been the subject of PIL.

In 1998 the noted environmentalist lawyer M.C. Mehta moved a petition in the Supreme Court drawing its attention to air pollution by automobiles and the thermal units generating power for the Delhi Electric Supply Undertaking (D.E.S.U)

The pollution was caused by the increase in, the use of petrol and diesel. The petitioner suggested that the Ministry of Environment could consider the pollution reducing device developed by the National Environment Engineering Research Institute (NEERI), Nagpur.

The deliberations in the course of this hearing took concrete shape and the Ministry of Environment appointed an ad-hoc committee to look into the problem of vehicular pollution and the current technology available for its prevention. The ad-hoc committee was later on superseded in 1998 by the Environment Pollution (Prevention and Control) Authority for the National Capital Region consisting of Shri Bhurelal and four other persons. This committee was appointed under the Environment (protection) Act., 1986, and invested with powers and functions specified there in.

In the cases on vehicular pollution,[27] time bound directions were issued to implement, in phases, several solutions and restrictions for the prevention of air pollution from vehicular traffic.

In one case,[28] the Supreme Court ordered that all commercial vehicles which were more than, 15 years old (later extended to 20 years) shall not be allowed to ply in the national capital territory with effect from 2nd Oct. 1998. Later on subject to certain conditions relaxations / exemptions weregiven upto 31.01.2002. The court also ordered (expansion of pre-mixed oil dispensers (petrol and 2T Oil) and ban on supply of loose 2 T Oil at petrol station and services garages.

In C.N.G. litigation titled M.C. Mehta Vs. Union of India[29] the Supreme Court treated air pollution in Delhi caused by vehicular emissions as violation of Art. 21. It directed all commercial vehicles operating in Delhi to switch to C.N.G. (Compressed Natural Gas) fuel mode for safeguarding health of the people from air pollution. Orders were passed On 28th July 1998, fixing the time limit within which the switch over to C.N.G. was to take place. The resulting disruption in bus services causing public hardships and the political nervousness and public discontent persuaded the Supreme Court to extend the time limit to 30 Sept. 2001, and then to 31, Jan. 2002. The court refused any further extension of time and directed that the owner of diesel buses beyond 31 Jan. 2002, shall pay fine of Rs. 500/- per bus per day, increasing to Rs. 1,000/- per day after 30 days of operation of the diesel buses.

The Supreme Court directed the Union of India to give priority to transport sector including private vehicles all over India with regard to the allocation of C.N.G. The Court clarified that C.N.G. would be made available first to the transport sector in Delhi and in other polluted cities of India only thereafter, the remaining quantity of C.N.G. would be allocated to public sector undertakings and power projects and then to industries.

Summing up

The Supreme Court has been intolerant of activities that caused pollution of the environment or disturb the ecology. At the same time it has been conscious of the imperatives of industrialization in the process of development. As such, it has tried to strike a balance between the two, and, applied the Polluter Pay Principle' and the 'Precautionary Principle' to reconcile the claims of Development with the demands of environment.

Instead of defining 'Sustainable development' in terms of inter generational equity, the Supreme Court has looked upon, 'Sustainable development' as equity between environment and development, and has activated the executive in its achievement. It was after its criticism of governmental inaction, in two cases,[30] that the government of India decided to constitute an authority to be known as the Environment Pollution (Prevention and Control) authority for the National Capital Region under the Environment (Protection) Act. 1986.

In two other cases the Supreme Court expressed the need for the establishment of environmental courts consisting of judicial and scientific experts. Justice Bhagwati in M.C. Mehta Vs. Union of India[31] pointed out the need for such specialized environmental courts in view of the increasing volume of environmental pollution and eclogical destruction cases. This view was reiterated in the A.P. Pollution Control Board vs. M.V. Nayudu.[32]

The Supreme Court is empowered under the Environment Protection Act to create special bodies to look into environmental issues, several such bodies were created in the past, which increased the role of judiciary and led to confrontations between judiciary and Environment Ministry. The Supreme Court has three committees on environmental issues in Delhi with overarching powers while a dozen odd regional authorities with area specific mandates are running, some of them for more than a decade.[33]

In 2009 the Kerala High Court has taken the initiative and decided to constitute a 'Green Bench' that will deal exclusively with cases relating to forests, conservation of trees and other cases pertaining to biodiversity from December 4, 2009.[34]

Earlier due to the personal, tireless efforts of Subhas Dutta a special "green bench" was established at the Calcutta High Court which the first dedicated bench of its kind in India. (Hindustan Times, 20 March 2011.)

Recently Parliament has passed a bill creating the National Green tribunal. The bill was cleared by the Rajya Sabha early May 2010. (Hindustan Times 06.05.2010 p. 6) opening the door for both individuals and organizations to seek fast track redressal and compensation for loss of life and property caused by environmental hazards.

The Supreme Court has crated a second special Green Bench to hear cases relating to forests and environment.

This briefly sums up the story of judicial activism in the area of environment and ecology.

References

1. The following Laws are the Principle Legislative majors relating to environment, - Wild Life (Protection) Act, 1972 Water (Prevention and Control fo Pollution) Act., 1974. Forest (Conservation) Act., 1980 Air (Prevention and Control of Pollutioin) Act., 1981, Environment (Protection) Act., 1986. This act provides for establishment of control and state pollution control Boards.
2. Gurdip Singh Environmental Law in India, Macmillan, India, 2005, p. 19.
3. *Ibid* p. 22.
4. *Ibid*– pp. 234-235.
5. People united for better living in Calcutta – Public vs. State of West Bengal, AIR 1993 CAL, 215.
6. M.C. Mehta vs. Union of India (1992) 3 SCC 25.
7. Rural Ligigation and entitlement Kendra, Dehradun vs. State of U.P. (1985) 2 SCC 431; AIR 1985 SC 652.
8. Kinkri Devi and another vs. State of Himanchal Pradesh and others, AIR, 1988 H. p. 4.
9. Krishna Nagar Gram Panchayat Tadepaeli vs. State of A.P. and another, 1983 (2) SCALE 125 (735).
10. Mukthi SangarshMovement vs. State of Maharashtra and others, 1990 (Supp.) SCC 37.
11. Tarun Bharat Sang. Alwar vs. Union of India and others AIR 1992 SC 514, 1994 (2) SCALE 68 (516).
12. M.C. Mehta vs. Union of India (1996) 8SCC 463.
13. T. Damodar Rao vs. Municipal Corporation, Hyderabad, AIR 1987 AP 181.

14. M.C. Mehta vs. Kamalnath, AIR, 2000, SC 1997.
15. Gurdip Singh, Environmental Law in India, Macmillan India, 2005, p. 63.
16. M.C. Mehta vs. Union of India, (1996) 4 SCC 351.
17. M.C. Mehat vs. Union of India and others (Shriram gas leak) 1985 (2) SCALE 151 (1280) 1986 (1) SCALE 23 (153) (1986) 2 SCC 176, 325 (1987) 1 SCC 395.
18. M.C. Mehta (1) vs. Union of India (1986) 2 SCC 176.
19. Indian Council for Enviro-legal Actions vs. Union of India, AIR 1996 SC 1446.
20. A.P. Pollution Control Board vs M.V. Nayudu; (2001) 2SCC 62.
21. Vellore Citizens Welfare Forum vs. Union of India, AIR 1996 SC 2715.
22. M.C. Mehta vs. Mehta Union of India (Calcutta tanneries (1997) 2 SCC 411.
23. M.C. Mehta vs. Union of India (1988) 1 SCC 471.
24. M.C. Mehta vs. Union of India (AIR 1997) SC 734.
25. M.C. Mehta vs. Union of India (1988) 1 SCC 471.
26. *The Times of India,* 27.08.2008.
27. M.C. Mehta vs. Union of Idnia (AIR 1998) SCC 617; (1998) 5 SCC 767, 6 SCC 63, 8 SCC 2006, (2001) 3SCC 756, AIR 1999 SC 291.
28. M.C. Mehta vs. Union of India AIR 1998 SC 2963; (1998) 2 SCC 63.
29. M.C. Mehta vs. Union of India AIR 2001 SC 1948; AIR 2002 SC (Supplement) 1696.
30. Vellore citizens Welfare Forum vs. Union of India, AIR 1996, SC: 2715, S. Jagannath vs. Union of India, AIR 1997, SC 811.
31. M.C. Mehta vs. Union of India AIR 1987, SC 965.
32. A.P. Pollution Control Bard vs. MV Nayudu, AIR 1999 SC 812. The Environment Minister Jairam Ramesh announced the decision to revitalize an old environmental tribunal bill. Currently Environment and Forest Ministry has prepared and

circulated a Green Tribunal Bill that would take the pressure off courts that are flooded with PILs on green issues. The cabinet note on the bills is under inter-ministerial discussions. (*Times of India*, Allhabad, 28.06.09).

33. *Times of India*, Allhabad, 28.06.09.
34. *Hindustan Times*, 01.11.09

PART–III

10

Judicial Overreach

In a Parliamentary system of government the task of controlling the executive is assigned to Parliament. Parliament controls the Political Executive directly by a number of well known devices, such as debates, discussions, questioning and voting on bills, resolutions, motions, financial proposals etc.

However, its control over the civil service (the administration) is indirect, exercised through the political executive. As such it remains flimsy, scanty and illusory. This led Ramsay Muir to remark, "Bureaucracy thrives under the cloak of ministerial responsibility".

In practice, the control over the administration has fallen to the lot of the judiciary which through the interpretative process of laws and the Constitution has so expanded its power and jurisdiction as to include every executive activity impinging upon the Rule of Law and the Fundamental Rights.

It has thereby sought to put a check on police excesses and atrocities, infirmities of the criminal justice system, administrative lapses, bureaucratrc acts of commission and omission and failure of municipal bodies in rendering services expected of them under Statutes and Regulations.

To this extent Judicial control over the administration has been hailed by the people as promoting the cause of Justice. This approach to judicial functioning is popularly described as judicial activism.

Judicial activism, in so far as it exercises control over the administration and keeps it within the bounds of law, is quite consistent with the theory of Constitutional Government. The difficulty arises when the judiciary proceeds to interfere in the sphere of the legislature or the political executive in the matter of laying down policy, suggesting legislative reforms or reviewing Constitutional amendments, or dictating them. Then the question arises about the sanctity of the principle of separation of powers and the judiciary is blamed for, violating this principle.

In the Ragging case[1] a divisional bench of the Himachal Pradesh High Court directed the state government to constitute an anti-ragging committee and called for its report within six months and subsequently issued directions to the government for implementation of the various recommendations of the committee. It further asked the Chief Secretary to file an affidavit within three months setting out the action proposed to be taken in the matter of anti - ragging legislation.

But the Supreme Court on appeal reversed the direction stating that, "It is entirely a matter for the executive branch of the government to decide whether or not to introduce any particular legislation. The court certainly cannot mandate the executive or any member of the legislature to initiate legislation, howsoever necessary or desireable the Court may consider it to be. If the executive is not carrying out any duty laid upon it by the Constitution or the law, the court can certainly, require the executive to carry out such duty and this is precisely what the court does when it entertains Public Interest Litigation. But at the same time the court cannot usurp the functions assigned to the executive and the legislature under the Constitution, and it cannot even indirectly require the executive to introduce a particular legislation, or, the legislature, to pass it or assume to itself a supervisory role over the law making activities of the executive and the legislature.

The same questions arose in Umed Ram vs. State of Himachal Pradesh[2] in which the P.W.D. was directed to proceed with the construction of a road and to complete the work within current financial year. It was also directed to apply for additional grants and to report back the progress in the matter.

The Supreme Court on appeal overruled these directives, while upholding that for residents of hilly areas access to road is implied in the right to life but held that the court could not direct the State Government to construct the road if there had been no allocation by the government for such construction. The Supreme Court agreed that the directives of the High Court brings about "Urgency, in Executive Lethargy" by encouraging the expenditure of already appropriated fund on construction, but the allocation of additional funds to complete the road to the village was entirely a matter within the discretion of the government. It directed the High Court not to require continuing reports from the State to determine what further action had been taken on the road and to leave it to the judgement and the priorities and initiatives, both of the executive and legislature, to pursue the matter.

In the Centre for Public Interest Litigation vs. Union of India[3] the Supreme Court held that in awarding a contract for development of the Panna and Mukta Oil fields, it was a matter of policy whether the oil wells should be developed on a stand alone basis by ONGS or not with which the court would not interfere.

Similarly in Kanhaiya lal Sethia vs. Union of India[4] the court refused to issue any direction to the Union of India to include Rajasthani language in Schedule VIII to the constitution on the ground that it was purely a policy matter. It said, "Generally, courts do not, in exercise of their power of judicial review, interfere in policy matter of the state, unless the policy so formulated either violates the mandate of the Constitution or any statutory provision or is otherwise actuated by malafides".

In another case, Ernakulam North Development Co-ordination Council vs. Union of India,[5] the Kerala High Court ruled that whether the Trivandrum - New Delhi Express should have a stoppage at Ernakulam Town Station is not a matter to be decided by the court. It is a policy decision to be decided by the Railways considering the convenience of the general public.

In the Foreign Adoption case[6] instead of adjudicating on a set of facts on the basis of existing law, the court proceeded to issue comprehensive guidelines carrying the force of law. It touched such controversial and sensitive policy issues as whether foreigners should be allowed to adopt Indian children, and, if so, under what circumstances.

It is such decisions of the court which have raised, eyebrows in the political circles. In a speech delivered on the AIR in 1982 at Pune justice Tulzapurkar expressed grave concern about "disturbing trends in the PIL stating that the court" in "the name of alleviating the grave public injury cannot arrogate to itself the role of an administrator or an overseer looking after the management and day to day working of all nonfunctioning or malfunctioning public bodies or institutions."

Pathak, J (as he was then) too, in Bandhua Mukti Morcha case[7] after cautioning the courts regarding the limits of their Constitutional Jurisdiction held," there is always the possibility, in Public Interest Litigation of succumbing to the temptation of crossing into territory which properly pertains to the legislature and the executive government. For in most cases the jurisdiction of the court is invoked when a default occurs in executive administration and sometimes where a void in community remains unfilled by legislative action.

"In the process of correcting executive error or removing legislative omission the court can easily find itself involved in policy making of a quality and to a degree characteristic of political authority and indeed run the risk of being mistaken for one."

In Sheela Barse vs. State of Maharashtra[8] the court assumed what Upendra Baxi calls, "creeping jurisdiction", It consists in taking over the direction of administration in a particular arena of the executive. The court's jurisdiction thus tends to 'creep' from the issues raised in the original petition to the larger social problems revealed by its activist inquiry. Thus in the Sheela Barse case relating to custodial violence to women prisoners in the Bombay city jail, the Supreme Court proceeped to issue guidelines applicable to the entire state of Maharashtra requiring the State—

(*i*) To work with the District Legal Aid Committee to assure that all undertrial prisoners receive free legal aid,

(*ii*) distribute pamphlets to prisoners on their right to bail,

(*iii*) Inform each prisoner's designated friend or relative of the arrest, and

(*iv*) Use only women police officers to guard and interrogate female suspects.

Policy Matters: Economic Issues

The Supreme Court on February 27, 2008, setting aside an Andhra Pradesh High Court order, upheld the validity of an Andhra Pradesh law enhancing stamp duty on sale of property. It advised the judges to exercise 'great restraint' in quashing economic statutes.

The Bench comprising Justices H.K. Sema and Markanday Katju said that as economic policies involve planning by experts, court's should refrain from interfering until the policies are unconstitutional. It said, "The court does not consist of economic or administrative experts. It, has no expertise in these matter and in this age of specialization, when policies have to be laid down with great care after consulting specialists in the field, it will be wholly unwise for the court to encroach into the domain of the executive and the legislature"[9]

Similarly in a case[10] decided in 2000 the Supreme Court refused to interfere with a contract awarded by government to consortium led by RIL - Enron for development of medium sized oil fields on a fixed royalty basis. It opted for it in preference to a varying rate based, on an ad valorem rate of oil. The court said that it could not be said that this decision was arbitrary or unreasonable. It said, "Where price fixation involve highly technical and complex procedure and depends upon various variables, it will be very difficult for a court to decide whether a particular price agreed to be paid under the contract was fair and reasonable or not.

Policy Matters: Law Enforcement Options

The maintenance of law and order is the function of the Executive, and its sole responsibility. Therefore it must have the discretion based upon the means and measures to secure this objective. It is not for the courts to decide whether the force employed to quell a riot or control an unruly violent mob was excessive and disproportionate. The observations of the Calcutta High Court declaring the police firing in Nandigram on March 14, 2007 as "wholly unconstitutional and illegal" are apparently "interference in the State and Centre's Jurisdiction."

The CPI (M)'s West Bengal Secretary, Biman Bose, who is the Left Front's Chairman and, a CPM Politburo member, took a strong exception to the High Courts, orders. He addressing a Party rally in Kolkata on Nov. 17, 2007 questioned, "will the court decide the government's course of action ? If the court tries to rule over the two other pillars of democracy, what is the need of the legislature and the executive?"

He asked, "If the High Court has the last word on everything what is the use of the legislature and the executive?"

The CPM leaders in West Bengal criticized both the Governor, Gopal Krishna Gandhi, and the High Court, for playing a partisan role on the Nandigram issue. The Senior CPM leader Benoy Konar said," Rajbhawan and the court have joined hands against the democratically elected government in the state. It is because of the Governor that the High Court took up the case on Nandigram.[11]

Another instance of the Media, Social activists and the court meddling into the strategy of the government in curbing indiscriminate violence by insurgent out laws and extremists is the denigration of the Salwa Judum role in Chhattisgarh. This is a Kind of a vigilante group promoted, funded and supported by the State government. Its main purpose is to Counter the Naxalite terror in the Dantewada region in Chhatisgarh by raising a force of private citizens and arming them to counter violence. Salwa - Judum is a force of some 3,400 special police officers (SPOs) comprising inmates of the relief camps and Naxalites, who had surrendered. They have been recruited legally and are under the command of the State police. It is certainly not a case of 'outsourcing' of law and order maintenance function by the State to a private group. It is a strategy of the State to fight Naxalite insurgency and extremism to save and protect the life and property of the people in Dantewada and Bijapur which are controlled by the Naxals.

The State Government claimed, "It is not State sponsored, but a people's initiative to combat the menace of naxalites. The State is committed to resolving the problem of naxalism, and any peaceful movement which resists violent methods definitely gets support of the state"[12]

In September 2008, the Supreme Court asked the Chhattisgarh government to implement some of the recommendations of the National Human Rights Commission relating to the activities of the Salwa - Judum.

In the face of these facts it seems to be an irresponsible and aggressive observation on the part of K.G. Balakrishnan, Chief Justice of India, who while admitting two PIL petitions, asked the respondent, "how can the State give arms to some persons? The State will be abetting in, a crime if these private persons kill others."[13]

The court may be right in assuming that the strategy followed by the State in Chattisgarh is prima- facie illegal but the ground reality is that terrorist violence, like Naxalite killing of innocent tribals and security forces cannot, be curbed by ordinary legal processes of the liberal state. The concern shown by the Chief Justice on the Salwa - Judum activities can only be interpreted as a case of judicial overreach.

This case exemplifies the intervention of the apex court with the, political executive in matters which are the exclusive jurisdiction of the political executive. However the Supreme Court in this, matter has been very cautious, It said, "When somebody (Salwa - Judum) is given arms, he claims to be a pseudo police. Once he is given arms, he will commit an offence though he has no right to do any such act. Some remedial measures have been suggested in the report and the state may, consider implementing them"[14] (The Hindu, 20 September, (2008)

Policy Matters: Pension

The Supreme Court has held that the payment of pension to eployees upon retirement is a social welfare measure. It is a right of the employee and not a discretionary, ex-gratia payment.

The Ministry of Finance issued an Office Memorandum liberalizing, the formula for the computation of pension applicable to those who retired on or after 31.03.1979.

The court held that the pensioners form a class and the division of pensioners into two classes, of those who retired after the date fixed (31.03.1979) was arbitrary and discriminatory. It ruled that all the pensioners would be covered by the revised scheme.[15]

In Rampyari vs. Union of India,[16] the court directed the payment of pension to the widow of a freedom fighter who had been seeking the pension due to her for four decades. This order was passed by the court on the basis of suo moto notice of an article appearing in a Rajasthani daily newspaper on 10, Sept. 1985.

Law Making : Judicial Initiatives

Law making is the function of the legislative branch of government. However, the judiciary in writing its judgement has often strayed into giving guidelines to the executive which have more or less the force of law. This amounts to judicial law making. This has happened specially in cases relating to Bonded Labour, Protective Home for women, sexual harassment of women at workplace, custodial violence against prisoners, adoption of Indian Children by foreigners and recently in the matter of food security bill.

In Bandhua Mukti Morcha case,[17] the court purported to develop, "a scheme for improving the living conditions for the workers in stone quarries", However in this case

Pathak J, cautioned the courts regarding the limits of their constitutional jurisdiction and warned it of the, "the temptation of crossing into territory which properly pertains to the legislature and the executive government,".

In the Foreign Adoption case[18] the petitioner requested the court to bar private agencies from arranging foreign adoptions, Instead the court went on to issue detailed directions regarding the adoption of Indian children by foreign parents. These directions were a set of principles and guidelines for evolving a procedure to prevent illegal sale of babies. This decision constitutes a virtual piece of judicial legislation. In the process, it resolved such controversial and sensitive policy issues as to whether foreigners should be allowed to adopt Indian children at all and if so, under what limited circumstances.

In Sheela Barse vs. State of Maharashtra[19] the court went on to lay down guidelines which should be followed in respect of women prisoners in police lock-ups.

In the Vishaka case[20] which was regarding sexual harassment of working women, the Supreme Court laid down eleven guidelines to be observed at all work places or other institutions until a legislation was enacted for the purpose. These guidelines were to be treated as the law declared by the Supreme Court under Art. 141 of the Constitution. What could be a more direct and patent case of judicial law making?

In several cases the court has given guidelines to check misuse of police powers to arrest, detain and interrogate.

Justice J.S. Verma is best remembered for rocking the political class in the 1990's with the Jain Hawala case,[21] without making pretense of steering clear of policy making. Justice Verma laid down the procedure for appointment of the CBI Director and, in a bid to insulate it from political pressure, placed the CBI under the supervision of the Central

Vigilance Commission (C.V.C.). The court issued several directions regarding C.V.C., CBI, Enforcement Directorate, etc., in order to ensure that the CBI and other governmental agencies carry out their public duty to investigate the crimes.

Earlier in the D.K. Basu[22] case Justice A.S. Anand came up with the law to check violations of Human Rights during and after arrest including any form of torture or cruel, inhuman or degrading treatment, whether it occurs during investigation, interrogation or otherwise. He regarded transparency of action and accountability as two possible safeguards against the abuse of police power and went on to issue eleven requirement, "to be followed in all cases of arrest or detention till legal provisions are made in that behalf as preventive measures."

The court said in the end that failure to comply with these riquirements shall render the concerned officials liable for departmental action and also liable to be punished for contempt of court. These requirements were aimed at curbing the use of questionable methods during interrogation and investigation leading sometimes to custodial violence or death in police lockup. These requirements constitute what has been called "Custodial Jurisprudence".

The Supreme Court on August 5, 2008 slammed the government for its refusal to amend the law (Section 441 IPC criminal trespass) for launching criminal prosecution against those illegally occupying official houses. The Bench was, told by the Additional Solicitor General that the Government had decided not to amend the IPC as it was of opinion that the existing provisions of the public premises Act were sufficient to evict those unauthoriselly occupying government accommodation. Moreover, it claimed that out of 99,100 government houses only 300-odd dwellings were under unauthorized occupation.

It is submitted that the function of the court is to implement the law as it is and not to fume or fret when the government refuses to yield to its Suggestions to amend the law. This attitude of the court is clear evidence of Judicial Overreach.[23]

The Supreme Court was approached by an NGO, Common Cause, to examine whether persons suffering from terminal diseases and likely to go into a permanent vegetative state have the right to die with dignity, subjecting themselves to voluntary euthanasia. It was argued on behalf of the petitioner, "Those at the end of their natural life span and likely to go into a state of terminal illness or permanent vegetative state are deprived of their right to refuse cruel and unwanted treatment like feeding through hydration tubes, being kept on ventilator, and other life supporting machines in order to artificially prolong their natural life span."[24]

The Supreme Court issued notice to the Centre on a petition seeking a direction to have a fresh look at the Medical Termination of Pregnancy Act. 1971, which allows abortion of foetus only upto 20 weeks, when there is substantial risk of abnormalities if the child was born. The petition was filed against a Bombay High Court judgement refusing to interfere with the provision. The SLP raised fundamental issues – the right of a woman to self determination over her body and whether ought to be any legal impediment at all to a woman's right to an abortion and whether the state right to interfere by way of legislation with such a fundamental personal decision, especially when a child was likely to undergo treatments, surgeries and might lead to subnormal life."[25]

Taking suo muto cognisance of the vandalism and destruction of property during the Gujjar agitation in Rajasthan, the Supreme Court in March, 2009 said that it would lay down guidelines for payment of damages, for destruction of public property during agitations and demonstrations by political parties and other organizations. The court earlier constituted a committee to suggest measures to tighten the law and make political parties accountable for such damage. After considering the reports of the committee Justice Arjit Pasayat observed that the existing Prevention of Damages to Public Property (P.D.P.P.) Act was grossly inadequate to deal with the huge losses in the course of an agitation. He said a large number of private property too suffered loss during such agitations to the tune of crores of rupees. The Judge indicated that the Bench would frame guidelines and would also set up a Damage claim Authority to fast track damage claims. The mechanism would remain in place till comprehensive changes were made in the Act. The committee had suggested that the leaders of political parties and organizations should be made guilty of abetment of the offence, and exemplary damages might be awarded, the object of which was to punish those indulging in vandalism.[26]

A recent case of Supreme Court trespass into the forbidden sphere of high policy making is its intervention in the matter of legislation aimed at fighting hunger (April 2010).

A Supreme Court report released in March 2010 by former Supreme Court Judge D.P. Wadhwa widens the definition of poverty adding about 500 million people to the ranks of the poor and will demand about Rs. 52,100 crore above the Rs. 1,18,535 crore the government plans to spend fighting poverty in 2010-2011. The report came at a time when the union cabinet was likely to clear this week (last week of March 2010), the seminal food security bill 2010. Based on such reports the Supreme Court has virtually taken over India's hunger policy for the past 9 years, passing more than 50 orders in what is now one of the world's most remarkable cases of judicial intervention – a public interest litigation commonly called the right to food case.

The Wadhwa report could become law if Supreme Court accepts it in hearing lated for next month (April 2010). (Hindustan Times 24.03.2010).

The proposed bill was withdrawn for a major overhaul as it was found wanting by the congress leadership in several respects.

(*a*) It down sizes people's food entitlement from 35 to 25 k.g.

(*b*) It has no provision by which the homeless – those without a fixed address can benefit.

(*c*) It estimates of the number of BPL families has been disputed.

The bill is the flagship initiative of the UPA government and therefore has been sent back to the empowered group of Ministers headed by finance minister Pranab Mukherjee (Hindustan Times, 03.04.2010).

Rotting Grain

On July 27, 2010, the Supreme Court took notice of the report published in Hindustan Times on the 140 million tonnes of grain rotting in the country for want of proper storage facilities and said it was a crime to waste food in a poor country where millions went hungry. A Bench headed by Justice Dalveer Bhandari, hearing a PIL filed by advocate Colin Gonsalves on behalf of the P.U.C.L. suggested that the grain should under no circumstances be allowed to rot, but instead, should be distributed among the hungry.

"If you cannot store the grain, give it to the people to eat" the bench told additional solicitor general Mohan Parasaran, representing the Centre. (Hindustan Times, 28.07.2010).

On August 12, 2010, the Court asked the Centre to consider free distribution of food grains to the poor instead of allowing it to rot in godowns. The Supreme Court had "directed" and not "advised" the Centre to distribute free food grains to the poor.

On August 19, 2010 the Agriculture Minister Sharad Pawar said that it was not possible to distribute grains for free. Reacting to this statement of Sharad Pawar the Supreme Court virtually reprimanded the Minister for not acting on its advice and clarified that the advice was part of his order and not just a suggestion. After the reprimand the Minister retracted his statement and declared that the court's orders would be "honoured". The court also issued orders for fresh poverty estimates and asked the government not to rely on old figures to allot subsidized grains to the poor. (Hindustan Times, 01.09.2010),

It is clearly a case of the Supreme Court going beyond the judicial function.

Reacting on the Supreme Court's order to distribute free grains to the poor that is rotting in the open, the P.M. Dr. Manmohan Singh on September 6, 2010 commented that it was not possible to distribute the grain, for free.

He said that he respected the sentiments behind the suggestion that a way should be found to ensure useful disposal of food grains to meet needs of the people but it was not possible to distribute the grain for free.

How can food grains be distributed free to an estimated 37 per cent of the population which lives below the poverty line"

He further said, "at the same time making food available free would destroy incentives to farmers to produce more. If there was no food available, there would be nothing to distribute".

Then he suggested that the Supreme Court not get into "the realm of policy formulation" (Hindustan Times 07.09.2010).

These decisions have gone down in history for trenching on executive or legislative domain. They set a healthy precedent for across the board police reforms, which were ordered in sept. 2006 by another bench of the apex court.

The Legislative Proceedings

The Supreme Court has not only legislated in the form of directives and guidelines but has also overlooked the constitutional provisions relating to immunity of the legislative proceedings from judicial review. As J.S. Verma, former Chief Justice remarks, "It was not a matter amenable to judicial intervention."

However, in two cases relating to assembly proceedings in U.P. in 1998 and Jharkhand in 2005 the court gave directions to the Speaker as to how to conduct the proceedings relating to the No Confidence Motion in the House. The interim order dated 9 March 2005 made by the Supreme Court in the Jharkhand Assembly case makes aweful reading. By its order, the court fixed the date for the session of the assembly, its one point agenda to have a floor test, issued directions to the Speaker relating to the conduct of the proceedings, and ordered video recording of the proceedings with direction to send a copy to the court. In making this order the court followed an earlier non – speaking order in Jagadambika Pal case,[27] relating to the U.P. Assembly which was a mere adhoc orderwith no precedent value.

Later on, in a decision rendered on 10.12.2007, a two member bench of the apex court comprising Justices A.K. Mathur and Markandey Katju held these directions given in the assembly proceedings in U.P. in 1998 and Jharkhand in 2005 as "glaring examples of deviations from the clearly provided constitutional scheme of separation of powers." Even Justice J.S.Verma[28] is in agreement with this adverse comment.

In the recent judgement dated 10.01.2007 in the matter relating to expulsion of 11 members of Parliament, for taking bribes to put questions in Parliament, the Supreme Court held that legislature must have the power to expel members for misconduct but added that the legislature cannot claim immunity from limited judicial review of the exercise of that power. Mr. Justice J.S.Verma, former C.J.I. remarks," .....This causes concern, Howsoever limited be the judicial scrutiny, availability of judicial review in that area erodes the separation of powers and immunity of the proceedings asserted by the constitution."[29]

The intervention of the Supreme Court has been sought in various cases involving policy matters, privileges of legislature and the like, notably the following,

M.P. Local Area Development Scheme (MPLADS), under which every M.P. is sanctioned Rs. 2 Crore for development of his / her constituency. It was alleged that the scheme interfered with the concept of federalism and division of powers between the Centre and the States.[30]

The expulsion of former Punjab Chief Minister Captain Amarinder Singh on September 10, 2008, by the State legislative assembly, who was held guilty of corrupt practices in the Amritsar land scandal while he was Chief Minister.

Setting aside the expulsion of Capt. Amrinder Singh for alleged breach of privilege in connection with an alleged land scam, the Supreme court on Monday 26.04.2010 criticised the State Assembly for having "exceeded its powers".

Holding the exercise of legislative privileges under Article 194 (3) of the Constitution as "not proper" in the case, a five judge constitution bench headed by Chief Justice of India K.G. Balakrishnan cautioned against arbitrary exercise of power of legislative privilege, saying would frustrate the objective of a parliamentary democracy.

"It is our considered view that the Punjab Vidhan Sabha exceeded its powers by expelling the appellant (Singh) on the ground of breach of privilege when there existed none. The allegedly improper exemption of land was an executive act attributable to the appellant and it did not distort, obstruct or threaten the integrity of legislative proceedings in any manner, the Bench said in its 89 pages judgement.

"If we were to permit the legislature to exercise privileges for acting against members for their executive acts during previous terms, the courts are likely to be flooded with cases involving political rivalries" the bench said. (Hindustan Times, Dated 27.04.2010).

One cannot find fault with the judgement of the court, but it is debatable if the court should admit petitions involving legislative jurisdiction.

Case of Judicial Overreach: Removal of Governors

The Constitution stipulates in Art. 156 that:

(1) "The Governor of a State shall hold office during the pleasure of the President". The provision in Art. 156 (3) which fixes a five year tenure for Governors is thus subject to Art. 156 (1). The Supreme Court on 7 May 2010 in a landmark judgement on a PIL filed in 2004 by the the BJP MP, B.P. Singhal, challenging the removal of Governors of U.P., Haryana, Gujarat and Odisha by the previous U.P.A government, held that the replacement of Governors with the change of power at the Centre was

arbitrary and capricious. It held that the decision on removal of Governors would be subject to judicial scrutiny and the court may seek the reasons and explanation behind the action. A five judge Constitution bench headed by C.J.I. Balakrishnan held that a Governor could be replaced only under "compelling" circumstances or reasons such as for proven misconduct or other irregularities. Removal of Governors cannot be on political ground or malafide. (Hindustan Times. 08.05.2010).

Later, speaking at the National Conference on "Law and Governance" Prime Minister ManMohan Singh indirectly criticised the encroachment of the judiciary into the executive sphere. He emphasised the importance of separation of powers, saying that the doctrine was acknowledged as one of the basic features of India's Constitution and that all the organs of the state – the Legislature, the judiciary and the executive are bound by and subject to the provisions of the Constitution, which demarcates their respective powers, jurisdiction, responsibilities and relationship with one another. It is to be assumed that neither of the three organs of the State, would exceed its powers as laid down in the Constitution". The constitutional expert, Mr. Subhash Kashyap said, "The Supreme Court has gone beyond the basic provision under Art. 156 (1) of the Constitution.......the apex court has clearly exceeded its jurisdiction". "He lamented that unless there was a strong government at the Centre "this judicial overreach can't be checked". (Hindustan Times. 9 May, 2010)

Party-Less Civic Polls

Two Public Interest petitions (PIL) have been filed before the Allahabad High Court challenging the recent order of the state government whereby it declared that mayoral and civic bodies elections will not be held on party symbols.

In both the PILS it has been contended that true democracy cannot exist without political parties as they educate people on issues.

Further, participatory democracy cannot exist without the backing of political parties.

In recent months, intense judicial pressure has led to the resignation and arrest of former Telecom Minister A. Raja (02.02.2011) and the unseating of CVC P.J. Thomas 03.03.2011. The government has also been at the receiving end of the SC's strictures in several other cases, mostly public interest litigations, in recent times. These have severely embarrassed the government.

Speaking at the 10th Moot Court competition organized by Amity University in NCR on 05.03.2011 Justice A.K. Ganguly of the Supreme Court said, "courts are widening their jurisdication and are now functioning as institutions of governance and not merely as arbitrators of disputes".

He called this expansion of "judicial jurisdiction a major transformation." (Hindustan Times, 16.03.2011)

Setting aside the expulsion of Capt. Amrinder Singh for alleged breach of privilege in connection with an alleged land scam, the Supreme court on Monday criticised the state assembly for having "exceeded its powers".

Holding the exercise of legislative privileges under Article 1947 (3) of the constitution as "not proper" in the case, a five judge constitution bench headed by Chief Justice of India K.G. Balakrishnan cautioned against arbitrary exercise of power of legislative privilege, saying it would frustrate the objective of a parlimentary democracy.

It is our considered view that the Punjab Vidhan Sabha exceeded its powers by expelling the appellant (Singh) on the ground of breach of privilege when there existed none the allegedly improper exemption of land was an executive act attributable to the appellant and it did not distort, obstruet or threaten the integrity of legislative proceedings in any manner, the bench said in it 89 pages judgement.

"If we were to permit the legislatures to exercise privileges for acting against members for their executive acts during previous terms, the courts are likely to be rivalries" the bench said. (Hindustan Times, 27.04.2010)

Constitutional Amendment

Judicial activiam is most questionable in the matter of amendment of the Constitution. The two aspects of this enquiry are :—

(1) Judicial decisions have at times resulted in amending the provisions of the Constitution.

(2) The amendments enacted by the Parliament in accordance with Art. 368 have been struck down by the Supreme Court as invalid, on one ground or the other.

(i) The Supreme Court has evolved principles which have the effect of Amending the Constitution. One such principle advanced in Golaknath case[32] (1967) is the doctrine of Prospective overruling. The result of this ruling is that constitutional amendments already adopted before this ruling will be valid even if they purported to take away or abridge fundamental rights, but constitutional amendments adopted after this ruling will be invalid if they trench upon the provisions of fundamental rights. In this way the Golaknath decision subordinated the

Constitutive authority of Parliament under Art. 368 to the limitations contained in Art. 13 contrary to the will of the constitution makers. Parliament had to enact the 24th amendment (1971) to set aside the Golaknath decision.

(ii) The other principle advanced in the Keshavanand Bharati case[33] (1973) is the doctrine of Basic Structure of the Constitution or essential features thereof. The Supreme Court advanced this doctrine as an inherent limitation on the amending power of Parliament. It invalidated the 42nd amendment which sought to place Constitutional Amendments beyond the purview of judicial review. In this way. Parliament's Power of Constitutional amendment under Art. 368 has been limited by judicial interpretation. This is a direct assault on the principle of parliamentary sovereignty which is the bed rock of parliamentary system of government.

(iii) The Constitution subjects the right to life and personal liberty (Art. 21) to Procedure established by law.

The view held uniformly since the Gopalan decision[34] was that the law means positive law, that is, law enacted by the legislature. This was to leave no ground for judicial scrutiny of legislation depriving person of his life or liberty. The Censtitution, makers deliberately avoided the U.S. formula of subjecting these rights to "due process of law" which must satisfy the judicial notion of "reasonableness and fairness."

In Maneka Gandhi vs. Union of India[35] overturned the majority decision in the Gopalan's case. It laid down:

(b) Articles 19 and 21 are not mututually exclusive.

(c) In the result, a law coming under Art. 21 must prescribe a procedure for deprivation of personal lilrerty of a person, which must not be arbitrary, unfair and unreasonable.

(d) Once the test of reasonableness is imported to determine the validity of a law depriving a person of his personal liberty, such law, shall be invalid if it violates the principle of natural justice.

Comm enting on this judicial about turn, D.D. Basu remarks:

"From Gopalan to Maneka, thus the judicial exploration has completed its trek from the North to the South Pole. The decision in Maneka's case is being followed by the Supreme Court in subsequent cases."[36]

This is a good example of judicial decision virtually altering the will of Constitution makers as expressed in the provision of the Constitution.

(II) The Minerva Mills decision[37] implies that the Supreme Court has even dismissed Parliament's title to sovereignty which was an article of political faith with the Constituent Assembly. This is why the Constitution makers had vested in the Parliament unlimited constitutive authority.

Art. 368 is an exclusive code on amendment of the Constitution. It places no limitation on Parliament's amending power as if the Parliament is the continuing Constitute Assembly.

The Supreme Court has discovered that limitation on that power is 'implied' in the word' amendment itself. Amendment does not mean the power to destroy. To impair an essential feature of the basic structure is to destroy the Constitution, to denude it of its identity. Hence the power of constitutional amendment is inherently limited, limited by its basic structure, by the essential features of the basic structure.

Howsoever forceful or earnest this argument may be it is not relevant to constitutional theory and practice. No Constitution can be stagnant or static for all times to come. But the Basic Structure Theory creates a bar to any fundamental change in the Constitution or its basic structure.

The successful challenge to Parliament's sovereign constitutive power has encouraged the Supreme Court to extend its jurisdiction to other matters which have been left to the subjective satisfaction of the President. (Ordinances, emergency proclamations, mercy petitions) or concern only the internal legislative procedure (no confidence motion and discipline, expulsion of M.P's etc.)

This trend has provoked even the mild-mannered Prime Minister Manmohan Singh to warn the judiciary not to overstep its limits. He added that the dividing line between judicial activism and judicial overreach is a thin one. A take over of the functions of another organ may at times become a case of overreach. He cautioned the judiciary against substituting its power of mandamus with the take over of the functions of other organs.[28]

Even a Division Bench of the Supreme Court comprising Justices A.K. Mathur and Markandey Katju warned that judges should know their "limits" and not try to run the government, They said, "We are repeatedly coming across cases where Judges are unjustifiably trying to perform executive or legislative functions. In our opinion this is clearly unconstitutional. In the name of Judicial activism, Judges cannot cross their limits, and try to take over functions which belong to another organ of the state."

Finally they observed "If there is a law judges can enforce it. But Judges cannot create a law and seek to enforce it. "In this context, the Bench recalled the observations of the then Chief Justice of India, A.S. Anand that, "Judicial Activism does not become judicial, adventurism. The courts must act with caution and proper restrain.

It said "policy matters on fiscal, educational and other matters are best left to the judgement of the executive.[39]

In another case, Justices H.K. Sema and Markandey Katju, upholding the validity of an Andhra Pradesh law enhancing Stamp Duty on sale of property, said, that the courts must exercise great restraint" in quashing economic statutes.

Quoting extensively from American judgements and a theory propounded by Prof. James Thayer in 1893, Justice Katju, writing the judgement for the Bench said, "In the age of specialization, when policies have to be laid down with great care after consulting specialists in the field, it will be wholly unwise for the Court to encroach into the domain of the executive or legislature and try to enforce its own views and perceptions."[40]

In another judgement, the same Bench advocating a path of restraint for the judiciary said that courts were not the answer to all problems and people should exercise their democratic rights instead of rushing to courts straight away. "There are many evils that cannot be solved by courts but (they can be) by the public who can either use their creativity or resort to democratic methods like holding a peaceful march", the Bench said, during the hearing of a Public Interest Litigation (PIL) seeking directions for implementation of road safety measures on national highways, "This is democracy, where elections are held. You vote for a better's government if you are not satisfied with the governance. "Justice Katju" a known votary of judicial restraint said.[41]

The Parliament self has debated and discussed the trend of the judiciary trespassing into the executive and legislative fields on two occasions, 7 Dec. 2006, and 3. Dec. 2007.

The Lok Sabha debate on "harmonious functioning of the legislature, executive and the judieiary "held on 03.12.2007 highlights the concern and the frustration over the recurring interventions of the judiciary in the handling of routine executive business and the decision of the Parliament on policy matters and Constitutional issues.

The MPs saw in this trend the erosion of the principle of separation of powers which is the bedrock of any constitutional democracy. They were at their wit's end to understand how could the judiciary overrule the Parliament which was the supreme organ of the state representing the will of the people.

Many members were prompted to term such interventions as a case of "Despotism", K.C. Deo saw in it the "tyranny of the Judiciary".

Here is inherent a clash between the people's aspiration for change and the judicial insistence on an unalterable basic structure.

The only lawful and peaceful course left therefore is the restructuring of the judicial power so as to deny it the right of Judicial review and restrict it to the function of adjudication on the basis of the existing law. That alone will reinstate the principle of Parliamentary Sovereignty which was the starting point of our Constitution —Makers.

References

1. Parent of a student of medical college, Shimla vs. State of H.P. (1985) 3SCC 169: AIR 1985 SC 910.
2. Umed Ram vs. State of H.P. (1986) SCC 68 AIR 1986 SC 847.
3. Centre for Public Interest Litigation vs. Union of India (2000) 8 SCC 606.
4. Kanhaiya Lal Sethia vs. Union of India (1997) 6SCC 573.
5. Ernakulam North Development Co-ordination Council vs. Union of India, AIR 1999 Ker 131.

6. L.K. Pandey vs. Union of India (1984) 2SCC 244; AIR 1984 SC 469.
7. Bandhua Mukti Morcha vs. Union of India, AIR 1984 SC 843.
8. Sheela Barse vs. State of Maharashtra (1983) 2 SCC 96 : AIR 1983 SC 378.
9. *Times of India*, Allhabad, 28.02.2008.
10. Centre for Public Interest Litigation vs. Union of India, (2000) 8 SCC 606.
11. *Hindustan Times*, Lucknow, 18.11.2007.
12. *The Hindu* 20, September 2008.
13. See Dilip Simeon, "No quick fixes, please" *Hindustan Times*, Lucknow dated 29.04.2008 Also See Ramchandra Guha, "A History of Abuse" *Ibid*, 27.5.2008 and Ravi Shankar Parasad, "Believe it or not the Salwa Judum is working", *Ibid*, dt. 11.06.2008.
14. *The Hindu*, 20.09.2008.
15. D.S. Nakara vs. Union of India AIR 1983, SC 130, also see: Poonamal and other, vs. Union of India and others, 1985 (3) SCC 345.
16. Rampyari vs. Union of India, AIR 1988 Raj 124.
17. AIR 1984 SC 843.
18. Laxmi Kant Panday vs. Union of India (1987) 1 SCC 67.
19. Sheela Barse vs. State of Maharashtra (1983) 2 SCC 96; AIR 1983 SC 378.
20. Vishaka case (1997) 6 SCC 241; AIR 1997 SC 3011.
21. Vineet Narian vs. Union of India (1998) 1SCC 226; AIR 1998 SC 889.
22. D.K. Basu vs. State of West Bengal, 1997 1SCC 416; AIR 1997 SC 610.
23. *Hindustan Times*, Lucknow, 06.08.2008.
24. *The Hindu* 15.02.2009
25. *Ibid*.
26. *The Hindu*, 18.03.2009.
27. Jagadambika Pal case; AIR 1998, SC 998.

28. J.S. Verma; The Indian Polity; Separation of Power, South Asia Politics, Sept. 2007.11.
29. *Ibid* pp. 11-12.
30. *The Hindu,* 22.01.2009.
31. *The Hindu* 12.02.2009, 13.02.2009, 24.02.2009.
32. Golaknath vs. State of Punjab, AIR, 1967 1643.
33. Keshavanand Bharathi vs. State of Kerala, AIR 1973 SC 1461.
34. Gopalan vs. State of Madras (1950) SCR 88 ADM vs. Shukla, AIR 1976 SC 1207.
35. Meneka Gandhi vs. Union of India AIR 1978 SC 597.
36. D.D. Basu : Introduction to the constitution of India, 19th edition, Wadhwa Company & Company 2008 p. 110.
37. Minerva mills vs. Union of India, AIR 1980 SC 1787.
38. *Hindustan Times*, Lucknow 09.04.2007.
39. *Times of India*, Lucknow 11.12.07.
40. *The Times of India*, Allhabad 28.02.2008.
41. *Hindustan Times*, Lucknow, 03.04.2008.

11

Restructuring Judicial Power and Judicial Reforms

The mountain of pending cases in the courts, from the lowest to the highest would seem to suggest a sort of a collapse of the justice delivery system in India.

The latest tally of pending cases at various levels of courts, according to the Law Ministry, is as follows:[1]

Subordinate Courts	2,66,50,467
High Courts	39,10,858
Supreme Court	54,106
Total	3,06,15,431

These figures do not include the cases pending in various Consumer Courts and Tribunals. Justice V.V Rao of Andhra High Court said on March 6, 2610, that it would take 320 year to dispose off all pending cases in India. According to one estimate backlog of pending cases in the Supreme Court grows by 5,352 every year.

Even former President Pratibha Patil, former Loksabha Speaker, Somnath Chatterjee and Prime Minister Manmohan Singh have expressed grave concern at the decay and decline in the judicial system. The President has warned that congestion in courts could lead to people being tempted to take the law into their own hands.[2]

The Prime Minister Mr. Manmohan Singh, speaking at a National convention organized by the AICC's legal and human rights department, said on 27th March 2010 that the massive backlog of cases in courts at every level of the judicial system diminishes India's democratic frame work. He added that democracy will have little meaning for the common man if he could not secure basic rights and easy access to speedy justice."[3]

Earlier he singled outthe backlog of more than 3 crore cases pending in Indian courts as the highest challenge confronting the judiciary and appealed for a war against this scourge."[4]

The then Chief Justice of India, K. G. Balakrishnan addressing a seminar on "Alternative methods of dispute resolution – conciliation and mediation" at Bangalore warned that delay in justice delivery could trigger a popular revolt against the judiciary and pull down the entire legal structure.[5]

Delivering the valedictory address of the three day regional workshop on "planning and management for timely justice" organised by the National Judicial Academy, Hyderabad, Supreme Court Judge S.B. Sinha said "Not only outsiders but insiders in the system feel we are not able to manage ourselves. It is imperative we put our house in order for better.judicial governance" He added, "a judiciary which' should be healthy is suffering from many diseases." The solution was in enhancing the quality and responsiveness of judiciary to the needs of the litigant public.[6]

The judicial backlog has serious ramifications on India's economy. Finance Minister, Pranab-Mukherjee recently said, delays in resolving judicial disputes were impacting inflows of foreign direct investments. He said,

"Foreign investors always consider the additional costs resulting from courtroom delays (before deciding on committing investments); "not only are court room delays eating, up two per cent of India's gross domestic product (they are) also leading to corruption low investment and inflation."[7]

Law Minister, M. Veerappa Moily unveiled a vision document on October 25, 2009 on how to reduce pendency —legalese for pending or undecided cases - over the next three years.

The government is setting up an 11 member National Arrears Grid (NAG) to ascertain the exact arrears and ensure optimal utilization of infrastructure.[8]

Besides, the cost of litigation is mind boggling. It is so excessive and exhorbitant as to be beyond the reach of the common man, even the middle class. The judicial system appears to be meant only for the very rich and affluent.

Arguing in a PIL case filed by NGO "Janhit Manch" on various suggestions for judicial reforms before a Bench of the Supreme Court comprising CJI Balkrishnan and Justice P. Satnasivam the senior counsel, Prashant Bhushan admitted that the cost of litigation had sky rocketed in recent years and that legal aid committees which give free advice to poor litigants, were not functioning properly.[9]

Restructuring Judicial Power

It is suggested that judiciary should be restricted to the adjudication of disputes in accordance with existing law and not empowered to review the constitutionality of laws or the validity of Constitutional amendments.

The function of review may be entrusted to a quasijudicial body such as the Constitutional Council in France or the Federal Constitutional Court in Germany.

The principle of judicial review has not been accepted any where in continental Europe. In France the jurists "thought it improper for a court to decide whether an act of a legislature conflicted with the Constitution. In their view that was no part of the function of judges. They might decide questions of ordinary law, and in this sphere might..... impose effective checks upon administrative action but they were not expected to invoke the Constitution".[10]

This doctrine prevailed under the Fourth Republic and under the present Constitution. Under the Fourth Republic a Constitutional Committee composed of the President of the Republic, Presidents of the two Chambers of Parliament, and seven members chosen by the National Assembly from outside of thein own ranks, and three members chosen in the same way by the Council of the Republic was empowered to reviewlaws which conflicted with the Constitution.

Similarly under the fifth Republic (1958) there is provision for a Constitutional Council (Art 56-63), This Council consists of nine members uo be appointed by the President of the Republic and by the Presidents of the National Assembly and the Senate in equal numbers. The former Presidents of the Republic shall be ex-officio members of the Constitutional Council, for life.

The functions of the Constitutional Council are:

(1) to supervise the election of the President and decide all election disputes,

(2) supervise the conduct of referenda.

(3) to decide on the constitutionality of organic laws before their promulgation.

(4) Laws may be referred to the Constitutional Council, before their promulgation, by the President of the Republic, the Prime Minister or the President of either House of Parliament.

Art. 62 of the French Constitution declares: "decisions of the Constitutional Council shall be subject to no appeal. They shall be binding on the executive and Parliament and on all administrative and judicial authorities."

German Model

In Germany the Basic Law (1949) provides for a Federal Constitutional Court to decide on the interpretation of the Basic Law in the event of disputes concerning the rights and duties of a Federal organ or of other parties. It consists of Federal Judges and other members elected in equal numbers by the two Houses of Federal Parliament.

In the erstwhile U.S.S.R the power of determining the constitutionality of laws was vested in the Presidium of the Supreme Soviet of the U.S.S.R.

Therefore the suggestion of a quasi - Judicial organ determining the constitutionality of laws has the support of constitutional law in continental Europe and also in the former socialist countries. It is only in the U.S.A that the Supreme Court exercises the power of judicial review of laws enacted by the Congress. But even in the U.S.A the Court has not had many occasions to decide upon the validity of Constitutional amendments. There is not a single instance of a Constitutional amendment having been invalidated by the Court. The idea that the Constitution has an inviolable, and unalterable basic structure is certainly not recognised in constitutional theory or practice anywhere in the world.

Therefore if an alternative mechanism, other than the higher judiciary, is devised or proposed for review of laws it should not be looked upon as something of an innovation.

Justice P.N. Bhagwati, in the Minerva Mill's case agreed that effective alternative institutional mechanisms or arrangements for judicial review can be made by Parliament."[11]

In another case, S.P. Sampath Kumar vs. Union of India, the learned Judge affirmed that while judicial review cannot be dispensed with, "it would be within the competence of the Parliament to amend the Constitution so as to institute in place of the High Court another alternative institutional mechanism or arrangement for judicial review provided it is not less efficacious than the High Court."[12]

This provides the clue to the way out of the impasse in which the Constitution has been bogged down due to the basic structure theory.

An alternative mechanism must be evolved for review of the Constitutional cases including Constitutional amendments in the event of any dispute as to their validity and such a mechanism should be outside of the present framework of judicial review. Such a framework should ensure that no court is able to frustrate the will of the people. In this sense judicial review is un-democratic. As the then Law Minister Gokhale said, in course of debate on the 42nd amendment, "if there is any un-democratic feature in the Constitution, it is the feature of judicial review. It is undemocratic because what is democratically done and decided by the elected representatives is set at naught by people who are not as elected and who in that sense, do not represent the people."[13]

It is notable that during the debate on the 42nd amendment bill an amendment was moved by Shri Hari Kishore Singh in the Lok Sabha for insertion of a new provision after Art, 368. The said provision stipulated that.[14]

(1) Parliament shall have the power to constitute a constitutional panel consisting of 25 members of parliament to interpret the Constitution or decide any question of constitutional validity of any law enacted by Parliament or State legislature.

(2) neither the Supreme Court nor any other court shall have any power or jurisdiction in respect of matters referred to in cl. (1) above.

(3) Parliament may by law prescribe qualifications for the members of the panel which shall be requisite for appointment as members of the panel and the manner in which they shall be selected.

This proposal did not evoke any interest at that time in the Parliament or outside because it was thought to be quite out of place in view of the addition of cls (4) and (5) to Art. 368. Now that these two clauses have been struck down as null and void and the amending power is remanded back to judicial control the proposal of a Parliamentary Panel as the alternative mechanism for review of Constitutional cases may be the only way to get out of the present constitutional impasse.

The constitutional experience of several democratic countries like France and Germany lends support to it and there is evidence to show that judicial opinion will not be averse to it.

Recreating Primary Constituent Power

It is, however, possible — the possibility cannot be ruled out that the Supreme Court may place a spanner in this process of restructuring of judicial power. The Supreme Court has consistently held[15] that any abridgement of the power of judicial review is an attack on the basic structure of the Constitution and therefore, impermissible in view of the Keshavanand ruling (1973).

The Supreme Court may still resist and nullify any attempt to whittle down the power of judicial review by recourse to amendment of Art, 368. To overcome this resistance it may be necessary to devise ways and means to recreate the primary constituent authority for restructuring the judicial power. It has even been suggested that in order to debar judicial challenge to constitutional amendments a fresh Constituent Assembly be convoked and the Constitution rewritten, or, alternatively, the existing Parliament should convert itself into a Constituent Assembly and then proceed to delete the provisions relating to judicial review. It may set up a quasi-judicial organ to review and decide upon the constitutionality of laws.

The judiciary will be relieved of this task and will be free to engage exclusively in the work of adjudication of disputes according to the existing laws.

With the Supreme Court relieved of its burden of judicial review of laws and constitutional amendments, the *raison d'etre* for its existence will be lost. Its civil and criminal jurisdiction may be transferred to state High courts. The High Court will be the highest court of appeal on all matters, civil and criminal, arising under any law, Union or State.

Where conflicting views are expressed on the same law by the High Courts, the matter should be referred to the quasi-judicial review panel to be established for the discharge of the review functions of the Supreme Court.

It will further promote the cause of justice if circuit Benches of the High court move from district to district to hear and decide appeals from the District Courts, if any, so that the litigant may not have to rush to the headquarters of the High court.

Judicial Reforms

However the judiciary will retain the power of reviewing the legality of executive action, that is to ascertain if such acts are in accordance with law and constitution or not. Judicial activism will still remain intact in so far as control over the executive and its lapses are concerned.

It is a valuable supplement to Parliamentary control over the Executive. While the parliamentary control is political in nature and collective in operation, the judicial control will be legal and indiviaual. The political control is macro control while the judicial control is micro control. It is the latter which serves as watch dog of public interest over the routine activities and omissions of the Executive.

In order to make the judicial function more effective and efficient certain reforms are necessary in the judicial system. These reforms should aim at—

1. evolving alternative mechanism for dispute resolution.
2. to accelerate the speed of justice delivery.
3. to bring down the sky high cost of litigation so as to make it affordable for the common man.
4. regulating public interest litigation.
5. decentralization of judiciary.

Alternative Mechanism for dispute resolution

Besides the regular courts, alternative mechanisms for dispute resolution should be devised as supplements to justice delivery system. Lok Adalats and Fast Track courts have been welcome steps in this direction. So have been the consumer courts. The Panchayat Adalats or Nayay Panchayats at the village level are also note worthy.

Lok Adalat

The institution of Lok Adalats is a revolutionary step in the justice delivery system. It is an innovative mechanism for alternative disputes resolution in a spirit of conciliation and mediation outside the court. The Supreme court itself has organized three Lok Adalats in one year (2008) and the CJI has promised that "such Adalats will be held at regular intervals". As many as 29 cases were settled in the second Lok Adalat (September 2008) and 39 in the third Lok Adalat (06.12.2008).

In the country as a whole there were held 13,000 Lok Adalats until 31 March 1996, and around 5 million cases were settled by mutual consent of the parties. Out of these 2,78,801 were motor accident cases. By 31 march 2005 the number of Lok Adalats held all around the country had risen to 4,57,510, which settled by mutual consent of the parties over 1,70,00,000 cases of which 8,54,529 were motor accident cases.

The Lok Adalats have been held not only under the Supreme Court but also under the State High Courts. The latter have been organized by the respective State Legal services Authorities constituted under section VI of the Legal Services Authority Act, 1987.

In U.P. alone during the last 20 years (1981 to 2009) as many as 32,062 Lok Adalats have been held which have disposed off 77,51,675 cases, involving marital disputes, civil cases, revenue cases, labour disputes, motor accident cases and other cases.

Punjab

A mega Lok Adalat named "Samadhan" 2008 was held at Gurgaon in December 2008 to settle petty cases pending in Haryana, Punjab and Chandigarh numbering over 1 million. The court set for itself a megatask to clear a quarter of this massive backlog in two days flat (20 and 21 December 2008).[17]

In U.P. Lok Adalats have been held every year from time to time besides special Lok Adalats to settle cases pending in the courts under specific laws, such as the Negotiable Instrument Act, 1881, Indian Succession Act, 1925, Child Labour (Prohibition and Regulation Act, 1986 and to settle disputes pending with the Lucknow Development Authority.

Jharkhand

In Jharkhand the first ever Lok Adalat was convened in Latehar districton 07.02.2009 to settle cases relating to the National Rural Employment Guarantee Act.

Delhi

Delhi Legal Services Authority made another innovation when it held a Lok Adalat for on-line settlement of disputes in collaboration with ICICI Bank in February 2009. Thousands of credit card defaulters of ICICI Bank got an opportunity to settle their long pending cheque bouncing cases and recovery suits at a hundred courts on a single day.

In this way the Lok Adalat system is providing an alternative dispute resolution mechanism to the poor and helpless. However, this device is applicable only to compoundable cases. The Lok Adalat has no power to decide a case on "merit". This lacuna has now been filled in by an amendment adopted in 2002, in the National Legal Services Authority Act, 1987. The amended Act provides for setting up of Permanent Lok Adalats with power to decide compoundable cases involving a sum not exceeding Rs. 10 lakhs, "on merit". Specialized Tribunals functioning outside the regular court system.

The Fast Track Courts, Consumer Protection Forums, established under the Consumer Production Act, 1986. The Telecom Regulatory Authority of India. (TRAI) established under the Telecom- Regulatory Authority of India Act, 1995, and Panchayat Adalats or Nyaya Panchayats have also provided alternative mechanisms for dispute resolution to save the litigant's time and money.[18]

In 2008 Parliament enacted a law the Gramin Nayalayas Act 2008, for creating 5,000 Gramin Nayayalayas to make justice accessible for people living in rural areas.

The Law provides for setting up of mobile courts at Panchayat level, presided over by a Judicial Magistrate, with powers to decide, on Criminal and civil matters within six months.[19]

The Law Minister M. Veerappa Moily has describe the move to set up village courts as a "revolution in making speedy and affordable justice (available) to the majority of Indians. The law provides for deciding cases in these courts within six months (and) this will bring down the pending cases to 50 per cent".

In the first phase, 200 such courts are to be set up and all the 5,000 are expected to be functional over the next three years.

The proposed village courts will decide petty criminal cases where there can be a maximum imprisonment of two years and civil disputes arising out of purchase of village property, use of common roads and drawing water from wells.

Judges will have the power of a judicial magistrate and appears against their orders can be filed in district courts.

The courts will also have the powers to decide cases of minimum wages, bonded labour, domestic violence, money lending, etc.

It is reported that 30 million cases are pending in Indian courts, 25 million in lower judiciary. Law Minister Veerappa Moily says it takes 15 years on average to decide a case in India.[20]

However, the plan to open 5,000 Mobile Rural Courts (Gram Nayayalays) across the country has not found favour with the majority of states. The Gram Nyayalayas Act came into force on October 2, 2009. Only 95 courts have come up in four states of which merely half are functioning, Law Ministry figure show only 15 of 25 States have responded to the letters sent by the Law Ministry, seeking proposals for setting up the Gram Nyayalayas. Of the States which have responded to the proposal - Andhra Pradesh, Tamil Nadu, Uttrakhand and Delhi have turned it down. In nearly similar responses, these states have stated, "there is no need to set up the Gram Nyayalayas since the existing system is effective.

Meghalaya and Mizoram have sought changes in the Act before implementing it. Jharkhand has found a high level committee to look into the matter. U.P. and West Bengal agreed to set-up these courts, subject to 100 per cent financial assistance from the Center.[21]

Administrative Tribunals

The 42nd amendment (1976) introduced Administrative Tribunals to handle cases in specified areas of legal disputes. These areas are conditions of service of persons appointed to public services and posts and matters relating to –

(*a*) tax laws,

(*b*) custom's duties and foreign exchang,

(*c*) industrial and labour disputes,

(*d*) land reforms,

(*e*) ceiling on urban property,

(*f*) Election disputes,

(*g*) Food stuff and other essential gods,

(*h*) Rent control and tenancy issues.

Service tribunals have been set up under the Administrative Tribunals Act, 1985; such tribunals may be established for the Union and a separate tribunal for each State.

The state of West Bengal set up in 1987 a Taxation Tribunal to adjudcate disputes relating to taxation under any of the State Acts.

Besides the Service Tribunal (CAT), Labour conciliation Courts and Income Tax Tribunals are good examples of operating tribunals.

We need to have a tribunal of the nature of an OMBUDSMAN in every organization and department and its branches in every office or unit thereof.

Harold Laski is a defender of the administrative courts and believes that, "the growth of administrative law is implicit in the nature of the modern state".

He adds that "what is really involved in the jurisdiction of these ministerial tribunals is the evolution of adequate administrative standards, and the root of such standards is by its nature, far more a matter for the executive than for the courts."

Defending these administrative tribunals he writes, "very largely, they are concerned with technical matters the decision of which requires a special knowledge rarely available either to magistrates or Judges. Their work is swift and cheap......... the ordinary.........courts........lack the knowledge necessary for the construction of proper administrative standards. It must be remembered that most of this jurisdiction is concerned with questions of "reasonableness" in policy, and it is difficult to see why a judge's view of "reasonableness" is more likely to be right than that of a minister who may have to answer for his view in the House of Commons."[22]

It is regrettable that the administrative tribunals have been limited to few areas. We need to strengthen and widen the reach of these- tribunals not only at the union level but also in every state.

Recently the Law Commission of India in its 215th report submitted to the Center has suggested an amendment to the Administrative Tribunal Act to exclude the appellate jurisdiction of High courts against the decisions of Center and State administrative tribunals and provide for direct appeal to the Supreme Court.[23]

First Model E-Court

At about the same time the CJI K.G. Balakrishnan inaugurated the first e-court, which started functioning on a pilot bases at the Ahmedabad city civil and sessions court on 9th February 2009. It is the first Model e-court in the country that will make the judicial process transparent and justice delivery system speedier. The court will provide audio-video-recording of proceedings with multipoint video conferencing facilities linking the court room, central jail, the police commissioner's office and the forensic science laboratory.

It was inaugurated by the CJI K.G. Balakrishnan. Speaking on the occasion, he said, efforts would be made to open similar e-courts in Mumbai and in other parts of the country.

Three other major cities in Gujarat-Surat, Vadodara and Rajkot were expected to be covered under e-courts in the second phase of implementation after about a year.

The experiment in e-court adjudication has several advantages—

(1) The undertrials lodged in the central jail would not have to be brought to the court as they could be virtually presented through video conferencing.

(2) This would nullify the chances of escape of undertrials during transit.

(3) The entire proceedings would be video-recorded and available for review in case of any doubt.

(4) The biggest advantage would be when the witnesses turn hostile in the court rooms or in reviewing the statements of the lawyers.[24]

Summary General Courts Martial (S.G.C.M.)

It may be suggested that there ought to be a special court, a sort of military tribunal for handling antinational acts and individuals, such as those relating to terrorism, naxalism, militancy, insurgency, proxywar and armed rebellion. Anti-national acts (ANA)are being perpetrated by anti-national individuals (ANI) and groups and even by transnational groups and individuals indulging in such anti national acts as smuggling, drug trafficking, money laundering and counterfeiting of currency. All such acts should qualify as war crimes and be dealt with under domestic law and under the conventions on terrorism. An alternative method of dealing with ANA and ANI would be to try such cases by summary general courts martial (S.G.C.M.). An S.G.C.M. held under the Army Act, can award punishment upto death.

Such a court consists of a minimum of three officers and may have a judge advocate. The procedure is summary in nature but guarantees the minimum safeguards to an accused.

An appeal from the decision of the S.G.C.M. may be allowed to the Armed Forces Tribunal, and no more.

If necessary, the Constitution may be amended to provide for exclusive jurisdiction of the S.G.C.M. to try ANI and ANA cases.

Commercial Courts

Presently there is under consideration of the Law Ministry (GOI) a proposal to set-up commercial courts in the Mega cities of the country to deal with high value cases (cases involving monetary transactions of over Rs. 2 crore). Such specialized courts will take load off regular courts in dealing with commercial issues and help reduce pendency of cases.[25]

Special courts have also been envisioned (such as commercial courts, green courts) to deal with specified categories of cases to take the load off regular courts and to provide expertise to the adjudicating forum.

Evening Courts

The other experiments like the evening courts are being tried in some places. Addressing the legal fraternity of the Himachal Pradesh High Court at Shimla on 16.02.2009, C.J.I. Balakrishnan said that the Supreme Court had opened Evening Courts in some states on trial bases with a view to save time and money of serving classes.

He disclosed that evening courts were working in New Delhi and Gujarat and the Morning Courts in Andhra Pradesh. The primary objective of these courts is to ensure that daily wage earners involved in petty cases, such as traffic rule violations, did not lose their wages by attending the ordinary courts.

Arbitration and Conciliation

Another alternative method of dispute resolution outside the established court system, which is being currently tried and encouraged, is conciliation and arbitration.

Arbitration as a method of disputes resolution was recognized in the Indian Contract Act, 1872, as the only exception to litigation in court. In 1996 Parliament passed the Arbitration and Conciliation Act, which came into force in January 1996. There is statutory provision that the Arbitral tribunals should encourage the parties to settle disputes by using mediation, conciliation or other procedures of dispute resolution at any time during the arbitral proceedings.

By a recent amendment to the code of Civil Procedure 1908, civil courts are empowered to actively assist in a settlement and refer disputes either to arbitration, conciliation or to a Lok Adalat or for judicial settlement, or refer the same to mediation. The Law Commission had recommended that it should be obligatory for the court to refer the disputes for settlement by way of arbitration, conciliation, mediation, judicial settlement or to a Lok Adalat. But this recommendation was diluted and the discretion is left with the civil court to recommend to the parties the recourse to arbitration or conciliation or judicial settlement.

Fali S Nariman, a leading Constitutional Expert has expressed anguish and surprise that the Arbitration and Conciliation Act 1996 "has now been in the statute book for nearly nine years, but there is as yet no noticeable trend amongst lawyers to encourage clients to make use of the conciliation provisions in the Act: though parties are inclinded (and often encouraged by arbitral tribunals) to first attempt a settlement directly between themselves before proceeding with an arbitration.

He insists that, "for this new law to be effective, there has to be a change in attitudes, both on the part of arbitrators, and also on the part of judges and lawyers. Without such attitudinal change, the law will remain constrained and fettered by a court-controlled Mindset."[26]

Inaugurating a conference organized by the Associated Chambers of Commerce and Industry of India (ASSOCHAM) Union Minister for Law and Justice H.R. Bhardwaj on 17 January 2009, underlined the intention to amend the Arbitration and Conciliation Act and said a draft document had heen prepared which aimed at resolving civil and commercial disputes through mediation and conciliation. He said the Singapore model was being studied where the arbiter was required to return his fees if he failed to arbiter within 40 days.

At the conference, Delhi High Court Chief-Justice A.P. Shah said an arbitration center would be setup in the Delhi High court within six months. To be regulated, by a trust comprising judges, retired judges and lawyers, it would be required to solve the cases within 18 months.[27]

At Allahabad (U.P.) the High Court has set up a Mediation and Conciliation Center as an alternative dispute redressal system.

Mediation is a process in which a mediater, a neutral third party, helps the parties to the dispute to reach a settlement. This process saves time and costs. It is confidential and voluntary, that is – any party has the right to terminate the mediation at anytime. The High Court will refer appropriate cases for mediation to the Center. A mediator from the Center will be appointed to mediate the dispute. If the settlement is reached, this will be reported to the court and the court will pass enforcement orders. In case, the settlement is not reached the court will hear and dispose of the matter.[28]

In Rajasthan the State legal services Authority in July 2008 setup at Jodhpur an arbitration center to provide litigants with an alternative system of dispute resolution. Inaugurating the center Chief Justice Narain Roy said that an institutional arrangement for arbitration proceedings was the need of the hour "in view of a huge back log of undecided cases in the courts. Arbitration ensured speedy and inexpensive disposal of cases with full transparency thorough conciliation between the parties. Arbitration is best suited to help settle matrimonial, family and property disputes.[29]

These experiments will certainly give a new dimension to dispute settlement procedure and should in course of time proliferate in other parts of the country.

Plea Bargaining

The concept of plea bargaining was incorporated in the Criminal Law Amendment Act, 2005 assented to by the President in January 2006. According to Fali S. Nariman Plea bargaining is now seen as an alternative method to deal with the staggering arrears of criminal cases. It is also expected to alleviate the sufferings of undertrials prisoners.

In Odisha a scheme of plea bargaining has been introduced to bring about a substantial reduction of cases, other than cases involving capital punishment, life imprisonment for imprisonment for a term exceeding seven years. Under plea bargaining the complainant and the accused are given time to workout a mutually satisfactory disposition of the case. This may include giving compensation and other expenses to the victim by the accused.[30]

Itinerant Courts

One example of itinerant courts is the proposal to establish special tribunals for solving educational disputes to be established in universities and colleges. The H.R.D. Ministry has set up a committee to finalise the details of the proposed tribunals, with Mr. R.P. Agarwal, Higher Education Secretary as its Chairman. The tribunals will settle disputes relating to teacher's service conditions and issues relating to the institutions and their employees, besides disputes among teachers.

Another example of itinerant court would be setting up of special courts for deciding cases relating to bounced cheques.

The following observations of Ex. CJI V.R. Krishna Iyer are noteworthy in this connection.

"People want local justice, summary procedures, early finality and quick execution of decrees and orders. But our procedure code is exasperatingly supererogatory. And once a decree is passed, the difficulties of the winning litigant begin in protracted execution proceedings. All this must be scrapped and substituted with summary simplicity. We may innovate and experiment with evening courts, itinerant courts, circuit benches, dispute settlement organs, quick arbitrations, conciliations and socially fruitful reconciliation.[31]

Speedy Justice

The Supreme Court has held that speedy trial is a constitutional right implict in the right to life under Art. 21 of the Constitution and this includes not only the proceedings in the court but also the preceeding police investigations. Laying emphasis on speedy trials and disposal of cases by the court, prime Minister Manmohan Singh said, "Trials should be conducted expeditiously and judgements delivered quickly.[32]

In one case the Supreme Court quashed the charges filed by the Anti-corruption Bureau against Pankaj Kumar, a businessman who along with his parents was accused of entering into a clandestine deal for supply of spare parts to a milk dairy owned by the government. The offence was allegedly committed in 1981, the FIR was recorded in 1987, the charge sheet was submitted in 1991. In the meantime the parents of Pankaj Kumar who as a minor was charged along with his parents in 1987, had died. Pankaj Kumar was acquitted of the offence.[33]

The speedy trial requires that—

(1) There should be shedding of formal practices and redtapism in petition drafting, in examining witnesses, in submission of documents and the like and the whole procedure should be simplified and business like.

Secondly, there should be not more than one REVIEW (appeal, revision or what ever name be given to it) at what ever level or forum.

In this connection Justice V.R. Krishna Iyer writes, "One appeal is fair. But room for many such appeals is cruel, expensive and vagarious, as it is now. Never ending litigative prodigality is a national waste. It involves a bizarre Bench–Bar extravaganza, loquacious advocacy, arcane 'submissions', systemic corruption, logomachic legalism and dilatory and noxious features. This must end."[34]

The Supreme Court itself has frowned upon the practice of High court to entertain second appeals in a case. The court drew attention to section 100 of the Civil Procedure Code (as amended in 1976) according to which if the judgement by the appeal court and lower court is similar, a second appeal should be admitted only if a "substantial question of law" is involved. It said that the second appeal should not become third trial on facts or one more dice in the gamble. The Law Commission too, in its 54th report said that in civil cases there should be only two hearings on facts – one before the trial court and the other before the first appellate court. The suggestion made above in this paper endorsed by Justice Krishna lyer is that there should be one appellate court, whether the High Court or the supreme Court, or any other court to hear appeal from the judgement of the trial court. As the Supreme Court said, "A search for absolute truth in the administration of justice, however, laudable, must be put under some reasonable restraint. A search for truth has to be reconciled with the doctrine of finality."

Thirdly, unlike in most other sectors that have to adhere to deadlines, the judicial process can drag on for ever under one pretext or the other. All court proceedings should be governed by a realistic time frame, after which those in charge of the justice delivery procedure must be held accountable. A time limit should be fixed for the final disposal or decision of a case which in no case and under no circumstances should exceed a specified period (say, one year).

Fourthly, the role of lawyers in judicial proceedings should be minimised. In most cases the petitioner should be required to present and plead for his own case in person before the court. Neither the court nor the litigant should require the services of a middleman, as the lawyers are in the existing system.

However an exception may be made in favour of certain collective entities, such as the government departments and its agencies, corporate houses, business establishments, companies, Public Utilities and Institutions and the like.

Speaking at a Seminar on 'Speedy Justice' organized by the All India Bar Association at New-Delhi in October 2008, the chairman of the Law Commission, A.R. Lakshmanan said that the Commission had recommended that the criminal justice system be completely overhauled. It "exhorted a radical change in the working of the law enforcement agencies, especially the police and public prosecutors to contain such delays in the recent past."

Justice Lakshmanan said that the Commission recently mooted the concept of plea bargaining negotiations, between the accused and the prosecution in which if the accused agreed to plead guilty to the charges, he/she would get certain concessions as a quid pro quo, with courts taking a lenient view, particularly in cases of lesser gravity.

As a measure for speedy justice the Madras High Court had recently directed that bail bonds be executed at police stations, instead of before trial courts.

Several speakers at the Seminar called for cutting down adjournments, fixing a time limit for deciding cases, creating additional infrastructure to ensure speedy justice. Justice Lakshmanan favoured an alternative disputes resolution mechanism such as negotiations, conciliation and mediation. Chief Justice Balakrishnan in his message said, "it goes without saying that deliberations on strategies for ensuring speedy justice are of the utmost importance for our judicial system."

The Delhi High Court has approved creation of six additional courts of special judges exclusively for the Central Bureau of Investigation cases in the capital.

The agency is facing a backlog of 986 corruption cases that are pending in the court.

While 44 cases are over 20 years old, 39 are pending for the past 15 years.[36]

Speaking at the 17th Conference of the CBI anti-corruption Bureaux in New Delhi on 26.08.09, Mr. Ashwani Kumar, Director C.B.I. said that the agency had decided to complete all investigations within one year. He disclosed that there are more than 9,000 cases charge sheeted by the CBl presently pending in the courts. He said, "the trial of corruption cases should be completed within a specified time frame, say in a few years".

CJI K.G. Balakrishnan said at Kochi, while inaugurating a three day training programme in mediation for judicial officers and lawyers that more evening courts should be set up in the country, besides those working in New Delhi and Gujarat and the morning courts in Andhra Pradesh. The Karnataka Government readily agreed to his suggestion and promised to pay incentives for the judicial officers working in the evening court. The primary objective of these courts is to ensure that daily wage earners involved in petty cases, such as traffic rule violations, did not lose their wages by attending the ordinary courts.

At this meeting the acting chief justice of the Kerala High Court pleaded that mediation could effectively reduce the number of pending cases.[37]

Inaugurating the 126th annual day celebrations of the Coimbatore Bar Association on 21.12.2008, the C.J.I. made the following suggestions—

(1) Speedy filling up of the vacant positions of judicial officers,

(2) increasing the number of CBI courts,

(3) need for setting up of more and more of Family Courts.

(4) the creation of special courts for handling cases under the Negotiable Instruments Act.

(5) Mediation and Arbitration under the Alternative Disputes Redressal System (A.D.R.S.) be given greater impetus.

The CJI disclosed that computerisation of courts will be completed in two years. He said that High Court judges numbering 877, 26 Supreme Court Judges and 15,000 Judicial officers have been provided with Laptop computers with net connectivity.[38]

Public Interest Litigation

PIL should be given statutory recognition and support. Its sweep should be widened. How is this to be done, is for experts in the fields of law and politics to deliberate upon and decide.

As of now, it can be said that PIL has served a useful purpose in coming to the aid of the poor, helpless, ignorant classes of people in knocking at the doors of courts and receiving instant relief.

A Supreme Court bench headed by Chief Justice Balakrishnan said, "Nobody is prepared to protect the common man's right. Who will protect the rights of common man if the executive does not do its, duty? When authorities are not taking action, who will take the action? Do you expect that a common man who is denied admission in a hospital will go to the chief minister with a complaint?"[39]

The Chief Justice gave two examples to illustrate his point. He said," there are a number of unauthorised schools and colleges where a large number of students are being cheated in connivance with the State governments. Where will they go? There is a condition that hospitals which are given lands must provide 30 per cent of the beds to the poor. Are they doing so? Where will such people go if their rights are denied? Nobody is prepared to protect the common man's rights."

The Chief Justice further said," We will protect the rights of the common man. We are not straying into the domain of the executive. We will do so only if the executive fails to do its duty.[40]

The Chief Justice agreed that the court should not interfere in policy decisions and in trivial issues.

The Supreme Court has already taken the initiative to forame broad guidelines and parameters for itself and for High Courts to regulate public interest litigation so as to keep at bay false, frivolous and malafide petitions.

On April 10, 2008 it issued notice to the Supreme court Bar Association and asked Senior Counsel Fali Nariman to render assistance in the matter.[41]

In this regard one suggestion is that the letter petition for certain catagories of persons and cases (to be specified by law) may be made the accepted norm for the court.

Such petitions should be shorn of any technicalities and drafted in plain, straight, simple language, state facts and the prayer and possibly the provisions of law.

There should be set up administrative courts in everydistrict for entertaining and deciding upon such pettitions and the courts should deal with them as would any executive office with any application, but within a defined time frame.

The appeal from its decision may be to the district court whose decision shall be final and conclusive of the matter.

Decentralisation of Judiciary

The administration of law is top heavy. It should be decentralised as much as possible. The steps in adjudication process should be reduced to two-the original petition and one and only one appeal (or review, revision or whatever it may be called).

The Supreme Court ought to be relieved of its burden of judicial review of laws and constitutional amendments. The *raison d'etre* for its existence will be lost. Its civil and criminal jurisdiction may be transferred to state High courts. The High Court will be the highest court of appeal on all matters, civil and criminal, arising under any law, Union or State.

It will further promote the cause of justice if circuit Benches of the High court move from district to district to hear and decide appeals from the District Courts, if any, so that the litigant may not have to rush to the headquarters of the High court.

Suggestions of L.K. Advani

L.K. Advani, former Dy. P.M. suggested that there should be created zonal benches of the Supreme Court in Delhi, Kolkata, Mumbai and Chennai.

He made this suggestion at a conference of the B.J.P legal cell last month (August 2008). Advani had said that the Supreme Court's principal bench should hear only inter-state disputes, constitutional matters and other important cases while zonal benches would hear appeals arising from High Courts.

In justification of this suggestion, he said, "citizens and the legal fraternity across the country feel that the Supreme Court has become too remote, too inaccessible, and too burdened with all kinds of cases".

Responding to Advani's suggestion for the creation of four zonal benches of the Supreme Court, Balakrishnan, C.J.I. agreed that these could be appellate forums with powers to hear appeals from High Court under Art. 136 and writ petitions under Art, 32.

Balakrishnan said that there could be zonal benches of the Supreme Court, if the prinicipal bench hears only constitutional matters and inter-state disputes.[42]

He added, "Our Supreme Court in the strict sense is not a constitutional court, that is the court dealing with just constitutional matters. We hear appeals under Art, 136; Cases come under various subjects. We have got original jurisdication, Art 32 (writ jurisdiction)...... We also hear public interest litigation."

The CJI said if such a decision is taken, the Supreme Court should be "be a complete constitutional court ...only constitutional matters and disputes between the states would be considered by the court. Disputes related to water, disputes about other such matter". The CJI said such system was functional in South Africa, Canada and U.S.A.

The suggestions made by the C.J.I, in brief are:

1. The supreme Court should be made the constitutional court dealing with constitutional matters and inter-state disputes.
2. There should be zonal benches of the Supreme Court in Delhi, Kolkata, Mumbai and Chennai to hear appeals from High Court under Art. 136 and writ petitions under Art. 32.

It may be added that the constitutional court as envisaged by the C.J.I. may be a quasi-judicial body with representations of the Parliament, the Bar and the academic community.[43]

Recommendations of the Parliamentary Panel

The Parliamentary Committee on Law and Justice in its 28th report submitted to the Parliament in October 22, 2008 reiterated its earlier recommendations that the Constitution be amended to make a provision for establishment of regional benches of the Supreme Court in the West, North, East and South for easy accessibility of justice to the poor and needy. As an experimental measure, a Bench could be set up in Chennai.[44]

The Committee reiterated this suggestion in its 32nd report submitted to Parliament in the third week of December 2008 also.

The committee also said that, "The High Court benches in various places in addition to the state capital is much appreciated by people for easy accessibility of justice to the poor and the needy, on reasonable expenditure". The committee noted that," even the Constitution makes provision under Act, 130 that the Supreme Court can meet in any other place or places as the Chief Justice of India may with the approval of the President, allow." The committee also recommended the introduction of regional languages as the language of the respective High Courts.[45]

However in a total volte face, presumably under pressure from legal lobby, the same CJI, on 16.08.09 rejected the Law Commissions recommendations for creation of four zonal benches of the Supreme Court to deal with the mounting arrears and make justice available to litigants at the nearest place possible. He said, "It will undermine the institutional integrity of the Supreme Court; we cannot split the Supreme Court". These are lame excuses and laconic arguments. How will the creation of zonal benches split the Supreme Court. Does the Supreme Court not function in benches? How will zonal benches be different from Supreme Court benches in New Delhi?

As for integrity of Supreme Court it must be underlined that the benches of the Supreme Court often divide in their decision and it is quite common for a subsequent bench to reverse the decision of its predecessor.[46]

In view of the wide gap between political Ideology and the vested interests of the Bar, it will require strong will and firm determination on the part of political and party leadership to go in for judicial reforms that would result in the decentralisation of justice delivery at the level of the High Courts and the Supreme Court.

These are some of the suggestions for judicial reforms. They are tentative suggestions based only and exclusively on the personal experience, observation and study of the researcher. They need, to be examined in depth by jurists, politicians and academicians and verified empirically by research scholars in Indian Universities.

References

1. *Hindustan Times,* 28.12.2009.
2. The August and September 2007, 27 people lost their lives in Mob lynching in Bihar. On 23rd February, 2008 a Mob dragged out a murder accused and beat him almost to death in Bihar, Hindustan Times, Lucknow 25.2.2008.
3. *Hindustan Times,* 28.03.2010, *Times of India* 29.03.2010.
4. *Hindustan Times,* 17.08.2009.
5. *Hindustan Times,* 28.12.2009.
6. *The Hindu,* 09.02.2009.
7. *Hindustan Times,* Lucknow, 22.03.2010.
8. *Hindustan Times,* Lucknow, 22.03.2010.
9. *Times of India,* Allahabad, 08.02.2009.

10. K.C. Wheare : Modern Constitutions, O.U.P. (HUL Series) 1956, P-150.
11. Minerva Mill's vs. Union of India, AIR 1980 SC 1789 at P-1836.
12. S.P. Sampath Kumar Vs. Union of India, AIR 1987, SC at P-389.
13. Rajya Sabha Debates, 09.11.76, Col.15.
14. Lok Sabha Debates, 01.11.1976 Col-167-169.
15. Keshavanand Bharati Vs. State of Kerala, AIR 1973,SC 1461, Indira Gandhi Vs. Raj Narain, AIR 1975 SC 2299, Minerva Mills vs. Union on India, AIR 1980 SC 1787.
16. Fali Nariman, India's Legal System: Can it be saved? Penguin Books, 2006, p. 48.
17. *The Hindu* 08.09.2008, 13, 10, 2008, 17.12.08, 21.12.08.
18. *The Hindu* 08.02.09 and (*The Times of India* 24.02.09) Another device currently mooted is the institution of Gram Nayalayas (village courts).
19. *Hindustan Times* 03.04.2010.
20. *Hindustan Times*, 02.10.2009.
21. *Hindustan Times* 03.04.2010.
22. Harold J. Laski, Parliamentary Government in England, Allen and Unwin, 1938, pp. 353-354.
23. *The Hindu*, 31.12.2008.
24. *The Hindu*, 10.02.2009.
25. *Hindustan Times*, Lucknow, 28.10.2010.
26. Fail S. Nariman, India's Legal System; cant be saved? Penguin Book India, 2006 pp. 44-47.
27. *The Hindu* 18.01.2009.
28. See *Hindustan Times* (Live) 25.06.2007.
29. *The Hindu*, 12 July 2008.
30. *Hindustan Times* Luknow, 02.04.2008.
31. *The Hindu*, 12.09.2008.
32. *Hindustan Times*, 27.06.09.
33. *Hindustan Times*, Lucknow, 14 July 2008.

34. *The Hindu,* 12 Sept. 2008, page 11. Also see V.R. Krishna Iyer, Law and Life, Universal Law Publishing Company, Delhi, 2008, p.61.
35. *Hindustan Times,* 07.04.09.
36. *The Hindu,* 21.12.2008.
37. *The Hindu,* 21.12.2008.
38. *The Hindu,* 22.12.2008.
39. *Hindustan Times,* Lucknow 10.04.2008.
40. *The Hindu,* Delhi 11.04.2008.
41. *Hindustan Times,* 11.04.2008.
42. In what appears to be preparing the ground for retracting his views on the setting up ofregional Benches of the Supreme Court, the C.J.I., K.G. Balakrishnan, in an interview granted to *The Hindu* on January 08, 2009, said indifferently, "I think most of the judges subscribe to the resolution passedin 1999 by the Full court of the Supreme Court that locating regional Benches, whether in Chennai or Kolkata or Mumbai, will affect the unity and integrity of the judiciary. The Supreme court is a national court and it should be in the (national) capital, which is in the central part of India". *The Hindu,* 10.01.2009.
43. *Hindustan Times,* Lucknow 15.09.2008.
44. *The Hindu,* 23.10.2008.
45. *The Hindu,* 29.12.2008.
46. *Hindustan Times,* 12.08.2009.

Bibliography

Abraham, Henry J., Freedom and the Court: Civil Liberties in the United States, New York: Oxford University Press, 1967.

Agrawala, S.K., Public Interest Litigation In India A Critique, Bombay, N.M. Tripathi, 1985.

Ahuja, Sangeeta, People, Law and Justice: A Case Book on PIL, Vol. I, II, New Delhi,Orient Longman Ltd., 1997.

Alexander, P.C., Indian in the New Millennium, Mumbai : Somaiya Publications, 2001.

Alexander, P.C. Through the Corridors of Power: An Insider's Story, New Delhi: Harper Collins, 2004.

Anand, C.L., Constitutional Law and History of Government of India, New Delhi, Universal Law Publishing Co., 2008.

Andhyarujina, T.R. : Judicial Activism and Constitutional Democracy in India, Bombay, N.M. Tripathi, 1972.

Antony, M.J., Social Action Through Courts: Landmark Judgments in Public Interest Litigation, New Delhi: Indian Social Institute, 1993.

Antulay, A. R. Appointment of a Chief Justice Perspectives on Judicial Independence, Rule of law and Political Philosophy Underlying the Constitution, Bombay; Popular Prakashan, 1973.

Arora, Tirlok Nath, Judicial Strictures: Liberty of Expression and Restraint, Delhi, Universal Law Publishing Co., 2001.

Austin, Granville, The Indian Constitution : The Corner Stone of a nation, New Delhi, Oxford University Press,1979.

Austin, Granville, Working a Democratic Constitution : A History of the Indian Experience, New Delhi, O.U.P., 2008.

Bains and Jain, Contemporary Political Theory, New Delhi, Radiant Publishers, 1980.

Bakshi, P.M., the Constitution of India, New Delhi, Universal Law Publishing Co., 2010.

Banerjee, Anil Chandra; The Constitutional History of India, Vol. I., Delhi, Macmillan, 1977.

Banerjee, Anil Chandra; The Constitutional History of India, Vol. II., Calcutta, A. Mukherjee and Co., 1978.

Bansal, J.P. : Supreme Court : Judicial Restraint Vs Judicial Activism, Jaipur, Unique Publications, 1985

Barker, Ermest Principles of Social and Political Theory, London, Oxford University Press, 1961.

Barry, Briand, The Liberal Theory of Justice, Oxford, 1973.

Basu, Durga Das, Introduction to the Constitution of India, 19th Edition, Reprint 2008, Nagpur, Wadhwa and Company, 2008.

Basu, Durga Das, Constitutional Law of India, New Delhi, Prentice Hall of India, 1978.

Baxi, Upendra : The Indian Supreme Court and Politics, Lucknow, Eastern Book Company, 1980.

Baxi, Uependra : The Crisis of the Indian Legal System, New Delhi, Vikas Publishing House, 1982.

Baxi, Upendra, Liberty and Corruption : The Antulay Case and Beyond, Lucknow : Eastern Book Company, 1989.

Baxi, Upendra : Courage, Craft and Contention : The Indian Supreme Court in eighties, Bombay, N.M. Tripathi, 1985.

Baxi, Upendra (ed), : K.K. Mathew on Democracy, Equality and Freedom, Lucknow, Eastern Book Co., 1978.

Bealey Frank : The Blackwell Dictionary of Political Science, Oxford, Blackwell, 1999

Becker, Theodore L, Comparative Judicial Politics Chicago: Rand Me Nally, 1976.

Berger, Raoel, Government by Judiciary: The Transformation of the Fourteenth Amendment, Cambridge, Mass, : Hardvard University Press 1977.

Bhagwan Vishnoo, Select Political Systems (A Comparative Study of the Constitutions of U.K., U.S.A., China and Bangladesh). New Delhi Sterling Publishers Pvt. Ltd. 2004.

Bhandari, M.K., Basic Structure of the Indian Constitution, New Delhi; Deep and Deep Publications, 1993.

Bhargava, Rajeev Politics and Ethics of the Indian Constitution, New Delhi O.U.P., 2008.

Bhushan, Shanthi, Courting Destiny – A Memoir, New Delhi, Penguin Viking, 2008.

Bickel Alexander M., The Least Dangerous Branch : The Supreme Court at the Bar of Politics, Delhi: Universal Law Publishing Co., 1998

Bluhm, William, T. : Theories of the Political System, New Delhi, Prentice Hall, 1981.

Brownlie Ian, Basic Documents In International Law, Oxford, 1967.

Cardozo, B., The Nature of the Judicial Process, Yale University Press, New Heaven, 1921.

Chandrachud, Y.V., The Basics of Indian Constitution: Its Search for Social Change and the Role of Judges, New Delhi, Publications Division, Ministry of Information and Broadcasting, 1989

Chaudhary, V.K.S., The Ivory Tower: 51 years of the Supreme Court, Universal Publishing Co. 2002.

Chopra, Pran, The Supreme Court Versus the Constitution, The Challenge to Federalism, New Delhi, Sage, 2008.

Cox, Archibald, The Role of the Supreme Court in American Government, New York: Oxford University Press, 1957.

Das, Cyrus and K. Chandra, ed, Judges and Judicial Accountability, Delhi: Universal Law Publishing Company, 2003.

Das, Gobind, Supreme Court in Quest of Identity, Lucknow, Eastern Book Company, 2000.

Desai, D.A., Rule of Law and Judiciary in Transformation of Society: India – G.D.R. Experiments, New Delhi : Kalamkar Prakashan, 1984.

Dhavan, Rajeev, Contempt of Court and the Press, Bombay, N.M. Tripathi Ltd. 1982.

Dhavan, Rajeev, "The Supreme Court as Problem Solver : The Mandal Controversy" in V.A. Pai Panandiker (ed)., The Politics of Backwardness; Reservation Policy in India, Delhi, Konark Publishers, 1997.

Dhavan, Rajeev, Reserved: How Parliament Debated Reservations 1995 -2007, New Delhi, Rupa & Co. 2008.

Dhavan Rajeev, R, Sudarshan and Salman Khurshid, ed., Judges and the Judicial Power, Bombay. N.M. Tripathi, 1985.

Dhavan, Rajeev : The Supreme Court of India and Parliamentary Sovereignty, Delhi : Sterling Publishers, 1976.

Dhavan, Rajeev, The Supreme Court of India: A Socio-Legal Critique of its Techniques, Bombay: N.M. Tripathi, 1977.

Dhavan, Rajeev et. al. (eds) : Judges and the Judicial Power, Bombay, N.M. Tripathi, 1985.

Dhokalia, R.P., International Law, Allahabad Central Book Depot 1963.

Dicey, A.V., An Introduction to the Study of the Law of the Constitution, Delhi, Universal Law Publishing (10th ed), 2008.

Divan, Shyam and Armin Rosencranz, Environmental Law and Policy in India; Cases, Materials and Statutes, Delhi: OUP, 2001.

Dubey, M.P. Role of Supreme Court in Indian Constitution, New Delhi, Deep and Deep Publications, 1987.

Dworkin, Ronald, Justice in Robes, Delhi, Universal Law Publishing Co., 2007.

Farrelly, Colin, Contemporary Political Theory, A Reader London, Sage, 2007.

Friedmann, W. Legal Theory, Delhi, Universal Law Publishing Co., 2008 (Fifth edition).

Friedmann, W. Law in a Changing Society, London, Stevens & Sons, 1959.

Gadgil, Madhav; Guha Ramchandra : Ecology and Equity, New Delhi, Penguin India, 1995.

Galanter Marc, competing Equalities : Law and the Backward classes in India, New Delhi, O.U.P., 1984.

Gauba, O.P. Dimensions of Social Justice, New Delhi, National Publishing Co., 1983.

Gaus Gerald F., Kukathas Chandran, (eds); Handbook of Political Theory, London, Sage, 2004.

Germino Dante : Beyond Ideology: The Revival of Political Theory, New York, Harper and Row, 1967.

Gettell Raymond G. : Political Science, Calcutta, The World Press, 1961.

Ginsberg, Morris: Law and Opinion in England in the 20th Century, Berkeley, University of California Press, 1959.

Ginsburg, Tom, Judicial Review in New Democracies: Constitutional Courts in Asian Cases, Cambridge, U.K., Cambridge University Press 2003.

Glazer, Nathan and Kristol Irving (Eds), The American Commonwealth 1976, New York, Basic Books, 1976.

Godbole, Madhav, The Judiciary and Governance in India, New Delhi, Rupa & Co., 2009.

Graham Keith (ed.) : Contemporary Political Philosophy : Radical Studies Cambridge, Cambridge University Press, 1982.

Griffth, J.A.G., The Politics of the Judiciary, Glasgow Fontana/ Collins, 1977.

Grover, Virender, Courts and Political Process in India, New Delhi: Deep & Deep Publications, 1989.

Gupta, Vijay K., Decision-Making in the Supreme Court of India, Delhi, Kaveri Books, 1995.

Gupta, Dutta, S. : The Supreme Court and Indian Capitalism 1950-67. In : Kumar Mukhopadhya (ed.) Society and Politics in Contemporary India, Calcutta, Council for Political Studies, 1974.

Hidayatullah, M : Democracy in India and the Judicial Process, Bombay, Asia Publishing House, 1966.

Hayek, F.A., The Constitution of Liberty, Chicago, 1960.

Hegde, K.S. Crisis in Indian Judiciary, Bombay, Sindhu Publications, 1973.

Hegde Rama Krishna, The Judiciary Today: A Plea for a Collegium, Government of Karnataka, 1988.

Hegde, K.S. Crisis in Indian Judiciary, Bombay, Sindhu Publications Pvt. Ltd. 1973.

Heffner, Richard D., A Documentary History of the United States, A Mentor Book, New York, 1952.

Hidayatullah, M., A Judge's Miscellany, Third Series, New Delhi, : Arnold Heinemann, 1982.

Hidayatullah, M., A Judge's Miscellany, Second senes, Bombay, N.M. Tripathi, 1979.

Hobhouse, L.T. The Elements of Social Justice, London, George Allen & Unwin, 1922.

Hurra, Sonia, Public Interest Litigation : In Quest of Justice, Ahmedabad: Mishra and Company, 1993.

Imam, M. The Indian Supreme Court and the Constitution, Lucknow, Eastern Book Co., 1973.

Irish, Marian D., (Ed.), Continuing Crisis in American Politics, U.S.A. Prentice Hall, Engle Wood Cliffs, 1963.

Jagmohan Reddy, P. : Liberty and Property under Indian Constitution, Calcutta, University of Calcutta, 1984.

Jai, Janak Raj, Commissions and Omissions in the Administration of Justice, New Delhi Regency Publications, 2003.

Jain, M.P., Indian Constitutional Law, 5th edn. Nagpur Wadhwa and Co. 2003.

Jain, Sampat, Public Interest Litigation, New Delhi: Deep & Deep Publications, 2002.

Jennings, Ivor : Some Characteristics of the Indian Constitution, London, Oxford University Press, 1953.

Jones, W.T., Masters of Political Thought, Vol. II, London, George G. Harrap, 1961.

Kapur, Devesh and Bhanu Mehta, Pratap Public Institutions in India: performance and design, New Delhi, O.U.P. 2005.

Kashyap, Subhash, C., Blue Print of Political Reforms, New Delhi, Shipra, 2003.

Kashyap, Subhash, C., Constitutional Law of India, New Delhi, Universal Law Publishing Co., 2008.

Kashyap, Subhash, C., ed., The Citizen and Judicial Reforms, New Delhi, Universal Law Publishing Co., 2003.

Kashyap Subhash C., ed., Reforming the Constitution, New Delhi: UBS Publishers Distributors, 1992.

Kashyap, Subhash C., Constitution of India - Review and Reassessment, New Delhi, Universal Law Publishing Co. 2010.

Kashyap, Subhash, Our Parliament, New Delhi, National Book Trust, India, 2005.

Keck, Thomas M. : The Most Activist Supreme Court in History: The Road to Modern Judicial Conservatism, Univ. of Chicago Press, 2004.

Kirpal B.N., et al; ed. Supreme But Not Infallible: Essays in Honour of Supreme Court of India, New Delhi, OUP, 2002.

Kothari, Rajni : Rethinking Development — In search of Humane Alternatives, Delhi, Ajanta, 1988.

Kozlowski, Mark, The Myth of the Imperial Judiciary: Why the Right is wrong about the courts, New York, University Press, 2003.

Krishna Iyer, Justice V.R., Some half hidden aspects of Indian Social Justice, Lucknow, Eastern Book Co., 1980.

Krishna Iyer, Justice V.R., A New Focus Towards Social Justice, Bombay, N.M. Tripathi, 1985.

Krishna Iyer, Justice V.R., At Crossroads, New Delhi, Deep & Deep Publications, 1992.

Krishna Iyer, Justice V.R., Constitutional Miscellany, Lucknow, Eastern Book Company, 2007.

Krishna Iyer, Justice V.R., Rhetoric Versus Reality: Essays on Human Rights, Justice and Democratic Values, Gurgaon : Hope India, 2004.

Krishna Iyer, Justice V.R., Law & Life, Delhi, Universal Law Publishing Co., 2008.

Kumaramangalam, S. Mohan; Judicial Appointments : An analysis of the recent controversy over the appointment of the Chief Justice of India, New Delhi : Oxford and I.B.H. Publications Co. 1973.

Laski, Harold J., Parliamentary Government in England, London, Allen & Unwin, 1952.

Laski, Harold J., A Grammar of Politics, New Delhi Anamika Publishers & Distributors Ltd., 2010.

Laxminath A., Basic Structure and Constitutional Amendments: Limitations and Justiciability, New Delhi : Deep & Deep Publications, 2002.

Locke, John, Two Treaties of Civil Government, London, Everyman's Library, 1949.

Madhava Menon, N.R., Rule of Law in a free Society New Delhi, OUP., 2009.

Malhotra, V.K. Welfare State and Supreme Court in India, New Delhi, Deep & Deep Publications, 1986.

Malhotra, G.C. (ed.) Fifty years of Indian Parliament, New Delhi, Lok Sabha Secretariat, 2002.

Malik, S. (ed.) Complete digest of Supreme Court Cases, Lucknow, Eastern Book Co.

Malik, S. (ed.) The Fundamental Rights Cases 1951-73, Lucknow, Eastern Book Company, 1973.

Malik, S. (ed.) Fundamental rights cases The Critics Speak, Lucknow, Eastern Book Co. 1975.

Markandan, K.C., Directive Principles in the Indian Constitution, New Delhi, Allied Publishers, 1996.

Mathew, K.K., Democracy, Equality and Freedom, Lucknow, Eastern Book Company, 1978.

Mathew, K.K., The right to equality and property under the Indian Constitution, New Delhi, National Publishing House, 1980.

May Erskine, Treatise on Law, Privileges, Proceedings and Usage of Parliament, London, Butterworths, 1976.

May, Erskine, Parliamentary Practice (21st ed.) London Butterworths 1989.

Miller, David (ed.): Liberty, Oxford, Oxford University Press, 1991.

Miller, David (ed) : The Blackwell Encyclopedia of Political Thought, Oxford, Blackwell Reference, 1987.

Miller, David (ed); Social Justice, Oxford, Clarendon Press, 1976.

Mohan, Arun, Justice, Courts and Delays, New Delhi, Universal Law Publishing Co., 2009

Morrison, Ken, Marx, Durkhem, Weber, Formations of Modern Social Thought, New Delhi, Sage., 2008.

Mridul, Marudhar, PIL, A Profile, Jaipur, Bharat Law House, 1986.

Narayana, P.S., Public Interest Litigation, Hyderabad : Asia Law House, 1999.

Naresh Kumar : Constitutional rights of prisoners, Delhi, Mittal Publications, 1986.

Nariman, Fali S., India's Legal System: Can it be saved? New Delhi, Penguin Books, 2006.

Nayar, Kuldip, Ed., Suppression of Judges, New Delhi: Indian Book Company. 1973.

Noorani, A.G., Ed., Public Law in India, New Delhi: Vikas Publishing House, 1982.

Palkhivala, Nani A., Our Constitution defaced and defiled, Delhi, Macmillan, 1974.

Pylee, M.V., Constitutional Amendment in India, New Delhi, Universal Law Publishing Co., 2010.

Pylee, M.V., Constitutions of the World, (3rd ed., 2 Vols)., New Delhi, Universal Law Publishing Co. 2006.

Pylee, M.V., India's Constitution, New Delhi, S. Chand & Co., 2005.

Ramakrishnan, P.S., Ecology and Sustainable Development, New Delhi, National Book Trust, 2001.

Rao, B. Shiva, ed., The Framing of India's Select Documents Constitution, (Set of Six Books) Bombay; N.M. Tripathi, 1967.

Rao, Mamta, Public Interest Litigation. A Renaissance in Social Justice, Lucknow, Eastern Book Company, 2002.

Reddy, O. Chinnappa, The Court and the Constitution of India – Summits and Shallows, New Delhi, O.U.P., 2009.

Rizvi, Syed Iqbal Hadi, Public Interest Litigation, Liberty and Justice for all, New Delhi, Renaisance Publishing House, 1991.

Robertson, Pat : Courting Disaster : How the Supreme Court is usurping the power of congress and the people, Integrity Publishers, 2004.

Roosevelt (III), Kermit, The Myth of Judicial Activism, Delhi, Universal Law Publishing Co. Pvt. Ltd., 2008.

Sabine, George Thomas L Thorson, A History of Political Theory (Fourth edition), New Delhi, Oxford & IBM Publishing Co. Pvt. Ltd. 1973.

Sager, Lawrence : Justice in Plain Clothes : A Theory of American Constitutional Practice, Yale Univ. Press, 2004.

Sathe, S.P. Judicial Activism in India: Transgressing Borders and Enforcing Limits, Mumbai, OUP, 2002.

Sathe, S.P., The Tribunal System in India, Bombay, N.M. Tripathi, 1996.

Savant, P.B., Judicial Independence : Myth and Reality, Pune Board of Extra-Mural Studies, University of Poona, 1988.

Schmidhauser, John R., ed., Comparative Judicial Systems; Challenging Frontiers in Conceptual and Empirical Analysis, London, Butterworth, 1987.

Schwarzmantel, John. J., Ideology and Politics, London, Sage, 2008.

Seervai, H.M., Constitutional Law of India, Vol.- I, II, & III, Delhi, Universal Law Publishing Co., 2010.

Seervai, H.M. The Position of Judiciary under the Constitution of India, Bombay, University of Bombay, 1970.

Sen, Amartya, The Idea of Justice, Allen Lane, Penguin Books, 2009.

Sen, Amartya : Inequality Re-examined, Oxford, Clarendon Press, 1992.

Sharma, Sri Ram : The Supreme Court in the Indian Constitution, New Delhi, Rajpal and Sons, 1959.

Sharma, Ram Avtar, (ed) Justice and Social Order in India, New Delhi, Intellectual Publishing House, 1984.

Shastri, S.C. Environmental Law, Lucknow, Eastern Book Company, 2005.

Shourie, Arun : Falling over Backwards: An Essay against reservations and Judicial populism, Delhi Asia Publications and Rupa, 2006.

Shourie, Arun : Worshipping False Gods : Ambedkar and the facts which have been erased, New Delhi; Asia Publications, 1997.

Shourie, Arun, Courts and their judgments: Premises, prerequisites, Consequences, New Delhi, Rupa and Co., 2001.

Shukla, B.M. (ed.) Law and Social Justice; A critical review of Justice D.A. Desai's important judgements, Jaipur, Rawat Publications, 1998.

Shukla, V.N. The Constitution of India (Eighth ed.), Lucknow, Eastern Book Company, 1990.

Simmonds, N.E. Central Issues in Jurisprudence: Justice, Law and Rights, 2003.

Singh B., The Supreme Court of India as an instrument of Social Justice, New Delhi, Sterling Publishers, 1976.

Singh, Gurdip, Environmental Law in India, New Delhi, Macmillan India, 2005.

Singhvi, L.M. (ed.) Fundamental Rights and Constitutional Amendments, New Delhi, National Publishing House, 1971.

Sinha, J.M.L. Constitution, the Judiciary and the People, Bombay, Popular Prakashan, 1983.

Sorabjee, Soli J., ed., Law and Justice, An Anthology, Delhi. Universal Law Publishing Company. 2003.

Spencer, J.R., Jackson's Machinery of Justice, Delhi, Universal Law Publishing Co. Pvt. Ltd., 2005 (Indian Reprint).

Subba Rao, K. : Social Justice and Law, New Delhi, National Publishing House, 1974.

Tope, T.K. : The Constitution of India, Bombay, Popular Prakashan, 1971.

Tormey, Simson & Townshend, Jules; Key Thinkers from critical theory to post-rnarxism, Sage, 2006.

Tripathi, P.K., Some insights into fundamental rights, Bombay, University of Bombay, 1973.

Tripathi, Shrish Mani, The Human Face of the Supreme Court of India, Varanasi, Ganga Kaveri Publishing House, 1993.

Veeraswami, K., Whither Law and Justice, New Delhi: Eastern Law House, 2001.

Verma S.K. and Kusum ed., Fifty years of the Supreme Court of India, Its Grasp and Reach, New Delhi, OUP, 2002.

Verma (Justice), J.S. New Dimensions of Justice, Delhi Universal Law Publishing Co., 2000.

Vidya Bhushan : Prison administration in India with special reference to Uttar Pradesh, New Delhi, S. Chand, 1970.

Wadehra, B.L. Public Interest Litigation: New Delhi, Universal Law Publishing Co., 2nd ed. 2009 (pb.)

Weisbrod, Burton A. (ed.), Public Interest Law, Los Angeles, University of California Press, 1978.

Wheare, K.C., Modern Constitutions, HUL Series, OUP, 1956.

Willington, Harry H., The Supreme Court and the Process of Adjudication; interpreting the Constitution New-Delhi Universal Law Publishing Co., 2008.

List of Cases

13.	Bearer Bonds Case, (1981) 4 SCR 675; R. K. Garg Vs. Union of India, Known as bearer bonds case.	71
14.	Berubari Union., (1960) SCR 250; Air 1960 SC 845.	64
15.	B. L. Wadehra Vs. Union of India, (1996) 2 SCC 594 and Almitra H. Patel Vs. Union of India, (2000) 2 SCC 679	182
16.	Bombay Hawkers' Union Vs. Bombay Municipal Corporation. AIR 1985 Sc 1206, (1985) 3 SCC 528	149
17.	Brij Bala Vs. State of H. P. and Others, (1984) 2 SLR 408	131
18.	B. R. Kapoor Vs. Union of India, AIR 1990 SC 752	78
19.	Centre for Public Interest Litigation Vs. Union of India (2000) 8 SCC 606	211, 214
20.	Chhotelal Vs. U. P. AIR 1979 All, 135.	167, 173
21.	Common Cause Vs. Union of India, (1996) 1 SCC 753	181
22.	Consumer Education and Research Centre Vs. Union of India, (1995) 3 SCC 42	181
23.	D. D. Vyas Vs Ghaziabad Development Authority, AIR 1993 All 57	182
24.	Deoki Nandan Prasad Vs. State of Bihar, AIR 1983 SC 1134	109
25.	Devadasan Vs. Union of India, AIR 1976 Sc 490	164
26.	Dhirendra Chamoli Vs. U. P. 1986 1 SCC 637.	146
27.	D. K. Basu Vs. State of West Bengal, (1997) 1 SCC 416; AIR 1997 SC 610	219

No.	Case	Page
109.	Sanjay Suri and another Vs. Delhi Administration, 1987 (2) SCALE 276 (1257)	136
110.	Sanjit Roy Vs. State of Rajasthan, AIR 1983 SC 328, 382,	131, 145
111.	Scheduled Caste and weaker Section Welfare Association and another Vs. State of Karnataka and others, 1991 (2) SCC 604	149
112.	Sebastian M. Hongray Vs. Union of India, AIR 1984 SC 1026	109
113.	Self-employed Women's Association Vs. Municipal Corporation of Ahmedabad, 1986 (2) SCALE 291 (1254)	150
114.	Sheela Barse Vs. State of Maharashtra, (1983) 2 SCC 96; AIR 1993 SC 378	79, 127,213,218
115.	Sheela Barse Vs. Union of India, 1987 (3) SCJ 543	127
116.	Sheela Barse Vs. Union of India, AIR 1988 SC 2211.	135
117.	Sheela Barse Vs. Union of India, AIR 1986 SC 1773; (1986) 3 SCC 596.	136
118.	Special Courts Bill 1978, AIR 1979 SC 478	65
119.	S.P. Gupta and other Vs. Union of India, AIR 1982 SC 149	72
120.	S.P. Gupta Vs. Union of India, AIR 1981 SC 149	95
121.	S.P. Sampat Kumar Vs. Union of India, AIR 1987 SC at page 389	241
122.	State of Madras Vs. Darshana Devi, AIR 1979 SC 766, 855	84
123.	State of Madras Vs. Champakam Dorairajan AIR 1951 SC 226.	156
124.	Sunil Batra (I) Case, (1978) 4 SCC 494	80

Index